The Gospel According to Jesus

By Stephen Mitchell

POETRY
Parables and Portraits

PROSE
The Gospel According to Jesus

TRANSLATIONS AND ADAPTATIONS
A Book of Psalms
Variable Directions: The Selected Poetry of Dan Pagis
Tao Te Ching
The Book of Job
The Selected Poetry of Yehuda Amichai (with Chana Bloch)
The Sonnets to Orpheus
The Lay of the Love and Death of Cornet Christoph Rilke
Letters to a Young Poet
The Notebooks of Malte Laurids Brigge
The Selected Poetry of Rainer Maria Rilke

EDITED BY STEPHEN MITCHELL
Into the Garden: A Wedding Anthology (with Robert Hass)
The Enlightened Mind: An Anthology of Sacred Prose
The Enlightened Heart: An Anthology of Sacred Poetry
Dropping Ashes on the Buddha: The Teaching of Zen Master Seung Sahn

FOR CHILDREN
The Creation (with paintings by Ori Sherman)

BOOKS ON TAPE
The Gospel According to Jesus
The Enlightened Mind
The Enlightened Heart
Letters to a Young Poet
Parables and Portraits
Tao Te Ching
The Book of Job
The Selected Poetry of Rainer Maria Rilke

THE GOSPEL ACCORDING TO JESUS

A New Translation and Guide
To His Essential Teachings
For Believers and Unbelievers

STEPHEN MITCHELL

HarperPerennial
A Division of HarperCollins*Publishers*

Designed by David Bullen
Compositor Wilsted & Taylor

The Library of Congress has catalogued the hardcover edition as follows:
Mitchell, Stephen, 1943–
    The gospel according to Jesus : a new translation and guide to his essential teachings for believers and unbelievers / by Stephen Mitchell. — 1st ed.
        p.   cm.
    Chiefly commentary on biblical excerpts.
    Includes bibliographical references.
    ISBN 0-06-016641-X
    1. Jesus Christ—Words.   2. Jesus Christ—Buddhist interpretations.
3. Jesus Christ—Jewish interpretations.   4. Bible. N.T. Gospels—
Criticism, interpretation, etc.   I. Bible. N.T. Gospels. English.
Selections.   II. Title.
BT306.M55   1991.
226'.1—dc20   90-56390

ISBN 0-06-092321-0 (pbk.)
93 94 95 96 97 RRD 10 9 8 7 6 5 4 3 2 1

CONTENTS

Introduction   *1*
    Notes   *62*

The Gospel   *99*

Commentary   *127*
    Baptism   *129*
    He Begins to Teach   *131*
    The First Disciples   *133*
    At Capernaum   *134*
    First Healings   *136*
    He Heals a Leper   *138*
    The Kingdom of God (1)   *139*
    The Kingdom of God (2)   *140*
    The Kingdom of God (3)   *145*
    The Inner Light (1)   *147*
    With the Wicked   *148*
    The Twelve   *156*
    He Heals a Paralytic   *157*
    The Beatitudes   *158*
    The Inner Light (2)   *161*
    Fulfilling the Law   *162*
    Charity   *173*

Prayer	174
The Inner Light (3)	181
Trust	182
Providence	186
You Receive Exactly What You Give	186
The Narrow Gate	190
Hearing and Doing	191
Jesus' Family (1)	192
Accusations of Sorcery	192
Jesus' Family (2)	195
Two Healings	196
Rejection in Nazareth	203
The Syrophoenician Woman	206
He Heals a Deaf Man, a Blind Man	209
An Exorcism	210
You Must Become Like Children (1)	214
Forgiveness	217
The Good Samaritan	218
The Lost Sheep and the Lost Coin	221
The Prodigal Son	223
You Must Become Like Children (2)	230
The Rich Man	232
Let the Dead Bury Their Dead	241
First Days in Jerusalem	243
The Tax to Caesar	246
The Greatest Commandment	247
The Woman Caught in Adultery	250
Gethsemane	255
The Arrest	257
Peter's Denial	263
The Trial Before Pilate	264
The Crucifixion	268

CONTENTS

Appendixes
Appendix 1: On Jesus 277
Appendix 2: On Healing 295
Appendix 3: On Miracles 301
Sources 307

Acknowledgments *311*

INTRODUCTION

I

One of the icons on the walls of my study is a picture of Thomas Jefferson, an inexpensive reproduction of the portrait by Rembrandt Peale. The great man looks down over my desk, his longish, once-red hair almost completely gray now, a fur collar draped softly around his neck like a sleeping cat, his handsome features poised in an expression of serenity, amusement, and concern. I honor his serenity and understand his concern. And I like to think that his amusement—the hint of a smile, the left eyebrow raised a fraction of an inch—comes from finding himself placed in the company not of politicians but of saints.

For among the other icons on my walls are the beautiful, Jewish, halo-free face of Jesus by Rembrandt from the Gemäldegalerie in Berlin; a portrait of that other greatest of Jewish teachers, Spinoza; a Ming dynasty watercolor of a delighted bird-watching Taoist who could easily be Lao-tzu himself; a photograph, glowing with love, of the modern Indian sage Ramana Maharshi; and underneath it, surrounded by dried rose petals, a small Burmese statue of the Buddha, perched on a three-foot-tall packing crate stenciled with CHUE LUNG SOY SAUCE, 22 LBS.

Because Jefferson was our great champion of religious freedom, he was attacked as a rabid atheist by the bigots of his day. But he was a deeply religious man, and he spent a good deal of time thinking about Jesus of Nazareth. During the evening hours of one winter month late in his first term as president, after the public business had been put to rest, he began to compile a version of the Gospels that would include only what he considered the authentic accounts and sayings of Jesus. These he snipped out of his King James Bible and pasted onto the pages of a blank book, in more-or-less chronological order. He took up the project again in 1816, when he was seventy-three, eight years after the end of his second term, pasting in the Greek text as well, along with Latin and French translations, in parallel columns. The "wee little book," which he entitled *The Life and Morals of Jesus of Nazareth*, remained in his family until 1904, when it was published by order of the Fifty-seventh Congress and a copy given to each member of the House and Senate.

What is wrong with the old Gospels that made Jefferson want to compile a new one? He didn't talk about this in public, but in his private correspondence he was very frank:

> The whole history of these books [the Gospels] is so defective and doubtful that it seems vain to attempt minute enquiry into it: and such tricks have been played with their text, and with the texts of other books relating to them, that we have a right, from that cause, to entertain much doubt what parts of them are genuine. In the New Testament there is internal evidence that parts of it have proceeded from an extraordinary man; and that other parts are of the fabric of very inferior minds. It is as easy to separate those parts, as to pick out diamonds from dunghills. (To John Adams, January 24, 1814)

> We must reduce our volume to the simple Evangelists; select, even from them, the very words only of Jesus, paring off the amphibologisms into which they have been led by forgetting often, or not understanding, what had fallen from him, by giving their own misconceptions as his dicta, and expressing unintelligibly for others what they had not understood themselves. There will be found remaining the most sublime and benevolent code of morals which has ever been offered to man. (To John Adams, October 12, 1813)

Jefferson's robust honesty is always a delight, and never more so than in the Adams correspondence. The two venerable expresidents, who had been allies during the Revolution, then bitter political enemies, and who were now, in their seventies, reconciled and mellow correspondents, with an interest in philosophy and religion that almost equaled their fascination with politics—what a pleasure it is to overhear them discussing the Gospels sensibly, in terms that would have infuriated the narrow-minded Christians of their day. But Jefferson, too, called himself a Christian. "To the corruptions of Christianity," he wrote, "I am, indeed, opposed; but not to the genuine precepts of Jesus himself. I am a Christian in the only sense in which he wanted anyone to be: sincerely attached to his doctrines, in preference to all others; ascribing to himself every *human* excellence; and believing he never claimed any other." It is precisely because of his love for Jesus that he had such contempt for the "tricks" that were played with the Gospel texts.

Tricks may seem like a harsh word to use about some of the Evangelists' methods. But Jefferson was morally shocked to realize that the words of Jesus had been added to, deleted, altered, and otherwise tampered with as the Gospels were put together. He might have been more lenient if he were writing today, not as a member of a tiny clear-sighted minority, but in an age when textual skepticism is, at last, widely recognized as a path to Jesus, even by devout Christians, even by the Catholic church. For all reputable scholars today acknowledge that the official Gospels were compiled, in Greek, many decades after Jesus' death, by men who had never heard his teaching, and that a great deal of what the "Jesus" of the Gospels says originated not in Jesus' own Aramaic words, which have been lost forever, but in the very different teachings of the early church. And if we often can't be certain of what he said, we can be certain of what he didn't say.

In this book I have followed Jefferson's example. I have selected and translated, from Mark, Matthew, Luke, and (very sparingly) from John, only those passages that seem to me authentic accounts and sayings of Jesus. When there are three accounts of the same incident, I have relied primarily on Mark, the oldest and in certain ways the most trustworthy of the three Synoptic Gospels. I have also included all the teachings from Matthew and from Luke that seemed authentic. And I have eliminated every passage and, even within authentic passages, every verse or phrase that seemed like a later theological or polemical or legendary accretion.

Gospel means "good news." While the Gospels according to Mark, Matthew, Luke, and John are to a large extent teachings *about* Jesus, I wanted to compile a Gospel that would be the teaching *of* Jesus: what he proclaimed about the presence of God: good news as old as the universe. I found, as Jefferson did, that when the accretions are recognized and stripped off, Jesus surprisingly, vividly appears in all his radiance. Like the man in Bunyan's riddle, the more we throw away, the more we have. Or the process of selection can be compared to a diamond cutter giving shape to a magnificent rough stone, until its full, intrinsic brilliance is revealed. Jefferson, of course, was working without any of the precision tools of modern scholarship, as if trying to shape a diamond with an axe. But he knew what a diamond looked like.

The scholarship of the past seventy-five years is an indispensable help in distinguishing the authentic Jesus from the inauthentic. No good scholar, for example, would call the Christmas stories anything but legends, or the accounts of Jesus' trial anything but polemical fiction. And even about the sayings of Jesus, scholars show a remarkable degree of consensus.

In selecting passages from the Gospels, I have always taken seriously the strictly scholarly criteria. But there are no scholarly criteria for spiritual value. Ultimately my decisions were based on what Jefferson called "internal evidence": the evidence provided by the words themselves. The authentic passages are marked by "sublime ideas of the Supreme Being, aphorisms and precepts of the purest morality and benevolence . . . , humility, innocence, and simplicity of manners . . . , with an eloquence and persuasiveness which have not been surpassed." As Jesus said, the more we become sons (or daughters) of God, the more we become like God—generous, compassionate, impartial, serene. It is easy to recognize these qualities in the authentic sayings. They are Jesus' signature.

To put it another way: when I use the word *authentic*, I don't mean that a saying or incident can be proved to originate from the historical Jesus of Nazareth. There are no such proofs; there are only probabilities. And any selection is, by its nature, tentative. I may have included passages which, though filled with Jesus' spirit, were actually created by an editor, or I may have excluded passages whose light I haven't been able to see. But much of the internal evidence seems to me beyond doubt. When we read the parables of the Good Samaritan and the Prodigal Son, or the saying about becoming like children if we wish to enter the kingdom of God, or the passages in the Sermon on the Mount that teach us to be like the lilies of the field and to love our enemies, "so that you may be sons of your Father in heaven; for he makes his sun rise on the wicked and on the good, and sends rain to the righteous and to the unrighteous," we know we are in the presence of the truth. If it wasn't Jesus who said these things, it was (as in the old joke about Shakespeare) someone else by the same name. Here, in the essential sayings, we have words coming from the depths of the human heart, spoken from the most intimate experience of God's compassion: words that can shine into a Muslim's or a Buddhist's or a Jew's heart just as powerfully as into a Christian's. Whoever spoke these words was one of the great world teachers, perhaps the greatest poet among them, and a brother to all the awakened ones. The words are as genuine as words can be. They are the touchstone of everything else about Jesus.

For me, then, Jesus' words are authentic when scholarship indicates that they probably or possibly originated from him and when at the same time they speak with the voice that I hear in the essential sayings. This may seem like circular reasoning. But it isn't reasoning at all; it is a mode of listening.

No careful reader of the Gospels can fail to be struck by the difference between the largeheartedness of such passages and the bitter, badgering tone of some of the passages added by the early church. It is not only the polemical element in the Gospels, the belief in devils, the flashy miracles, and the resurrection itself that readers like Jefferson, Tolstoy, and Gandhi have felt are unworthy of Jesus, but most of all, the direct antitheses to the authentic teaching that were put into "Jesus'" mouth, doctrines and attitudes so offensive that they "have caused good men to reject the whole in disgust." Jesus teaches us, in his sayings and by his actions, not to judge (in the sense of not to condemn), but to keep our hearts open to all people; the later "Jesus" is the archetypal judge, who will float down terribly on the clouds for the world's final rewards and condemnations. Jesus cautions against anger and teaches the love of enemies; "Jesus" calls his enemies "children of the Devil" and attacks them with the utmost vituperation and contempt. Jesus talks of God as a loving father, even to the wicked; "Jesus" preaches a god who will cast the disobedient into everlasting flames. Jesus includes all people when he calls God "your Father in heaven"; "Jesus" says "*my* Father in heaven." Jesus teaches that all those who make peace, and all those who love their enemies, are sons of God; "Jesus" refers to himself as "*the* Son of God." Jesus isn't interested in defining who he is (except for one passing reference to himself as a prophet); "Jesus" talks on and on about himself. Jesus teaches

God's absolute forgiveness; "Jesus" utters the horrifying statement that "whoever blasphemes against the Holy Spirit never has forgiveness but is guilty of an eternal sin." The epitome of this narrowhearted, sectarian consciousness is a saying which a second-century Christian scribe put into the mouth of the resurrected Savior at the end of Mark: "Whoever believes and is baptized will be saved, but whoever doesn't believe will be damned." No wonder Jefferson said, with barely contained indignation,

> Among the sayings and discourses imputed to him by his biographers, I find many passages of fine imagination, correct morality, and of the most lovely benevolence; and others again of so much ignorance, so much absurdity, so much untruth, charlatanism, and imposture, as to pronounce it impossible that such contradictions should have proceeded from the same being.   (To William Short, April 13, 1820)

Once the sectarian passages are left out, we can recognize that Jesus speaks in harmony with the supreme teachings of all the great religions: the Upanishads, the Tao Te Ching, the Buddhist sutras, the Zen and Sufi and Hasidic Masters. I don't mean that all these teachings say exactly the same thing. There are many different resonances, emphases, skillful means. But when words arise from the deepest kind of spiritual experience, from a heart pure of doctrines and beliefs, they transcend religious boundaries, and can speak to all people, male and female, bond and free, Greek and Jew.

The eighteenth-century Japanese Zen poet Ryōkan, who was a true embodiment of Jesus' advice to become like a child, said it like this:

> In all ten directions of the universe,
> there is only one truth.
> When we see clearly, the great teachings are the same.

What can ever be lost? What can be attained?
If we attain something, it was there from the beginning of
    time.
If we lose something, it is hiding somewhere near us.
Look: this ball in my pocket:
can you see how priceless it is?

II

What *is* the gospel according to Jesus? Simply this: that the love we all long for in our innermost heart is already present, beyond longing. Most of us can remember a time (it may have been just a moment) when we felt that everything in the world was exactly as it should be. Or we can think of a joy (it happened when we were children, perhaps, or the first time we fell in love) so vast that it was no longer inside us, but we were inside it. What we intuited then, and what we later thought was too good to be true, isn't an illusion. It is real. It is realer than the real, more intimate than anything we can see or touch, "unreachable," as the Upanishads say, "yet nearer than breath, than heartbeat." The more deeply we receive it, the more real it becomes.

Like all the great spiritual Masters, Jesus taught one thing only: presence. Ultimate reality, the luminous, compassionate intelligence of the universe, is not somewhere else, in some heaven light-years away. It didn't manifest itself any more fully to Abraham or Moses than to us, nor will it be any more present to some Messiah at the far end of time. It is always right here, right now. That is what the Bible means when it says that God's true name is *I am*.

There is such a thing as nostalgia for the future. Both Judaism and Christianity ache with it. It is a vision of the Golden Age, the days of perpetual summer in a world of straw-eating lions and roses without thorns, when human life will be foolproof, and fulfilled in an endlessly prolonged finale of delight. I don't mean to make fun of the messianic vision. In many ways it is admirable, and it has inspired political and religious leaders from Isaiah to Martin Luther King, Jr. But it is a kind of benign insanity. And if we take it seriously enough, if we live it twenty-four hours a day, we will spend all our time working in anticipation, and will never enter the Sabbath of the heart. How moving and at the same time how ridiculous is the story of the Hasidic rabbi who, every morning, as soon as he woke up, would rush out his front door to see if the Messiah had arrived. (Another Hasidic story, about a more mature stage of this consciousness, takes place at the Passover seder. The rabbi tells his chief disciple to go outside and see if the Messiah has come. "But Rabbi, if the Messiah came, wouldn't you know it in here?" the disciple says, pointing to his heart. "Ah," says the rabbi, pointing to his own heart, "but in here, the Messiah has already come.") Who among the now-middle-aged doesn't remember the fervor of the Sixties, when young people believed that love could transform the world? "You may say I'm a dreamer," John Lennon sang, "but I'm not the only one." The messianic dream of the future may be humanity's sweetest dream. But it is a dream nevertheless, as long as there is a separation between inside and outside, as long as we don't transform ourselves. And Jesus, like the Buddha, was a man who had awakened from all dreams.

When Jesus talked about the kingdom of God, he was not prophesying about some easy, danger-free perfection that will someday appear. He was talking about a state of being, a way of living at ease among the joys and sorrows of *our* world. It is possible, he said, to be as simple and beautiful as the birds of the sky or the lilies of the field, who are always within the eternal Now. This state of being is not something alien or mystical. We don't need to earn it. It is already ours. Most of us lose it as we grow up and become self-conscious, but it doesn't disappear forever; it is always there to be reclaimed, though we have to search hard in order to find it. The rich especially have a hard time reentering this state of being; they are so possessed by their possessions, so entrenched in their social power, that it is almost impossible for them to let go. Not that it is easy for any of us. But if we need reminding, we can always sit at the feet of our young children. They, because they haven't yet developed a firm sense of past and future, accept the infinite abundance of the present with all their hearts, in complete trust. Entering the kingdom of God means feeling, as if we were floating in the womb of the universe, that we are being taken care of, always, at every moment.

All spiritual Masters, in all the great religious traditions, have come to experience the present as the only reality. The Gospel passages in which "Jesus" speaks of a kingdom of God in the future can't be authentic, unless Jesus was a split personality, and could turn on and off two different consciousnesses as if they were hot- and cold-water faucets. And it is easy to understand how these passages would have been inserted into the Gospel by disciples, or disciples of disciples, who hadn't understood his teaching. Passages about the kingdom of God as coming in the future are a dime a dozen in the prophets, in the Jewish apocalyptic writings of the first centuries B.C.E., in Paul and the early church. They are filled with passionate hope, with a desire for universal justice, and also, as Nietzsche so correctly insisted, with a festering resentment against "them" (the powerful, the ungodly). But they arise from ideas, not from an experience of the state of being that Jesus called the kingdom of God.

The Jewish Bible doesn't talk much about this state; it is more interested in what Moses said at the bottom of the mountain than in what he saw at the top. But there are exceptions. The most dramatic is the Voice from the Whirlwind in the Book of Job, which I have examined at length elsewhere. Another famous passage occurs at the beginning of Genesis: God completes the work of creation by entering the Sabbath mind, the mind of absolute, joyous serenity; contemplates the whole universe and says, "Behold, it is very good."

The kingdom of God is not something that will happen, because it isn't something that *can* happen. It can't appear in a world or a nation; it is a condition that has no plural, but only infinite singulars. Jesus spoke of people "entering" it, said that children were already inside it, told one particularly ardent scribe that he, the scribe, was not "far from" it. If only we stop looking forward and backward, he said, we will be able to devote ourselves to seeking the kingdom of God, which is right beneath our feet, right under our noses; and when we find it, food, clothing, and other necessities are given to us as well, as they are to the birds and the lilies. Where else but here and now can we find the grace-bestowing, inexhaustible presence of God? In its light, all our hopes and fears flitter away like ghosts. It is like a treasure buried in a field; it is like a pearl of great price; it is like coming home. When we find it, we find ourselves, rich beyond all dreams, and we realize that we can afford to lose everything else in the world, even (if we must) someone we love more dearly than life itself.

The portrait of Jesus that emerges from the authentic passages in the Gospels is of a man who has emptied himself of desires, doctrines, rules—all the mental claptrap and spiritual baggage that separate us from true life—and has been filled with the vivid reality of the Unnamable. Because he has let go of the merely personal, he is no one, he is everyone. Because he allows God *through* the personal, his personality is like a magnetic field. Those who are drawn to him have a hunger for the real; the closer they approach, the more they can feel the purity of his heart.

What is purity of heart? If we compare God to sunlight, we can say that the heart is like a window. Cravings, aversions, fixed judgments, concepts, beliefs—all forms of selfishness or self-protection—are, when we cling to them, like dirt on the windowpane. The thicker the dirt, the more opaque the window. When there is no dirt, the window is by its own nature perfectly transparent, and the light can stream through it without hindrance.

Or we can compare a pure heart to a spacious, light-filled room. People or possibilities open the door and walk in; the room will receive them, however many they are, for as long as they want to stay, and will let them leave when they want to. Whereas a corrupted heart is like a room cluttered with valuable possessions, in which the owner sits behind a locked door, with a loaded gun.

One last comparison, from the viewpoint of spiritual practice. To grow in purity of heart is to grow like a tree. The tree doesn't try to wrench its roots out of the earth and plant itself in the sky, nor does it reach its leaves downward into the dirt. It needs both ground and sunlight, and knows the direction of each. Only because it digs into the dark earth with its roots is it able to hold its leaves out to receive the sunlight.

For every teacher who lives in this way, the word of God has become flesh, and there is no longer a separation between body and spirit. Everything he or she does proclaims the kingdom of God. (A visitor once said of the eighteenth-century Hasidic rabbi Dov Baer, "I didn't travel to Mezritch to hear him teach, but to watch him tie his shoelaces.")

People can feel Jesus' radiance whether or not he is teaching or healing; they can feel it in proportion to their own openness. There is a deep sense of peace in his presence, and a sense of respect for him that far exceeds what they have felt for any other human being. Even his silence is eloquent. He is immediately recognizable by the quality of his aliveness, by his disinterestedness and compassion. He is like a mirror for us all, showing us who we essentially are.

The image of the Master:
one glimpse
and we are in love.

He enjoys eating and drinking, he likes to be around women and children; he laughs easily, and his wit can cut like a surgeon's scalpel. His trust in God is as natural as breathing, and in God's presence he is himself fully present. In his bearing, in his very language, he reflects God's deep love for everything that is earthly: for the sick and the despised, the morally admirable and the morally repugnant, for weeds as well as flowers, lions as well as lambs. He teaches that just as the sun gives light to both wicked and good, and the rain brings nourishment to both righteous and unrighteous, God's compassion embraces all people. There are no pre-conditions for it, nothing we need to do first, nothing we have to believe. When we are ready to receive it, it is there. And the more we live in its presence, the more effortlessly it flows through us, until we find that we no longer need external rules or Bibles or Messiahs.

For this teaching which I give you today is not hidden from you, and is not far away. It is not in heaven, for you to say, "Who will go up to heaven and bring it down for us, so that we can hear it and do it?" Nor is it beyond the sea, for you to say, "Who will cross the sea and bring it back for us, so that we can hear it and do it?" But the teaching is very near you: it is in your mouth and in your heart, so that you can do it.

He wants to tell everyone about the great freedom: how it feels when we continually surrender to the moment and allow our hearts to become pure, not clinging to past or future, not judging or being judged. In each person he meets he can see the image of God in which they were created. They are all perfect, when he looks at them from the Sabbath mind. From another, complementary, viewpoint, they are all imperfect, even the most righteous of them, even he himself, because nothing is perfect but the One. He understands that being human *means* making mistakes. When we acknowledge this in all humility, without wanting anything else, we can forgive ourselves, and we can begin correcting our mistakes. And once we forgive ourselves, we can forgive anyone.

He has no ideas to teach, only presence. He has no doctrines to give, only the gift of his own freedom.

> Tolerant like the sky,
> all-pervading like sunlight,
> firm like a mountain,
> supple like a branch in the wind,
> he has no destination in view
> and makes use of anything
> life happens to bring his way.
>
> Nothing is impossible for him.
> Because he has let go,
> he can care for the people's welfare
> as a mother cares for her child.

III

Jesus left us the essence of himself in his teachings, which are all we need to know about him.

We want to know much more, of course. What did he look like? What color were his eyes? Was he tall or short? What did his voice sound like, as he spoke the Aramaic words that were perhaps written down but never preserved? What were the details of the spiritual rebirth that transformed him from a village carpenter into the being whose portrait is in those words? Was he a disciple of John the Baptist? Who were his friends, and what did they talk about after dinner or as they walked through the

Galilean countryside? How skillful a teacher was he in his intimate relationships with his disciples? What really happened between Judas and him? Was he married? Was he ever in love? Did he have any premonition that his end would come at such a heartbreakingly early age, and with such great physical agony?

We know so little about his life. A very few facts, and no more. He was baptized by John the Baptist. He taught. He healed. He was crucified by the Romans. The rest is silence, probabilities, and hints. But anyone who can distinguish between the language of legend and the language of human experience knows that his life must have had a very different shape from the one into which it was molded by the piety of the early church.

This is an important matter not only for Jews, agnostics, Buddhists, and others who find their hearts touched by the authentic words of Jesus, but also for Christians. "Is it not time," Emerson asked, "to present this matter of Christianity exactly as it is, to take away all false reverence for Jesus, and not mistake the stream for the source?" We can't begin to see who Jesus was until we remove the layers of interpretation which the centuries have interposed between us and him, and which obscure his true face, like coat after coat of lacquer upon the vibrant colors of a masterpiece.

I understand how difficult even the thought of this may be for some Christians. It is always difficult to let go of our pieties, those small, familiar, comfortable alcoves which we enter when we need to be consoled or reassured that the world is safe. Of course, it is possible to be a traditional Christian, just as in first-century Palestine it was possible to be a scribe or a Pharisee, and live an entirely honorable, even a holy, life. But if we want to go further and enter the kingdom of God, we can't care about safety, or hold on to our beliefs. When the merchant found the pearl of great price, he went and sold everything he had in order to buy it.

We should set aside, first, the Christmas legend. We don't

have to eliminate it; it is beautiful and has its place; but we should realize that it is a fairy tale and, though it is suffused with the joyful spirit of Jesus, tells us nothing about his actual birth. Next, all concepts about Jesus, and all his traditional titles (Messiah, Savior, Redeemer, Son of Man, Son of God), which originated not in his own teaching but in the church's thoughts about him. Then, most of the stories about plots and opposition from Pharisees and others, because they are so deeply tainted by the Evangelists' anti-Semitism, which developed in the decades after Jesus' death, out of the growing mutual hostility between church and synagogue. And finally, the legends of the resurrection, those poignant whistlings in the dark, in which Jesus appears as an insubstantial ghost of himself. "If Christ was not raised," Paul said, "your faith is empty." But faith is larger than any *if*s; and when we trust God completely, we can trust death as well.

So. He was baptized. He taught. He healed. He was crucified by the Romans. What more can we intuit once the legends have been peeled away?

The focal point of a great spiritual Master, the point from which his teachings begin, tells us something important about him. Lao-tzu, like his fraternal twin Spinoza, begins with the vision of wholeness, the current of perfection that flows through all things, the God beyond God. The Buddha begins with the mind; he shows us, with infinite compassion, how to see through our neuroses, into the face we had before our parents were born. Jesus begins with the kingdom of God in the heart. His teachings have such a deep moral resonance that they take us beyond the realm of the moral and make righteousness seem like the most beautiful thing on earth. In this he is prototypically Jewish. What is required of us is to do justly, to love mercy, and to walk humbly with our God. Not "behind": "with."

But few people are ready to enter the kingdom of God. So Jesus has a second focal point: forgiveness. If Lao-tzu's teaching is a circle, Jesus' is an ellipse.

People who are familiar only with Christianity among the

great world religions don't realize how surprising this emphasis is. Other great Masters teach forgiveness, to be sure. But for them it is a secondary matter. When we center ourselves in the Tao, surrendering our own will to the will of God-or-Nature, when we purify our mind of the desires and aversions that arise from primal ignorance, then eventually, without any intention or effort on our part, we become the kind of person who finds it easy to forgive personal wrongs.

> When you realize where you come from,
> you naturally become tolerant,
> disinterested, amused,
> kindhearted as a grandmother,
> dignified as a king.

Why did Jesus place such emphasis on forgiveness? Perhaps partly because he felt that this was the most important lesson the people of his time and place needed to learn. But I think there was another reason. An insightful psychotherapist will notice that many of her patients are confronting, at a more acute stage, issues that she is currently confronting in herself. They are drawn to her as to a relatively clear mirror, and the mirroring is mutual: in them too she can see herself. Even a great Master teaches what he needs, or once needed, to learn.

The emotion that informs Jesus' teaching about forgiveness is so intense, so filled with the exhilaration of forgiving and being forgiven, that it must have come from a profound personal experience. I would like to feel my way into this experience by examining some hints that the Gospels give about his position in the original holy trinity: the father, the son, and the mother.

IV

The first thing we ought to realize about Jesus' life is that he grew up as an illegitimate child. On this point both traditional

Christians and non-Christians can fully agree, because even those who believe in the virginal conception don't believe that the angel Gabriel appeared to everyone else in Nazareth, to assure them that Mary's child had been fathered by God.

> We say that she was highly honored among women. . . . It is true that Mary conceived the child in a miraculous fashion, but she nevertheless did it "after the manner of women" [Genesis 18:11], and pregnancy is a time of anxiety, distress, and paradox. It is true that the angel was a ministering spirit, but he wasn't a meddler: he didn't appear to the other girls in Israel and say, "Don't despise Mary; the extraordinary is happening to her." The angel appeared only to Mary, and no one could understand her. Has any woman been as humiliated as Mary was, and isn't it true here also that the one whom God blesses he curses in the same breath? This is the spirit's view of Mary, and she is not—it is revolting that I have to say this, but it is even more revolting that people have inanely and sanctimoniously depicted her in this way—she is not a lady lounging in her gorgeous robes and playing with an infant god.
>
> (Søren Kierkegaard, *Fear and Trembling*)

If an angel appeared, he appeared only to Mary, and she was unmarried, and her too-early pregnancy was a scandal to the whole village. There would have been no corroboration of the miracle, no protection. She would have been exposed to the contempt of her neighbors, and not only for the six months after her swollen belly became visible—she would have had to eat derision and insult with her daily bread for as long as she lived. As for the social effects on a young child: growing up with the shame of being called a bastard must be almost as painful as being illegitimate in fact.

But let us suppose that Jesus was conceived and born in the ordinarily miraculous way:

> I, too, am mortal, like every human,
> Descended from the first man formed of the dust.

I was molded into flesh in a mother's womb;
For nine months I was compacted in blood
From the semen of a man and sexual pleasure.
I, too, breathed-in the common air,
Was laid on the earth that bears us all,
And my first sound was a wail, like everyone else.
No king is born differently; for there is just
One way into life, and one way out.

(Wisdom of Solomon 7:1–6)

For most people, and for Christians who don't accept the virginal conception literally but see it as a pious legend and a metaphor, the evidence of Jesus' illegitimacy is fairly clear. There are four passages in the official Gospels, and one in the Gospel of Thomas, that hint at it. (Of course, we have to read between the lines to realize their meaning; where the Evangelists want us to read black, we must read white.) This matter has been studied in great detail by contemporary scholars; the most exhaustive treatment is *The Illegitimacy of Jesus* by Jane Schaberg. I will just quote the five passages, with a few comments.

1. From the infancy narrative in Matthew:·

Now the birth of Jesus happened in this way. Mary, his mother, was engaged to Joseph, but before they came together to live, she was found to be pregnant by the Holy Spirit. And Joseph, being a just man and not wanting to put her to public shame, decided to divorce her quietly. But as he was considering this, behold, an angel of the Lord appeared to him in a dream, and said to him, "Joseph, son of David, do not be afraid to take Mary as your wife, for what has been begotten in her is of the Holy Spirit. And she will give birth to a son, and you shall name him Jesus."

Behind the author's (and the angel's) explanation that Mary was made pregnant by the Holy Spirit is an accusation that must have been current during Jesus' lifetime. As the Catholic scholar Raymond E. Brown writes:

Matthew tells us of the rumor that Mary's pregnancy was adulterous. The explanation given by the angel may have set Joseph's mind at ease; but in the implicit logic of Matthew's account there would have been no way to disguise the fact that Jesus would be born indecently early after Mary was taken to Joseph's home. Obviously, Matthew is facing a story that is in circulation, and factual data that he cannot deny: he does not and seemingly cannot reply that Jesus was born at the proper interval after Joseph and Mary came to live together. Traces of the rumor of irregularity of birth and illegitimacy appear elsewhere in the New Testament. . . . Since it is not easy to dismiss such a persistent charge, which may be as old as Christianity itself, those [Christians] who deny the virginal conception cannot escape the task of explaining how the rumor of illegitimacy and irregularity of birth arose and how they would answer it without accepting a very unpleasant [sic] alternative.

2. From the genealogy at the beginning of Matthew's Gospel:

Abraham begat Isaac, Isaac begat Jacob, Jacob begat Judah and his brothers, Judah begat Perez and Zarah out of Tamar, Perez begat Hezron, Hezron begat Ram, Ram begat Aminadab, Aminadab begat Nahshon, Nahshon begat Salmon, Salmon begat Boaz out of Rahab, Boaz begat Obed out of Ruth, Obed begat Jesse, Jesse begat King David, David begat Solomon out of Uriah's wife, . . .

The peculiar feature in this list is the mention of the four women (in the divergent genealogy in Luke 3:23ff., no women are mentioned). Morton Smith explains the significance of their presence here:

Matthew's genealogy of Jesus (1:2–16) refers to only four women besides Mary: they are Tamar, whose children were born of incest; Rahab, the madam of a brothel; Ruth, a non-Israelite, who got her second husband by solicitation, if not fornication, and so became the great-grandmother of David (Ruth 4:21f.); and Bathsheba ("the wife of Uriah"), whose relations with David began in adultery, though she became the mother of Solomon. That the author of a genealogy for a Messiah should have chosen to mention only these four women requires an explanation. The most likely one is that Matthew wanted to excuse Mary by these implied analogies.

3. From Mark's account of Jesus' failure at Nazareth:

And when the Sabbath came, he began to teach in the synagogue, and many people who heard him were bewildered, and said, "Where does this fellow get such stuff?" and "What makes *him* so wise?" and "How can he be a miracle-worker? Isn't this the carpenter, the son of Mary, the brother of James and Joseph and Judas and Simon, and aren't his sisters here with us?" And they were prevented from believing in him.

In English, "the son of Mary" gives no idea of the phrase's connotation in Aramaic or Hebrew. In Semitic usage, a man was normally called "[name] son of [father's name]"; if he was called "[name] son of [mother's name]," it indicated that his father was unknown and that he was illegitimate. According to a later Jewish legal principle, "A man is illegitimate when he is called by his mother's name, for a bastard has no father." That is why in my version of the Gospel I have translated *ho huios tēs Marias* — "the son of Mary" — as "Mary's bastard" (it is impossible to know exactly how crude an insult the Aramaic would have been).

4. In the Gospel of John we find the following debate between "Jesus" and "the Jews":

["Jesus" says:] "I know that you are Abraham's descendants, but you are trying to kill me, because my teaching has found no place in you. What I have seen with the Father, I speak; what you have heard from the father, you do."

They answered, "Our father is Abraham."

Jesus said to them, "If you are children of Abraham, do the works of Abraham. But now you are trying to kill me, a man who has spoken the truth to you, which I heard from God. Abraham did not do that. You are doing the works of your father."

They said to him, "*We* were not born of fornication. We have one father: God."

Jesus said to them, "If God were your father, you would love me. . . . Your father is the devil, and you want to do your father's will. He was a murderer from the beginning. . . ."

John is almost never a trustworthy witness to the historical Jesus, but in this accusation, as Jane Schaberg explains, he seems to have preserved an authentic strand of tradition. ("Jesus'" answer, in its hatred and demonization of the Jews, is, of course, anything but authentic.)

In the midst of this argument, the opponents say, "*We* were not born of fornication" (*Hymeis ek porneias ou gegennēmetha*), the emphasis on "we" implying "but you were," that is, implying that Jesus was illegitimate. The Jews meet Jesus' challenge to their religious or spiritual legitimacy by a challenge to his physical legitimacy. The suggestion of Jesus' illegitimacy here is subtle and is drawn from pre-gospel tradition.

5. Finally, there is a spine-tingling verse from the Gospel of Thomas: "He who knows his [true] Father [i.e., God] and Mother [i.e., the Holy Spirit] will be called the son of a whore." In this verse, which I think originates from Jesus (though it is tinged with Gnostic theology), we can hear the taunts and insults of the Nazareth villagers echoing down through the centuries.

If someone wished to choose the most difficult starting point for a human life, short of being born diseased or deformed, he might well choose to be born illegitimate. In the ancient world, both Jewish and Roman, illegitimacy was considered one of the most shameful of human conditions. The central biblical text is

Deuteronomy 23:3: "No *mamzer* shall enter the assembly of YHVH, even to the tenth generation" (*mamzer* is usually translated as "bastard," and interpreted as "the child of an adulterous union").

> The *mamzerim* were forbidden marriage with the priestly families, Levites, legitimate Israelites, and even with illegitimate descendants of priests. At the end of the first century C.E. their rights to inherit from their natural fathers were in dispute. They could not hold public office, and if they took part in a court decision, the decision was invalidated. Their families' share in Israel's final redemption was vigorously argued. The word *mamzer* was considered one of the worst insults to a man. *Mamzerim* were among those called the "excrement of the community."

This was by no means only a Jewish attitude; the contempt for illegitimate children was just as strong among Gentiles. We can see it clearly in the polemical treatise *Contra Celsum*, which the Christian theologian Origen wrote, in about the year 248, to refute the various refutations of Christianity put forth by the philosopher Celsus. In the following passage, Origen is responding to Celsus's accusation that Jesus was born illegitimate. I will quote this at some length, because it gives us an insight into the minds of the men who created Christian doctrine:

> It was inevitable that those who did not accept the miraculous birth of Jesus would have invented some lie. But the fact that they did not do this convincingly, but kept as part of the story that the virgin did not conceive Jesus by Joseph, makes the lie obvious to people who can see through fictitious stories and show them up. Is it reasonable that a man who ventured to do such great things for mankind in order that, so far as in him lay, all Greeks and barbarians in expectation of the divine judgment might turn from evil and act in every respect acceptably to the Creator of the universe, should have had, not a miraculous birth, but a birth more illegitimate and disgrace-

ful than any? As addressing Greeks, and Celsus in particular who, whether he holds Plato's doctrines or not, nevertheless quotes them, I would ask this question. Would He who sends souls down into human bodies compel a man to undergo a birth more shameful than any, and not even have brought him into human life by legitimate marriage, when he was to do such great deeds and to teach so many people and to convert many from the flood of evil? Or is it more reasonable (and I say this now following Pythagoras, Plato, and Empedocles, whom Celsus often mentions) that there are certain secret principles by which each soul that enters a body does so in accordance with its merits and former character? It is therefore probable that this soul, which lived a more useful life on earth than many men (to avoid appearing to beg the question by saying "all" men), needed a body which was not only distinguished among human bodies, but was also superior to all others. . . .

Suppose that all bodies conform to the habits of their souls; then for the soul that was to live a miraculous life on earth and to do great things, a body was necessary, not, as Celsus thinks, produced by the adultery of Panthera [a Roman soldier who was rumored to be Jesus' real father] and a virgin (for the offspring of such impure intercourse must rather have been some stupid man who would harm men by teaching licentiousness, unrighteousness, and other evils, and not a teacher of self-control, righteousness, and the other virtues), but, as the prophets foretold, the offspring of a virgin, who according to the promised sign should give birth to a child whose name was significant of his work, showing that at his birth God would be with men.

For people living in the first century, then, whether they were Jews, pagans, or Christians, it was inconceivable that an illegitimate child could grow up to be a decent man, much less a prophet or a great spiritual teacher. They didn't have a category for that. Most people still don't. Nor do they understand what

Jesus meant when he said, "Nothing can defile a man from the outside; it is only what comes out of a man that defiles him."

I don't think that we can fully appreciate who Jesus became unless we realize the overwhelming difficulties he must have had as an illegitimate child in a small provincial town, which one has to assume was fairly harsh and moralistic when it dealt with such matters. Mary may have been the most loving of mothers, and Jesus himself was no doubt an unusually gifted and joyful child; but even so, the atmosphere of public contempt and derision must have felt like a continual attack on his soul. When we imagine such a beginning, our admiration for him can only increase. Conventional piety, of course, would like to urge us, as it compelled Matthew and Luke, to give the infant Jesus the accoutrements of holiness that we see in all the paintings: angels, auras, sumptuous gifts, visiting dignitaries who worship him on bended knees. But there is a deeper piety of the actual. And that deeper piety shows us that God is to be found not in the *should be*, but in the *is*.

It is remarkable what an opposite and complementary shape the life of the Buddha had. He was born the son of a king, and in order to become himself, he had to overcome the difficulties that arise from being rich, all the temptations of luxury and power, the camel-and-the-eye-of-the-needle syndrome. We can see the respective beginnings of these two great men as opposite ends of the spectrum that is the human condition. Together, their meaning is that no life is so sheltered or so shamed that it can't be transformed into a vehicle of God's grace, a vessel filled with the deepest charity and wisdom. So capable are we of using whatever materials we are given; so irresistible is the phototropism of the human soul.

Even for Christians, I think, even theologically, it is appropriate for Jesus to have taken on the difficult karma of opprobrium, as Blake taught in his wonderfully perceptive late poem "The Everlasting Gospel":

Was Jesus born of a virgin pure
With narrow soul and looks demure?
If he intended to take on sin
The mother should an harlot been.
. . . .
Or what was it which he took on
That he might bring salvation:
A body subject to be tempted,
From neither pain nor grief exempted,
Or such a body as might not feel
The passions that with sinners deal?

What more powerful way could there have been for Jesus to become one with all the outcasts and despised of the earth than to be born illegitimate? Taking on this particular incarnation would mean experiencing, in his own body, at the most vulnerable time of a human life, the most intense shame, wretchedness, and separation, so that he could eventually include and invite everyone into the kingdom of God. Rather than the famous misinterpreted verse from First Isaiah about a "virgin" giving birth to a son, Second Isaiah's description of the despised figure known as the Suffering Servant seems truly prophetic of Jesus.

He is despised and rejected of men; a man of sorrows, and acquainted with grief: and we hid as it were our faces from him; he was despised, and we esteemed him not. Surely he hath borne our griefs, and carried our sorrows: yet we did esteem him stricken, smitten of God, and afflicted.

Prophetic not of his death, but of his birth.

V

Only one word has come down to us directly from the lips of Jesus in its original Aramaic: *abba*, "father." Mark quotes it in the context of the prayer at Gethsemane, which may or may not be historical; but it is certain that Jesus used the word often, and that it lies behind the *our father*'s and the *your father*'s of the authentic sayings. And while his teaching about the presence, here, now, of the kingdom of God is so simple that it may seem absurd to some and immoral to others—a stumblingblock to the Jews and to the Greeks foolishness—his description of God as an infinitely loving father is a teaching everybody can understand.

Few of us, though, can feel the intensity of what Jesus meant when he said *abba*. Actually, we don't have a word for it. Our word *father* reflects a personal and social reality which is a much diluted version of the reality a first-century Jewish father had for his children: a position of absolute power, for both good and evil, which commanded a fear or a respect that we can barely conceive of. To really translate the word, we would have to translate the culture.

For Jesus, the Father is pure generosity, pure creativity, the embodiment of the first hexagram of the I Ching, the archetypal power that generates the whole universe, that blesses and keeps and makes its face shine upon all its children and gives them peace. And not only absolute creative power, but also absolute mercy, a quality we associate more with mothers. The prophets, in fact, speak of God as feeling a kind of motherly love for Israel, since the Hebrew verb *rhm*, usually translated as "to have mercy or compassion," derives from a root that means "womb."

The Psalms and the prophets occasionally speak of God as a father, even as a mother. But the image is not a common one in the Bible. It became much more common in later Judaism; as the Aramaic scholar Gustaf Dalman said, "Jesus adopted this term for God from the popular usage of his time." Of Dalman's many examples, I will cite two. The first is from the Book of Jubilees:

> "Their [the Israelites'] souls will attach themselves to Me and
> to all My commandments, and My commandments will re-

turn to them; and I will be to them a father, and they will be My children. And they will all be called children of the living God; and every angel and every spirit will surely recognize that these are My children, and that I am their father in sincerity and righteousness, and that I love them."

The second is from the second-century rabbi Yehuda ben Tema:

Be bold as a leopard, quick as an eagle, swift as a gazelle, and strong as a lion to do the will of your heavenly Father.

So Jesus' teaching was not original, in the strict sense of the word. The subject of originality is a sore point with certain kinds of literal-minded Christian and Jewish scholars. The former try to prove that Jesus was, the latter that he wasn't, original; and the opposing idea, that he wasn't, or was, makes these scholars feel as squirmy as someone who has sat on an anthill at a picnic. They are looking in the wrong direction. Originality has nothing to do with priority. An image is like a musical key; just because someone used G-minor before doesn't make Mozart a copycat. When the Holy Spirit comes, all things are made new. Jesus wasn't the first to speak of God as a loving father, or even to say "Be like your Father." But his sayings, in their intimacy and passion, speak from the most profound experience of God's fatherness, and express the intimacy and passion with which he lived it.

VI

To appreciate Jesus' teaching about God as an infinitely loving father, we don't *have* to relate it to Jesus' life. But I think that the teaching gains in richness and poignancy when we do.

If there is one reality that marks what we might call the emotional life of Jesus, as glimpsed through his various sayings, it is the presence of the divine father and the absence of a human father. This is entirely in keeping with the probability that he grew up as an illegitimate child. We don't know if Mary ever married, though presumably she did, since she had four other sons and at least two daughters. The father, or stepfather, is never mentioned in the authentic verses of the Gospels. (References to Joseph occur only in Matthew's and Luke's infancy legends.) According to a later verse in Matthew, Jesus once said, "Don't call any man on earth 'father,' for you have just one father, and he is in heaven."

Every illegitimate child must feel intense longing for a father: not only the longing that orphans feel, for an adult male presence at the core of their life, but also for legitimation, for a father—for *the* father—to come and say, "Yes, you do belong to the human community. You are of infinite value, like every human being. You are my beloved child."

We know nothing about Jesus' enlightenment experience, which changed him from carpenter to Master, from "son of a whore" to a son of God. (We know nothing . . . we know nothing. . . . Even when I don't say it explicitly, this phrase will be a kind of silent ground bass that accompanies everything I try to intuit about Jesus' life.) The experience may have happened at any time: as he was hammering nails in his workshop, as he was walking on the pebbly shore of the Sea of Galilee, perhaps as he was fasting and meditating in the wilderness. The Gospel of Mark implies that it happened while he was being baptized by John the Baptist, and that may be the historical reality. Before I try to imagine the event more fully, I need to talk about the way it is used by the four Evangelists.

It is the first event that we know of in Jesus' life, and along with his crucifixion by the Romans, it is, as I said before, one of our very few historical certainties. But we have only the most meager information about it: "At that time Jesus came from Nazareth in Galilee, and was baptized in the Jordan by John." Just that sentence. We don't know what brought Jesus to be baptized or what kind of experience it was. The heavenly voice and the descent of the Holy Spirit in the form of a dove are explanations added by the early church. But it is possible that the mythological form both obscures and preserves something of the actual experience.

In almost all the ancient manuscripts of Mark and Luke, the heavenly voice says, "You are my beloved son; with you I am well pleased" (Matthew recasts the sentence in the third person). But at Luke 3:22, a few ancient manuscripts read, "You are my son; this day I have begotten you." This is a quotation from Psalm 2; since the verse is also quoted in Acts and Hebrews, it must have been current in the early church. Again, there is no way to know if this account is just Christology or if it actually contains some memory of Jesus talking about the event, telling about how he felt reborn, begotten by God, in and through this experience.

It is obvious that the Gospel writers felt uncomfortable with the fact of the baptism. One reason is Jesus' subordination to John the Baptist. How could the Messiah have bowed before the Messenger?

We know that during Jesus' life and in the early years after his death, there was intense competition between his disciples and the disciples of John. Luke says that Apollos, who later became an apostle, at first "understood only the baptism of John," implying that it was inferior to the Christian baptism. Similarly, according to Luke, when Paul arrived in Ephesus, he asked the congregation,

"Did you receive the Holy Spirit when you became believers?"

And they said, "No, we didn't even hear that there is a Holy Spirit."

And he said, "Then what were you baptized into?"

And they said, "Into John's baptism."

And Paul said, "John baptized with a baptism of repentance, and he told the people to believe in the one who was to come after him, that is, in Jesus."

And when they heard this, they were baptized into the name of the Lord Jesus.

(Since no texts from the Baptist's disciples have come down to us, we don't know what they thought of Jesus. They may not have thought of him at all. But if they did, given the ego investment that disciples have in the superiority of their teacher, it is likely that they put him in, at best, second place.)

So Jesus' baptism would have been an acute problem, except for a relatively mature disciple. To guard against the conclusion that John was somehow superior to Jesus, Mark puts these words into the Baptist's mouth: "One who is stronger than I is coming after me, and I am not worthy to stoop down and untie the thong of his sandals. I have baptized you with water, but he will baptize you with the Holy Spirit." Matthew adds a conversation in which John himself asks the troubling question about the baptism and confesses his inferiority directly to Jesus:

Then Jesus came from Galilee to the Jordan to be baptized by John. John, trying to prevent him, said, "Why are you coming to me? *I* need to be baptized by *you*!" But Jesus answered him, "Let it happen now; for it is proper that we fulfill all righteousness in this way." Then he let it happen.

Luke solves the problem by putting John in prison and having Jesus baptized in the passive voice, by an undesignated agent:

When all the people were being baptized, and when Jesus too had been baptized and was praying, the heavens opened. . . .

The Fourth Gospel never mentions that Jesus was baptized, and has John recognize him as the Son of God the moment he sees him.

The point of all this editorial activity is to explain an event which, according to the writers' beliefs, should not have taken place. The event is incontrovertible precisely because of their embarrassment. No writer would have invented a detail that was so troubling.

But there is an even more embarrassing aspect to the baptism. As Mark says, "All the people were baptized by [John] in the river Jordan, confessing their sins." If Jesus was "a man without sin," as the later, and probably the early, disciples thought—or even more, if he was the preexistent Son of God—how could he have had any sins to confess, and why did he feel the need for baptism? This question was posed explicitly in the fourth-century *Debates of Archelaus, Bishop of Mesopotamia, and the Heresiarch Mani*:

> *Archelaus:* If Jesus was not baptized, neither is any of us baptized. But if there is no baptism, neither will there be any remission of sins, but everyone will die in his sins.
>
> *Mani:* Therefore is baptism given for the remission of sins?
>
> *Archelaus:* Yes.
>
> *Mani:* But Christ was baptized: Had he therefore sinned?
>
> *Archelaus:* Not so; rather, "He was made sin for us," taking on our sins.

The Evangelists deal with the problem by immediately focusing attention on Jesus' vision (according to Mark, followed by Matthew, only Jesus could see the dove; Luke implies that everyone could see it; according to John, it was visible only to the Baptist). The writer of the Gospel of the Nazoreans, which probably dates from the early second century, acknowledges the problem by denying the baptism:

> The mother of the Lord and his brothers said to him, "John the Baptist baptizes for the forgiveness of sins; let us go and be baptized by him."

But Jesus said to them, "What sin have I committed, that I should go and be baptized by him? Unless what I just said is a sin of ignorance."

There is no problem about the baptism unless we hold on to the idea that Jesus is superhuman, an idea that he himself certainly didn't have. "Why do you call me good?" he once said to an earnest inquirer who called him "Good Rabbi"; "no one is good except God alone." It would be a childish view of him to think that he never caused suffering or made mistakes. (The Hebrew word for "sin" means "to miss the mark.") And in his own view of himself, he undoubtedly felt, like anyone who has spent a great amount of time in prayer or meditation, that he was just one partial expression of the divine whole: the moon reflected, however clearly, in a dewdrop. That he felt imperfect and fallible simply means that he was one of us.

If the account of the official Gospels does contain some authentic memory, what can the actual event have been like for Jesus? Here we have to look behind the mythologized language: the sky splitting apart, the Holy Spirit descending as a dove. What we are left with is the voice of God, in one of its myriad forms.

It isn't hard to imagine the external details of the baptism scene: the crowds of enthusiastic devotees, the fiery-eyed Baptist, unkempt, "clothed in camel's hair, with a belt of animal hide around his waist," and preaching with the greatest passion and urgency, the immersions, the cheers, the groans of emotional release, the clumps of friends and relatives who stand together, dripping, on the riverbank. For many of these people the baptism was undoubtedly a profound experience. But Jesus' experience must have been fundamentally different. Repentance can be a transitory emotion, and the revival meeting is notorious for ecstasies that vanish at the threshold of the ego.

I see him as a sincere young man who, on some unconscious level, was still struggling with the pain of his childhood, and who had not yet penetrated to the place of pure light. Perhaps it was the ferocious intensity of John, the first prophet he had ever met, that precipitated the experience. But as Jesus looked into his eyes, or as he was thrust under the surface of the Jordan River, something broke open, not in the heavens but in his own heart. He felt an ecstatic release, a cleansing of those painfully hidden childhood emotions of humiliation and shame, a sense of being taken up, once and for all, into the embrace of God. "You are my beloved son; this day I have begotten you."

The passage which, for me, sheds the most light on what this experience must have felt like is the parable of the Prodigal Son. The story, as Jesus tells it, is beyond praise; in its tenderness and compassion, it speaks to all of us. Its economy and pathos are unsurpassed in the literature of the world, and its artistry is even more apparent to those familiar with the similar parable in the Lotus Sutra of Mahayana Buddhism, which rambles on and on like a well-meaning, dimwitted uncle.

Jesus' parable was primarily intended for the righteous. Its lesson is that those who have always remained with God, as the older son remained with his father, shouldn't feel resentful toward those who have truly repented and returned, but should receive them openheartedly, with joy, as the father received his younger son. That is the ostensible teaching, and it is an extremely important and moving lesson. But most people, when they think of or talk about the parable, remember only its first part. The reason for this, it seems to me, is not only that most people identify themselves with the younger son, but also that the unconscious center of gravity of the parable itself, its most intense emotion, lies in the first part.

It begins with the father and his two sons, but quickly focuses attention on the younger one.

There once was a man who had two sons. And the younger one said to him, "Father, let me have my share of the estate." So he divided his property between them. And not many days afterward, having turned his share into money, the younger son left and traveled to a distant country, and there he squandered his inheritance in riotous living. And after he had spent it all, a severe famine arose in that country; and he was destitute. And he went and hired himself out to a citizen of that country, who sent him to his farm to feed the pigs. And he longed to fill his belly with the husks that the pigs were eating; and no one would give him any food.

Later I will examine the story in detail. For now, I want to consider its emotion. Jesus' interest here is not in telling how the younger son arrived at his destitute condition, but in describing that condition. There is an almost unbearable sense of degradation. The son is treated, and feels like, the lowest of the low. He is cut off from all human society, reduced to spending his days taking care of pigs, the unclean animal par excellence, and is too disgusted to eat the carob pods that they feed on in their contented piggish way.

Christian teaching identifies Jesus with the father in the parable. But in a parable, as in a poem or a dream, the teller is *all* the images and characters. And given the focus on the figure of the younger son, given the depth of emotion emanating from him, it is clear that Jesus has particularly, and wholly, entered into *him* at this point. Of course, this identification may be simply a matter of his general empathy with the poor, the bereft, and the downtrodden. But it is hard for me not to think that he has entered so deeply into the younger son because he himself had once felt that way. I am not suggesting that there is a correspondence of details between the story and his life, or that he ever lived prodigally. But any separation from God is painful to a young man of Jesus' gifts, and the smallest mistake appears huge under the microscope of his moral conscience. Not even the greatest Masters were spared the process of spiritual death and rebirth. For Jesus, the rebirth must have been particularly astonishing, because it had to include and overcome the sustained indignities of his childhood. "The way down and the way up are one and the same," as Heraclitus tells us. When we sink to the bottom of our lostness, we can begin to find ourselves.

> And when he came to himself, he said, "How many of my father's hired men have more than enough to eat, while I am dying of hunger. I will get up and go to my father, and say to him, 'Father, I have sinned against God and against you, and I am no longer worthy to be called your son. Let me be like one of your hired men.'" And he got up, and went to his father. And while he was still a long way off, his father saw him, and was moved with compassion, and ran to him, and threw his arms around him, and kissed him. And the son said to him, "Father, I have sinned against God and against you, and I am no longer worthy to be called your son." But the father said to his servants, "Quick, bring out the best robe we have and put it on him; and put a ring on his hand, and sandals on his feet. And bring the fatted calf, and kill it; and let us eat and make merry. For this son of mine was dead, and he has come back to life; he was lost, and is found."

Suddenly the younger son comes to himself, becomes himself, in realizing how lost he is, though he is not so lost as to feel that he can't return to his father. No sooner does he realize that he can return, than he *does* return; no sooner does he realize that he is unworthy to be called his father's son, than the father runs to him and embraces him and treats him like the most worthy of sons. "You are my beloved son; this day I have begotten you."

I don't want to suggest that Jesus be identified only with the younger son. It is also true that he is the father, that wonderful figure whose delicate, loving treatment of the older son calls for as much admiration as his unconditional acceptance of the younger son. And he is also the older son, whose grievances are stated harshly but fairly, and whom the parable treats with the tolerance and respect so disastrously lacking in the inauthentic Gospel sayings about the righteous. But if we look for the parable's center of gravity, we can recognize that Jesus is the younger son at least as much as he is the father. And when the son returns to the father, all his shame and sorrow and unworthiness are taken up into the father's uncontainable joy. At this point, the story steps out of the son's consciousness into the father's; in a sense, the son becomes the father. There is no longer any difference between the exhilaration of being forgiven and the joy of forgiving.

One further question about the parable cries out to be asked, and Erik Erikson has asked it acutely:

> Even lengthy parables can be summarized in a brief saying. I think the last dozen words of the Prodigal Son will do: "Your brother was dead, and is alive; he was lost, and is found." Again, then, the Way is "within" and "amidst you." And the Abba was steadfast in loving both these sons—so different in familial status and in personality. Almost a mother, some readers may be tempted to say, and, indeed, as one reviews this parable's theme of the healing of the generational process, one cannot help asking: was there, in this earthly vision of the comparison, no mother, either dead or alive? And if alive, was she not called to say hello, too?

As in the parable, so in Jesus' life. After he returned to his Father, was there no mother to greet him? I would like to consider this question next.

VII

Jesus gives us a most vivid example of what it feels like to live in the continual presence of love, in the present and only tense of the verb *God*. His teaching is lucid through and through. Or almost through and through. The one point of unclarity is the family; in particular, the mother. I don't mean this as a criticism of him, but as a simple perception. I would like to take a look at this unclarity, which allows us a rare insight into the workshop of his heart. But before I examine the relevant verses, I need to put them in perspective.

We can use different metaphors to describe the experience that changed Jesus. It is the kind of experience that all the great spiritual Masters have had, and want us to have as well. Jesus called this experience "entering the kingdom of God." We can also call it "rebirth" or "enlightenment" or "awakening." The images implicit in these words come from experiences that we all know: the birth of a child, the light of the sun, the passage from sleep to what we ordinarily call consciousness. Any of these images can be helpful in pointing to a realm of being which most people have forgotten. It *is* like being born into true life, or like the sun streaming into a room that has remained dark for a long time, or like waking up from a dream, or, as Jesus must have felt, like returning home to the Father. And each of these images contains a further truth, if we follow it attentively. Being reborn is only the first stage of a new life, and doesn't mean coming into full spiritual maturity: the infant has a lot of growing up to do before it is self-sufficient. Awakening doesn't necessarily mean arriving at full consciousness: the dreams are gone, but we may still be sleepy, and not truly alert. Or, to return to the image of sunlight passing through a window: the area that has been suddenly wiped clean of selfishness and self-protection—desires, fears, rules, concepts—may be the whole windowpane, or it may be a spot the size of a dime. The sunlight that shines through the small transparent spot is the same light that can shine through a whole windowpane, but there is much less of it, and if someone stands with his nose pressed to one of the other, opaque spots, he will hardly see any light at all.

Two examples. First, Paul of Tarsus, the greatest and yet the most misleading of the earliest Christian writers. It is obvious that Paul's experience on the road to Damascus was a genuine and powerful one. Who can deny the sunlight streaming through his famous praise of love in First Corinthians? And there are a number of other passages where his mind and heart are transparent. But Paul came to his experience with a particularly difficult character: arrogant, self-righteous, filled with murderous hatred of his opponents, terrified of God, oppressed by what he felt as the burden of the Law, overwhelmed by his sense of sin. In terms of the metaphor, his windowpane was caked with grime.

There are things I admire about Paul: his courage, his passion, his loving concern for the Gentiles, his great eloquence, the incredible energy with which he whirled around the Mediterranean for, as he thought, the glory of God. But in a spiritual sense, he was very unripe. The narrow-minded, fire-breathing, self-tormenting Saul was still alive and kicking inside him. He didn't understand Jesus at all. He wasn't even *interested* in Jesus; just in his own idea of the Christ. "Even though we once knew Christ according to the flesh," he wrote, "we no longer regard him in this way." In other words, it isn't relevant to know Jesus as a person of flesh and blood or to hear, much less do, what he taught; the only thing necessary for a Christian is to believe that Jesus was the Son of God and that he died in atonement for our sins. Like the writer of Revelation, Paul harbored a great deal of violence in his mind, which he projected onto visions of cosmic warfare, and onto an image of God as a punitive father. And he most ignorantly believed in what Spinoza describes as "a prince, God's enemy, who against God's will entraps and deceives very many men, whom God then hands over to this master of wickedness to be tortured for eternity." After his conversion, there was indeed a transparent area in his mind, but much of the window was still opaque. And since he thought he was in possession of the truth, he made no effort to clean the rest of the window. The experience that should have been just the beginning of his spiritual life became the beginning and the end of it. We can feel in the writings of Paul the Christian some of the same egotism, superstition, and intolerance that marred the character of Saul the Pharisee.

As a second and contrary example, perhaps the greatest example of patience and meticulousness in the history of religion, I would like to propose Chao-chou, who lived during the golden age of Zen in T'ang dynasty China. He experienced enlightenment in 795, when he was seventeen years old, then remained with his teacher for forty years, refining his insight and gradually dissolving his opacities and character flaws. Zen Master Kuei-shan, his contemporary, describes this process:

> Through meditation a student may gain thoughtless thought, become suddenly enlightened, and realize his original nature. But there is still a basic delusion. Therefore he should be taught to eliminate the manifestations of karma, which cause the remaining delusion to rise to the surface. There is no other way of cultivation.

Anyone who has undergone the experience of spiritual transformation knows how agonizing it can be. It is like cleaning the heart with a piece of steel wool. Or like that terrace in Dante's *Purgatorio* where the spirits who have stopped for a while to talk, dive back into the flames. They choose to return to the excruciating pain, to stand again in the pale blue archways of primal grief or rage where the heat is the greatest, because their most ardent wish is to be burned free of all self-absorption, and ultimately to disappear, into God's love. (The fire is consciousness.)

After his teacher died, Chao-chou remained in the monastery for a three-year mourning period; then he set out on a twenty-year pilgrimage to hone himself against the greatest Masters of his time. He said, in words that must have shocked the hierarchical and age-venerating Confucian mind, "If I meet a hundred-year-old man and I have something to teach him, I will teach; if I meet an eight-year-old boy and he has something to teach me, I will learn." Only when he was eighty years old did he feel mature enough to set up shop as a teacher. He taught for the next forty years, and his sayings are a marvel of lucidity, compassion, and humor.

Jesus must have undergone a good deal of spiritual development outside the story that has come down to us, before his enlightenment experience. After it, there was still one place of vivid pain and darkness left in his heart, a residual sorrow from his childhood: one area of dust on an otherwise transparent windowpane. I will suggest that he later came, at least unconsciously, to a resolution of his family drama. But even if the dust remained, it doesn't detract from him. All of us have our assignments to complete, whether they are big or little. That Jesus was unclear on one point, that he couldn't yet fulfill the commandment to honor father and mother, shouldn't be shocking, even for devout Christians. "Therefore he had to become like his fellow humans in every way," the author of the Epistle to the Hebrews says. He was so young when he died. And he had so little time.

From this perspective, then, of relative and complete clarity, I would like to examine Jesus' relationship with his family.

Just as there is no mother in the parable of the Prodigal Son, Mary of Nazareth is almost completely absent from Jesus' life and words. When she does appear, once, in the authentic accounts of him, the incident is a painful one. The few times that he mentions her, his words are cool, even hostile. Here again, the evidence is scattered across the Gospels; it needs to be assembled before we can see the connections.

To begin with, the relevant verses:

• When someone says to Jesus, "Your mother and your brothers are outside, asking for you," he refuses to let them enter the house and says, pointing to his disciples, "*These* are my mother and my brothers. Whoever does the will of God is my brother, and sister, and mother." This statement is usually seen as an admirable instance of Jesus' fellowship with the community of believers. It may be that; but it is also, and primarily, I think, a rejection of his actual mother and brothers.

• When a woman in a crowd calls out, "Blessed is the womb that bore you and the breasts that gave you suck," Jesus says, "No: blessed rather are those who hear the word of God and obey it." Again, there may be a lesson here for the pious. But we can hear the subtext, and we can almost feel Jesus bristling at the woman's remark.

• He laments that "a prophet is not rejected [dishonored, treated with contempt] except in his own town and in his own family and in his own house."

• His teaching about loyalty to parents is uniformly negative, and is so shocking, not only to religious sensibilities but to our ordinary sense of decency, that it is almost never mentioned in church. When it *is* mentioned, it is softened, interpreted, and bent into an appropriately pious shape. But Jesus' words themselves are unambiguous:

> And as they were traveling along the road, he said to a certain man, "Follow me."
> And the man said, "Let me first go and bury my father."
> But Jesus said to him, "Let the dead bury their dead." [That is, "Let the spiritually dead bury their relatives who are physically dead."]
> Another man said to Jesus, "I will follow you, sir, but let me first say good-bye to my family."
> And Jesus said to him, "No one who puts his hand to the plow and then looks back is ready for the kingdom of God."

Jesus' point here is that we have to be ready to give up everything if we want to enter the kingdom of God. That is quite true. He said the same thing elsewhere, wonderfully, in his image of the merchant who found the pearl of great price and went and sold everything he had and bought it. What is shocking here is his timing: the words "Let the dead bury their dead," addressed to a man whose father has just died, are like a slap in the face. Even Job's comforters knew when to remain silent. And surely Jesus could have allowed the second man to say good-bye to his wife and children.

This teaching about cutting off all family ties is epitomized by a verse in Luke: "If anyone comes to me and doesn't hate his own father and mother and wife and children and brothers and sisters and even his own life, he can't be my disciple." The sentiment is even stronger in a verse (with a Gnostic spin on it) from the Gospel of Thomas: "Whoever doesn't hate his father and his mother as I do can't become my disciple. And whoever doesn't love his true Father [God] and his true Mother [the Holy Spirit] as I do can't become my disciple. For my mother gave me death, but my true Mother gave me life."

The fairest and most positive summary of this aspect of Jesus' teaching was made by George Bernard Shaw, of all people:

> Get rid of your family entanglements. Every mother you meet is as much your mother as the woman who bore you. Every man you meet is as much your brother as the man she bore after you. Don't waste your time at family funerals grieving for your relatives: attend to life, not death: there are as good fish in the sea as ever came out of it, and better. In the kingdom of heaven, which, as aforesaid, is within you, there is no marriage nor giving in marriage, because you cannot devote your life to two divinities: God and the person you are married to.

All this is true in a certain way, true for certain people or at certain stages of life. It is especially appropriate for young adults, who often need a moratorium to sort out their various confusions, and for those extremely rare people who have arrived at a sense of wholeness with their sexuality and want to devote themselves to a life of contemplation. But it is also untrue. However much I see all women as my mothers, I have a special bond with my flesh-and-blood mother, and if I don't honor it with my full attention, the flow of my love will be obstructed, and a portion of my heart will remain opaque. Nor is it true to say that in the kingdom of heaven there is no marriage. Marriage is one of the most direct paths to and in the kingdom of heaven. When I can truly devote myself to my wife, I *am* devoting myself to God, because all love is the love of God. "For the mature person, the Tao begins in the relation between man and woman, and ends in the infinite vastness of the universe."

Of course, many men, in many religious traditions, have felt a powerful conflict between family life and religious life; that is why celibacy has traditionally been seen as the most direct path to God. But, as anyone who reads Paul or Augustine knows, it is one thing to give up sex with your body and quite another to give it up in your mind. In the same way, it is one thing to leave your parents and quite another to let go of them in your mind. Abraham is the symbol for the latter, complete liberation: because he is able to leave his father's house forever, he is given an eternal blessing from God.

A couple of months after I began studying with my old Zen Master, he said to me, "You have three jobs here. Your first job is to kill the Buddha." I had read that phrase in the old Zen teachings, and I knew what it meant—to let go of any concepts of a separate, superior, enlightened being outside myself. Then he said, "Your second job is to kill your parents."

"What does that mean?" I asked.

"As long as there is anything you want from your parents," he said, "or anything about them that upsets you, they will be an obstacle in your mind. 'Killing your parents' means accepting them just as they are. They enter your mind like an image reflected on the water. No ripples."

"It sounds very difficult."

"Only if you think it is," he said.

Then he said, "Your third job is to kill me."

It is, in fact, possible to leave everything without leaving anything. We learn this from the teachings of the great Masters, and we can know it for ourselves, through our own experience. It is only for people in the more arduous stages of transformation that there is a conflict. Even when we understand the concern for wholeheartedness that caused Jesus to teach as he did about family, we can recognize an extreme quality, a lack of balance, an off-centeredness, in the tone of these sayings that almost begs us to consider them in the realm not of spiritual teaching but of psychology.

The clearest statements I have found about attachment to home and family occur in the teaching of Ramana Maharshi. A beginner once said to him, "I want to give up my job and family and stay with you, sir, so that I can be with God." Maharshi said, "God is always with you, in you. That is what you should realize."

Questioner: But I feel the urge to give up all attachments and renounce the world.

Maharshi: Renunciation doesn't mean giving away your money or abandoning your home. True renunciation is the renunciation of desires, passions, and attachments.

Questioner: But single-minded devotion to God may not be possible unless one leaves worldly things.

Maharshi: No: a true renunciate actually merges in the world and expands his love to embrace the whole world. It would be more correct to describe the attitude of the devotee as universal love than as abandoning home to become a monk.

Questioner: At home the bonds of affection are too strong.

Maharshi: If you renounce home when you aren't ripe for it, you only create new bonds.

Questioner: Isn't renunciation the supreme means of breaking attachments?

Maharshi: That may be so for someone whose mind is already free from entanglements. But you haven't grasped the deeper meaning of renunciation. Great souls who have abandoned their homes have done so not out of aversion to family life, but because of their largehearted and all-embracing love for all mankind and all creatures.

Questioner: Family ties will have to be left behind sometime, so why shouldn't I take the initiative and break them now, so that my love can be equal toward all people?

Maharshi: When you truly feel this equal love for all, when your heart has expanded so much that it embraces the whole of creation, you will certainly not feel like giving up this or that. You will simply drop off from secular life as a ripe fruit drops from the branch of a tree. You will feel that the whole world is your home.

I have already quoted a verse from the one incident in which Mary appears. This incident requires closer attention. It begins with one of the most hair-raising verses in the Gospels:

> And when his family heard [about all this], they went to seize him, for they said, "He is out of his mind."

Hidden inside this verse is a world of misunderstanding and disappointment. Actually, it is a miracle that the verse survived at all, to speak to us. It appears only in Mark; both Matthew and Luke apparently found it so shocking that they deleted it from their accounts. (Even in Mark, the transcribers of two of the best ancient manuscripts were so embarrassed by it that they altered it to read, "And when *the scribes and the others* heard about him, they went to seize him, for they said, 'He is out of his mind.' ")

What is happening here? We can't be certain of the details, because we don't know what Mary and Jesus' brothers heard that troubled them so much. Perhaps it had to do with his healings and exorcisms at Capernaum; perhaps a neighbor had watched one of the treatments and had returned to Nazareth with a frightened report about the strange sounds Jesus had uttered or the physical contortions he had gone through. Or perhaps there were rumors of his bizarre and incomprehensible doctrines: that the pure in heart can actually see God, or that adults should be like children, or that the kingdom of God has already come. Whatever it was that they heard, they concluded that he had gone insane. So, like any responsible family, concerned for his well-being and wanting to prevent him from harming himself or others, they went out to "seize" him and bring him back home (the Greek verb is a strong one, and is used later in Mark, of the troops in Gethsemane, with the meaning "to arrest").

And his mother and his brothers arrived, and standing outside, they sent in a message asking for him.
And the people in the crowd sitting around him said to him, "Your mother and your brothers are outside and want to see you."
And Jesus said, "Who are my mother and my brothers?" And looking at those who sat in a circle around him, he said, "*These* are my mother and my brothers. Whoever does the will of God is my brother, and sister, and mother."

When Jesus' mother and brothers arrive at Capernaum, he is in a house, teaching, with a crowd of disciples and sympathizers around him. The crowd is so large that Mary and the brothers can't enter, so they send in a message, asking him to come out; their intention is to "seize" him and take him home to Nazareth. When he is told that they are waiting for him, Jesus' response is, in effect, to disown them. Of course, it isn't difficult to see Jesus' point: that he loves those who do God's will more than he loves even his own mother (if she were not to do God's will). We can realize the truth of this teaching, on the absolute level—it is true in the same sense in which the primal commandment to love

God with *all* one's heart is true — and at the same time recognize, on the relative level, the lack of wholeness, of healedness, in its antagonistic tone. This note of irritation was already pointed out by the heretic Mani in the fourth-century *Debates of Archelaus, Bishop of Mesopotamia, and the Heresiarch Mani*:

> Mani said, "Someone once said to Jesus, 'Your mother and your brothers are outside,' and Jesus did not kindly receive the person who said this, but indignantly rebuked him, saying, 'Who are my mother and my brothers?'"

Christian scholars have felt such a compelling need to justify Jesus' conduct that they haven't really taken it in. The Jewish scholar C. G. Montefiore is more objective, though in his comment there is an element of blame:

> It has been urged that the harsh bearing of Jesus towards his mother and family may be explained and justified on the grounds (a) that his family did not understand or believe in his mission, (b) that his whole soul was so filled with this mission that there was no room in it for family ties and interests, and (c) (the most important of all) that his special work implied and demanded a separation from, an abandonment of, all worldly connections and occupations.
>
> Yet when all is said, there is a certain violation or *froissement* of Jewish sentiment as to parents in this passage, and it is strange to find Jesus, who acts so dubiously towards his own mother, afterwards [Mark 7:9ff.] reproaching the Pharisees with not honoring father and mother! Even if the explanations of his conduct given above are adequate, Jesus might have explained matters to his mother and family quietly and in private, whereas he, in order to score a point, put them to open shame and humiliation. . . . No Jew who remains a Jew can well believe that the conduct of Jesus in this story, however justified in its essential issues, was justified in detail, blameless and exquisite in method.

But there is no reason to blame Jesus for his conduct. What is important is to see it clearly. His rejection of his mother seems to me an early, inadequate response to what he must have felt as her rejection of him, her incomprehension of who he had become. Or perhaps it goes back further, to his childhood. Perhaps it contains an unconscious or half-conscious element of blame for the stigma of his birth, and was part of his distancing himself from his shame and everything connected with it.

When someone undergoes a spiritual transformation, he or she is truly reborn. The shape of the personality may be the same, and a residue of unfinished karmic business may still be there, but in the depths, the old, self-preoccupied self is dead and there is a wholly new awareness. Integration of this new self into one's life and family and society is the greatest and most difficult challenge in spiritual practice. (The work may take seven years or seven lifetimes, but people who are in love with God do it gladly; as in the story of Jacob and Rachel, the years "seemed to him only a few days, so great was his love for her.") It is particularly difficult with parents, who are deeply invested in creating us in their own image, and see only the former self who was their child. How can they understand that one's roots have grown deeper than the family, have penetrated beyond birth and death? Incomprehension is a given, except in very rare instances. The question is how one deals with the incomprehension.

While no other great spiritual teacher I know of had to face such a difficult childhood as Jesus did, all others had to give up their attachments to personal relationships, especially to the powerful centrifugal force of the family. Departures are often painful, and those who are left behind feel betrayed or abandoned. We can't help that. But if, like Abraham, we live in the place from which it is impossible to depart, we can make our departure an act of love. We are "ahead of all parting," as Rilke put it, and not only for ourselves. How poignant is the moment in the life of the Buddha when Gautama, knowing he has to leave his beloved wife and set out to solve the great question of life and death, leans over her sleeping body and kisses her on the cheek, one last time. But if he hadn't left, he could never have awakened and helped countless others to awaken, including her.

Jesus' return to his family after his baptism experience must have been as painful as his subsequent return to Nazareth. We have an account of the latter, and it is a story of rejection:

> From there he went to Nazareth, his native town, and his disciples followed him.
>
> And when the Sabbath came, he began to teach in the synagogue, and many people who heard him were bewildered, and said, "Where does this fellow get such stuff?" and "What makes *him* so wise?" and "How can he be a miracle-worker? Isn't this the carpenter, Mary's bastard, the brother of James and Joseph and Judas and Simon, and aren't his sisters here with us?" And they were prevented from believing in him.
>
> And Jesus said, "A prophet is not rejected except in his own town and in his own family and in his own house."
>
> And he was unable to do any miracle there, because of their disbelief.

In this story, the people of Nazareth can't believe that the Jesus whom they knew as an illegitimate child has been transformed into a prophet. They see him through the distorting lens of the past, and therefore are completely unaware of his presence. We aren't told whether Mary or any of Jesus' brothers or sisters were in the synagogue on this occasion. But the reaction of the townspeople is similar to the family's reaction. (In a different context, the Gospel of John says that "even his own brothers didn't believe in him.")

There is a striking comment on the Nazareth incident by Zen Master Ma-tzu (709–788), who of course had never heard of Jesus:

> Don't return to your native town:
> you can't teach the truth there.
> By the village stream an old woman
> is calling you by your childhood name.

This little poem is both lovely and poignant in its acceptance of a psychological given: that even the greatest Master may still appear to his family as the child he was—small, needy, untransformed.

With both his family and the people of Nazareth, Jesus' reaction is to depart and shake off the dust from his feet. But this seems to me a provisional attitude, and I think he held to it as a matter of protection, while he was coming to full inner ripeness. There is a traditional Hindu metaphor that clarifies two appropriate stages:

> When the young plant is just sprouting out of the seed or is still weak and tender, it requires seclusion and the protection of a strong thorny fence to keep off cattle that might otherwise eat it or trample upon and destroy it. But the same shoot, when it develops into a large tree, dispenses with such protection and itself affords shade, sustenance, and protection to cattle and men, without detriment to itself.

At this later stage, detachment and filial piety aren't mutually exclusive. When someone has found freedom in his heart, everything that was once an obstacle—parents, money, sex—becomes an opportunity for a further degree of surrender. We can sense this freedom in Jesus' parables, when he speaks of Samaritans and sinners. And we feel that someone as largehearted and compassionate as he was would surely have been able to fulfill both the commandment to love God with all his heart and the commandment to honor his mother. John the Evangelist was so convinced of this that he imagined Mary at the foot of the Cross, and imagined Jesus, in almost his final words, placing her in the care of the "disciple whom he loved." That is what gives his account a sense of personal closure that the other three Gospels don't have. When we love someone, we wish him all possible peace and wholeness in his heart. And we want him, before he dies, to have finished his earthly business, which is, after all, his Father's business as well.

VIII

Before I return to Jesus and Mary, I would like to say a little more about forgiveness.

It is Jesus' most important teaching for those who aren't ready to enter the kingdom of God, as Blake recognized:

> There is not one moral virtue that Jesus inculcated but Plato and Cicero did inculcate before him. What then did Christ inculcate? Forgiveness of sins. This alone is the gospel and this is the life and immortality brought to light by Jesus, even the covenant of Jehovah, which is this: if you forgive one another your trespasses, so shall Jehovah forgive you, that he himself may dwell among you.

Forgiveness is a sign pointing us toward that kingdom. We ask Jesus, *How should we live?* He says, *Love God, love your neighbor.* We ask, *What is that like?* He says, *Let go.* Letting go of an offense means letting go of the self that is offended.

There are only a few passages in which Jesus mentions forgiveness, but they are central. In all of them, he is teaching *us* forgiveness; it is never a question of *his* forgiving sins. The two passages in which Jesus himself is said to forgive sins—the stories of the man sick with palsy, and of the repentant sinner who wets Jesus' feet with her tears—probably derive from the church's image of him as a divine being. The most that Jesus could have taught these two unhappy people would be to forgive them-selves. Or he could have said, as a provisional teaching, that God had forgiven them. But actually, forgiveness is an experience that happens only outside the kingdom of God. If you have to let go, then there was something to hold on to. Where there is no offense to begin with, there is nothing to forgive. It is more ac-curate to say that inside the kingdom of God there is only accep-tance.

In Jesus' sayings, it may seem as if God's forgiveness is depen-dent on ours. "Forgive us our wrongs, as we forgive those who have wronged us." "For if you forgive others their offenses, your heavenly Father will forgive you." "If you don't judge, you will not be judged; if you don't condemn, you will not be con-demned; if you forgive, you will be forgiven." But these *ifs* have only one side, like a Möbius strip. Jesus doesn't mean that if you do condemn, God will condemn *you*; or that if you don't forgive, God won't forgive *you*. He is pointing to a spiritual fact: when we condemn, we create a world of condemnation for ourselves, and we attract the condemnation of others; when we cling to an of-fense, we are clinging to precisely what separates us from our own fulfillment. Letting go means not only releasing the person who has wronged us, but releasing ourselves. A place opens up inside us where that person is always welcome, and where we can always meet her again, face to face.

In these sayings of Jesus, God is a mirror reflecting back to us our own state of being. We receive exactly what we give. The more openhearted we are, the more we can experience the whole universe as God's grace. Forgiveness is essentially openness of heart. It is an attitude, not an action.

> Peter once asked him, "Sir, how often should I forgive my brother if he keeps wronging me? Up to seven times?"
>
> And Jesus said to him, "Not just seven: seventy times seven."

It doesn't arise from morality, but from vision; it doesn't require effort, but is itself the inexhaustible energy of life.

> Why did the ancient Masters esteem the Tao?
> Because, being one with the Tao,
> when you seek, you find;
> and when you make a mistake, you are forgiven.
> That is why everybody loves it.

This is the vivid experience of everyone who lives in harmony with the way things are. What does it mean to say that when we are at one with the Tao we are forgiven? As soon as we make a mistake, we become aware of it, we admit it, and we correct it, on the spot. Thus there is no residue.

Attitude precedes action and generates it. The Buddhists are particularly adept at cultivating the mind of universal compassion, and have a scripture, the Metta Sutta (the Scripture of Lovingkindness), which could be seen as a meticulous commentary on the above-quoted verse from the Lord's Prayer: "Forgive us our wrongs, as we forgive those who have wronged us." It includes a directed meditation in which the meditator is asked to open his heart and, first, forgive himself for any wrong he has ever committed, in thought, word, or deed. Then he is asked to forgive anyone who has ever wronged him and to let go of the offense completely. Finally he is asked to send lovingkindness to his enemies and all those he dislikes, and to all beings in the universe, humans and animals and plants and paramecia and all other unimaginable life forms, and to wish them perfect joy. (Anyone who finds it difficult to forgive should try the effects of doing this meditation every day, for ten or twenty years.)

Jesus' most profound and moving statement on forgiveness is, again, the parable of the Prodigal Son. There is no explicit mention of forgiveness in it. But its point is obvious: the father's heart has always been open. When he runs to embrace the younger son, he is not *doing* anything; he is simply expressing what he has always felt. And once the son returns, he doesn't have to do a thing to earn his father's forgiveness. Forgiveness is already fully there, in the embrace, before the son can even open his mouth to beg it.

This teaching about forgiveness is not new to Judaism, but in the parable of the Prodigal Son it is stated with the greatest clarity and depth. As with any image or metaphor that tries to illuminate a three-dimensional human truth, the light shines on just one side. Jesus' emphasis is on the father's joy, which we can feel bursting through every vessel in his body as he forgets his patriarchal dignity and rushes out to welcome his returning son.

The prophets illuminate another side. They portray Israel as a wife, and God as a husband who forgives her. In Second Isaiah, the wife has been abandoned for a long time (we aren't told why); but God ultimately has compassion on her and takes her back "with eternal love." Jeremiah's image is more detailed, and more shocking: Israel has betrayed God and is like an unfaithful wife; she has been promiscuous; she has acted like a whore. But God's love, says Jeremiah, is unfailing. Though Israel has been unfaithful, God is not unfaithful. If only Israel will return to him, he will take her into his arms again, as a beloved wife.

The prophets' image doesn't express the profound joy that we feel in Jesus' image of the father. But the father hasn't been wronged directly and personally, as the God of the prophets has. The aspect of the truth which this image illuminates is that God's love, and therefore ours, can forgive anything. Imagine the worst offense possible: imagine being betrayed by the person you loved and trusted the most, imagine the most painful sexual wound you can possibly experience. Even this, the prophets are saying, can be transformed into absolute forgiveness. All Israel, all each of us, needs to do is to return to the love that is always ready to receive us.

The most powerful of the prophetic images occurs at the beginning of Hosea. "Go take a whore as your wife," God tells the prophet abruptly. The voice comes out of nowhere. There is no prologue, and only the starkest of explanations to soften the shock and urgency of the command. "Marry her and have children with her, because this land has acted like a whore." Here the image is hair-raising not only because of its savage bluntness but, even more, because its intent is not to stay in the realm of images. Hosea is commanded to enact it; the word has to become flesh. In surrendering everything, he allows his whole life to become a metaphor. And eventually, through his love for his unfaithful wife, he is able to fathom God's forgiveness in the depths of his own heart, and to become its perfect embodiment.

> "I will marry you to myself forever; I will marry you to myself in righteousness and justice, in love and compassion; I will marry you to myself in faithfulness; and you will know the Unnamable."

IX

In Jesus' sayings, and in his one recorded meeting with his mother, it is apparent that he hasn't yet forgiven her. His gruffness, his resistance to anything that has to do with family, indicate that he hasn't let go.

We have no explicit information about how or whether he came to a more mature resolution of the relationship. In the Synoptic Gospels, Mary simply disappears from the picture.

But there is a hint: the story of the Woman Caught in Adultery.

> The next morning, as Jesus was teaching in the Temple, the scribes brought a woman who had been caught in adultery, and they stood her in the middle. And they said to him, "Rabbi, this woman was caught in adultery, in the very act. Moses in the Law commanded us to stone such women to death; what do *you* say?"

But Jesus stooped down and with his finger wrote on the ground.

And as they continued to question him, he stood up and said to them, "Let whoever of you is sinless be the first to throw a stone at her." And again he stooped down and wrote on the ground.

And when they heard this, they went out one by one, the older ones first. And Jesus was left alone, with the woman still standing there.

And Jesus stood up, and said to her, "Woman, where are they? Has no one condemned you?"

And she said, "No one, sir."

And Jesus said, "I don't condemn you either. Go now, and sin no more."

This famous passage has the strangest history of any text in the Gospels. It doesn't appear in any of the most ancient manuscripts, and seems to have been circulating as a free-floating piece of oral tradition until the end of the fourth century, when it began to be added to the written Gospels. Most scribes ineptly tacked it on to the Gospel of John, after 7:52 (this is where it appears in the Textus Receptus, and hence in the King James version), though some placed it after 7:36 or 7:44 or 21:25. One insightful scribe placed it after Luke 21:38, recognizing that the passage is written in a style very different from John's, and more like Luke's. On external evidence, then, the story has only a shaky claim to authenticity. Nevertheless, the best scholars agree that it "has all the earmarks of historical veracity."

Three details seem to me especially convincing. The first is Jesus' gesture of writing on the ground, which has eluded scholars and theologians for at least sixteen centuries. The very fact that it has no obvious meaning is evidence for its authenticity, since subtlety of this kind is never present in the church's stories, in which "Jesus" becomes more and more supernatural as the decades go on. I can't imagine any disciple inventing a Jesus who has to think and doodle on the ground. This gesture was, in fact, so irritating or baffling to some Christian exegetes that they converted it into another superhuman display: according to them, what Jesus wrote on the ground was the sins of all the accusing scribes.

The second detail is the statement "Let whoever of you is sinless be the first to throw a stone at her." Here Jesus is including himself with all human beings, as capable of making mistakes. He is certainly not saying, "Only I, who am sinless, have the right to throw a stone at her," but rather "None of us has the right." Blake, in "The Everlasting Gospel," makes this point explicit by prefacing it with Jesus' statement in Mark 10:18 that "No one is good except God alone":

> "Thou [God] art good and Thou alone,
> Nor may the sinner cast one stone."

The third detail is the final statement, "I don't condemn you either." If this were a creation of the early church, like Luke's story of the repentant sinner, it would have had Jesus say, "Your sins are forgiven," and make the story's focal point the doctrine that "the Son of Man has the authority on earth to forgive sins." Here, Jesus correctly understands that forgiveness is not the issue, since the woman has committed no offense against him. "I don't condemn you" doesn't mean "I forgive you." Only her husband was in a position to forgive her, since only he was wronged.

In the story of the adulteress, Jesus is brought face to face with a woman who symbolically and psychologically stands for his mother. She too has committed adultery, and he is being asked to judge her. Since our attitudes and actions toward people of the opposite sex are a reflection of our unconscious attitudes toward our parent of the opposite sex, I feel that Jesus couldn't have treated the adulteress as he did, with love and absolute nonjudgment, if he hadn't first, somewhere in his depths, forgiven Mary. If such a transformation took place, before this incident or during it, it was as important as the one he underwent at his baptism. There, he felt forgiven by his Father; here, he was able to forgive his mother. And if the one insightful scribe was correct in placing the incident after Luke 21:38, it has even greater significance. It is the last event we are told about in the authentic accounts of Jesus, before his arrest and crucifixion. It may have been the last teaching he ever gave.

When John the Evangelist has Jesus look down from the cross and place his mother in the care of the "disciple whom he loved," he is describing a scene which has no basis in historical reality, a scene imagined by his own very touching piety, out of his desire for it to be true. Perhaps that is what I have done here. Perhaps the story of the adulteress never actually took place. Or if it did, it is possible that Jesus was able to see her with a nonjudgmental love and still, in some hidden corner of his heart, keep holding on to his rejection of his mother.

But I don't think that someone who had experienced forgiveness as Jesus had, someone whose teachings about it have the depth and beauty that his teachings do, would himself have been unable to forgive. If this story gives us no historical information, it can nevertheless serve as a symbolic reminder of how we must come to peace with parents, lovers, friends and enemies, and with the most difficult, unlovable parts of ourselves. The more fully we accept them and thus let them go, the more light we allow into our hearts. And as Paul said about each of us, in one of his most transparent insights, "When all things are made whole in the Son, then he will be wholly included in the Father, so that God may be All in all."

NOTES

General Note: All translations in this book are mine unless otherwise indicated. The Lao-tzu translations come from my *Tao Te Ching: A New English Version*, Harper & Row, 1988. If no source is indicated, the translation comes from *The Enlightened Mind: An Anthology of Sacred Prose*, HarperCollins, 1991, or is published here for the first time.

p. 3, Ming dynasty watercolor: "Bird-watching," by the Zen-Taoist monk Tao-chi. (See Marilyn Fu and Wen Fong, *The Wilderness Colors of Tao-chi*, Metropolitan Museum of Art, 1973.) Actually, this watercolor was painted between 1697 and 1700, five decades after the fall of the Ming dynasty in 1644; but I think of it as Ming because Tao-chi was a member of the Ming imperial family.

p. 4, version of the Gospels:

> On 4 February 1804 he received two sets of the New Testament . . . and by 10 March the compilation was finished and bound. (Dickinson W. Adams, ed., *Jefferson's Extracts from the Gospels*, Princeton University Press, 1983, p. 27)

p. 4, He took up the project again:

> I made, for my own satisfaction, an extract from the Evangelists of the text of his morals, selecting those only whose style and spirit proved them genuine, and his own: and they are as distinguishable from the matter in which they are embedded as diamonds in dunghills. A more precious morsel of ethics was never seen. It was too hastily done however, being the work of one or two evenings only, while I lived at Washington,

overwhelmed with other business: and it is my intention to go over it again at more leisure. This shall be the work of the ensuing winter. (To Francis Adrian Van der Kemp, April 25, 1816)

p. 4, The Life and Morals of Jesus of Nazareth: Commonly known as *The Jefferson Bible*.

p. 4, private correspondence: For some of Jefferson's other statements on Jesus, see Appendix 1, pp. 278ff.

p. 5, To the corruptions of Christianity: To Dr. Benjamin Rush, April 21, 1803.

p. 5, added to, deleted, altered, and otherwise tampered with: Additions: Most of what "Jesus" says in the Gospels, from his first words to his words on the cross. Deletions: The most important example of a deleted passage is Mark 3:21, absent in both Matthew and Luke. Alterations: Jesus in Mark 10:18 says, "Why do you call me good? No one is good except one: God"; Matthew (19:17) changes this to "Why do you ask me about the good? There is One who is good." (See Commentary, pp. 232f.)

As for the "tricks" played with the texts of other books relating to the Gospels, Jefferson may have been referring to the Testimonium Flavianum. This famous paragraph about Jesus, which has been recognized as a Christian forgery since the sixteenth century, was inserted into the text of the first-century Jewish historian Josephus's *Jewish Antiquities* to replace Josephus's own account of Jesus, now lost to us.

p. 5, the official Gospels were compiled: The probable dates are: Mark, 65–70 C.E.; Matthew, c. 80–85; Luke, c. 85–90; John, c. 100. It seems to me certain that Matthew and Luke used the text (or *a* text) of Mark's Gospel as one source of their versions. But the relationship among the three is very complex. The best introduction to the subject is E. P. Sanders and Margaret Davies, *Studying the Synoptic Gospels*, Trinity Press International, 1989.

p. 5, teachings of the early church: How did Jesus' teaching get so distorted in the Gospels? This is a complicated story, and would require a book in itself to explain. (The most insightful study of the "Easter experience" is Thomas Sheehan, *The First Coming: How the Kingdom of God Became Christianity*, Random House, 1986.)

Briefly, what must have happened was this: Sometime after the crucifixion, Peter had an experience in which he became convinced that Jesus was somehow still alive, that he had been "raised" by God. Or perhaps the experience was Mary Magdalene's, and she told it to Peter and the other apostles. It may have been a sudden realization, which was later expressed in mythological terms as a physical resurrection and ascension into the sky. Or it may have been some kind of occult phenomenon, like the many documented apparitions of what we call ghosts. Whatever it was, it lifted the apostles from the depths of their grief and from some of their guilt at having abandoned Jesus after his arrest, and changed them into men and women of great courage and faith: the first Christians.

This transformation of the apostles is one of the cornerstones of Christian apologetics; and it is, to be sure, impressive and deeply moving. But we need to be aware of the *quality* of the transformation. It was what I would call a religious rather than a spiritual experience. That is, although it took the apostles from doubt and despair to faith, it didn't take them into the kingdom of God. "Every disciple who is fully taught will be like his teacher" (Luke 6:40). But they were nowhere near being fully taught. They only believed in, they hadn't experienced, God. And they still didn't understand Jesus' teaching. They thought that the kingdom of God was an external event, and that it was still to come; soon, very soon, but in the future. At first they believed that it would certainly come within their own lifetimes (Mark 9:1, I Thessalonians 4:15ff.). As their hope was gradually disappointed, they came to believe that the kingdom would come only after death, that, as Paul said,

"Flesh and blood can't inherit the kingdom of God" (I Corinthians 15:50), i.e., you can't enter the kingdom of God while you are alive.

The gospel they preached was not the good news which Jesus proclaimed. Instead of teaching God's presence, they preached "that Christ died for our sins, in accordance with the Scriptures; and that he was buried; and that he was raised on the third day, in accordance with the Scriptures; and that he appeared to Peter, and then to the Twelve" (I Corinthians 15:3ff.), and that he would soon return to judge the living and the dead. Instead of God's absolute love and forgiveness, they preached a god who condemned most of humankind to eternal damnation and would save only those who believed that Jesus was the Son of God.

p. 5, followed Jefferson's example: Tolstoy, too, compiled a Gospel harmony, which he called *The Gospels in Brief.* In describing his work, he used a metaphor strikingly similar to Jefferson's "diamonds from dunghills," though less harsh in its elaboration:

> When, at the age of fifty, I first began to study the Gospels seriously, I found in them the spirit that animates all who are truly alive. But along with the flow of that pure, life-giving water, I perceived much mire and slime mingled with it; and this had prevented me from seeing the true, pure water. I found that, along with the lofty teaching of Jesus, there are teachings bound up which are repugnant and contrary to it. I thus felt myself in the position of a man to whom a sack of garbage is given, who, after long struggle and wearisome labor, discovers among the garbage a number of infinitely precious pearls. This man knows that he is not blameworthy in his distaste for the dirt, and also that those who have gathered these pearls along with the rest of the sackful, and who have thus preserved them, are no more to blame than he is, but, on the contrary, deserve his love and respect.

See Appendix 1, pp. 288ff.

p. 6, Synoptic Gospels:

> Matthew, Mark, and Luke are called "synoptic" because they
> tell basically the same story in the same sequence, and often in
> the same precise wording. They can be studied side by side, in
> a book called "a synopsis" — "seeing together" — and from this
> type of aid for study they get their collective title.
>
> (Sanders and Davies, *Studying the Synoptic
> Gospels*, p. 3)

p. 6, Like the man in Bunyan's riddle: This simile comes from
George Bernard Shaw; see Appendix 1, p. 292.

p. 6, a remarkable degree of consensus: The most interesting con-
temporary project is the Jesus Seminar, which has already
published *The Parables of Jesus: Red Letter Edition*, Robert W.
Funk, Bernard Brandon Scott, and James R. Butts, eds., Pole-
bridge Press, 1988, and *The Gospel of Mark: Red Letter Edition*,
Robert W. Funk with Mahlon H. Smith, eds., Polebridge
Press, 1991. Seven further books are scheduled for publica-
tion: *The Wit and Wisdom of Jesus According to the Jesus Seminar*,
The Five Gospels: Red Letter Edition, *The Sayings Gospel Q: Red
Letter Edition*, *The Gospel of Thomas: Red Letter Edition*, *The
Gospel of Luke: Red Letter Edition*, *The Gospel of Matthew: Red
Letter Edition*, and *The Gospel of John: Red Letter Edition*.

In the Seminar, a hundred Gospel scholars have been discussing and voting on the authenticity of every saying of Jesus
that appears in the Gospels of Mark, Matthew, Luke, and
Thomas. Each saying receives a vote from each scholar, in the
form of a colored bead dropped into a voting box. Red means
that "Jesus undoubtedly said this or something very like it";
pink, that "Jesus probably said something like this"; gray, that
"Jesus did not say this, but the ideas contained in it are close to
his own"; black, that "Jesus did not say this; it represents the
perspective or content of a later or different tradition." Then
the scores are tabulated and the sayings ranked in order. Red
votes are worth three points, pink votes two, gray votes one,
and black votes zero. The parable of the Good Samaritan, for

example, the second-highest-ranking parable, received an average vote of 2.43, or 81 percent; while the fourth-lowest-ranking, the parable of the Dragnet, received an average vote of 0.36, or 12 percent.

Of the thirteen parables that the scholars ranked highest, as being most probably authentic, I have included nine in my Gospel; of the lowest-ranking twenty, I have included none.

As an example of an inauthentic parable, here is the above-mentioned parable of the Dragnet:

> The kingdom of heaven is like a net that was thrown into the sea and gathered fish of every kind; when it was full, the men pulled it ashore and sat down and put the good fish into baskets and threw the bad ones away. That is how it will be at the close of this age. The angels will come and separate the wicked from the righteous, and will throw them into the fiery furnace, where there will be wailing and gnashing of teeth. (Matthew 13:47ff.)

It doesn't require much insight to recognize that we are confronting a very different consciousness here than in, say, the parable of the Prodigal Son. The teller of the parable has no comprehension of the God who sends sun and rain to the unjust as well as to the just. He has split the universe into good and bad. When he contemplates the punishment of the wicked, he feels a moral titillation, the schadenfreude which later culminates in the doctrine that one of the principal amusements of the saints in heaven is looking down and watching the agony of the wicked. And his metaphor is amusingly inaccurate, since from the fish's (= the human's) viewpoint, being chosen for the basket is death, while being thrown back is life. (Or if the fish are being thrown not into the sea but onto a heap on the shore, it doesn't matter whether they are chosen or thrown away.)

p. 6, the strictly scholarly criteria: See Sanders and Davies, *Studying the Synoptic Gospels*, pp. 301ff.

p. 7, sublime ideas of the Supreme Being: To William Short, August 4, 1820.

p. 8, have caused good men to reject the whole: Jefferson to Dr. Benjamin Rush, April 21, 1803.

p. 8, the archetypal judge: Some scholars think that by "the Son of Man," "Jesus" meant an apocalyptic figure other than himself. Whether or not "Jesus" was referring to himself, he said that this figure will come "in the clouds with great power and glory. And then he will send out the angels and gather together the elect from the four winds, from the end of the earth to the end of the sky" (Mark 13:26f.). In one of Matthew's most moving and at the same time foulest parables, "Jesus" says that the Son of Man "will tell those on his left: 'Depart from me, cursed ones, into the everlasting fire that was prepared for the devil and his angels'" (Matthew 25:41).

This teaching about hell, which the church took over from a fierce, apocalyptic strand of Judaism, and which it here put into "Jesus'" mouth, proceeds from a very impure consciousness, filled with fantasies of hatred and revenge and of an unforgiving, unjust god whose punishments are insanely disproportionate to the offenses. There have always been theologians to justify this doctrine, though none of them has, like Dante, walked among the damned with horror and pity in his heart. Even Dante's exquisite music is sometimes too morally ugly to bear, as when he makes his sign over the Gates of Hell read *Justice was what moved my high Maker; / I was made by divine Might, / by supreme Wisdom and primal Love.*

If hell means anything in reality, it is the world of torment that humans create for themselves and for one another out of their own greed, hatred, and ignorance. It is not a physical place; it is a psychological metaphor.

There is a compassionate and very funny comment on hell in one of the dialogues of Zen Master Chao-chou:

A monk asked Chao-chou, "Is there any possibility, Master, that you will go to hell?"

Chao-chou said, "I'll be the first to go."

The monk said, "Master, why should you, a good and wise man, go to hell?"

Chao-chou said, "If I don't go, who will be there to teach you?"

p. 8, love of enemies: Matthew 5:44f.

p. 8, vituperation: For example, in Matthew 23:33.

p. 8, sons of God: Jesus never thought of himself as *the* son of God, much less as "the only-begotten Son of God."

Like the poet of Psalm 2, who has God say to the king, "You are my son; today I have begotten you," Jesus meant something entirely metaphorical when he said "son of God": someone who takes after God as a son takes after his father. If you truly love God, and treat your fellow human beings with respect and compassion, then you are a son (or daughter) of God. "Blessed are the peacemakers, for they will be called sons of God." "Love your enemies, do good to those who hate you, bless those who curse you, and pray for those who mistreat you, so that you may be sons of your Father in heaven." The more you are like God, the more you are a child of God.

This same sense of "son" or "child" of God, and of "begotten" as meaning "spiritually reborn," occurs in the Epistles, side by side with the later, Christological sense. We find it in the following passages:

To all who received him [the Word] and believed in his name, he gave the ability to become children of God—those who were begotten [or, born], not by blood, nor by the will of the flesh, nor by the will of a male, but by God. (John 1:12f.)

All who are led by the spirit of God are sons of God. (Romans 8:14)

In Christ Jesus I have begotten you through the Gospel. (I Corinthians 4:15)

I appeal to you about my child Onesimus, whom I have begotten in prison. (Philemon 1:10)

Of his own will he [God] gave birth to us by a word of truth. (James 1:18, where the image is of a mother rather than a father)

Praised be the God and Father of our Lord Jesus Christ, who in his great mercy has begotten us anew into a living hope . . . (I Peter 1:3)

See how great the love is that the Father has given us, so that we may be called children of God. (I John 3:1)

We know that everyone begotten by God does not sin. (I John 5:18)

And finally in Galatians 4:6, one of the most sincere and moving statements that Paul ever made:

And because [or, to show that] you are sons, God has sent forth the spirit of his son into our hearts, crying "Abba! Father!"

p. 8, reference to himself as a prophet: Mark 6:4 (also Luke 13:33, though the authenticity of this verse is doubtful). There are also several indications that he was regarded as a prophet by people who were open to his teachings (Mark 6:15, 8:28, Matthew 21:11, Luke 7:16,39).

p. 8, talks on and on about himself: Most of Jesus' self-referential sayings ("I am the bread of life," "I am the light of the world") occur in John's Gospel, though in the Synoptic Gospels we have such statements as "No man knows the Father but the Son" (Matthew 11:27). The most startling of all is from the Gospel of Thomas (Thomas, 77): "I am the light that shines over everything. I am the All. From me the All came forth, and to me the All has returned. Split a piece of wood, and I am there. Pick up a stone, and you will find me there." We should understand that the "I" of these passages is not the personal "I," but the great, transpersonal "I" of the Atman, the "I" of Buddha-consciousness.

But even if we read these expressions as they should be read, without confusing the speaker with the personal Jesus, we may very well sense an inflation in them, and feel like a mischievous four-year-old creeping up to a balloon with a pin.

We find similar statements in the Mahayana Buddhist tradition. Probably the best known is the one the infant Buddha is supposed to have uttered immediately after issuing from his mother's womb: "Above the heavens, below the heavens, only I am the Honored One." The tenth-century Zen Master Yunmen, famous for his deadly humor, was unwilling to let the tradition get away with this cosmic piety, and commented, "If I had been there when the Buddha said that, I would have chopped him into little pieces and fed him to a hungry dog."

p. 9, whoever blasphemes against the Holy Spirit: Mark 3:29. This sentence is probably responsible for more mental anguish than any other sentence in world literature.

For a brave, loving, and relatively clear nineteenth-century Christian attempt to reconcile it with the essential teachings of Jesus, see George MacDonald's sermon "It Shall Not Be Forgiven," in *Creation in Christ*, ed. Roland Hein, Harold Shaw Publishers, 1976, pp. 47ff. Along the same lines (and not considering its context in Mark), my friend the Benedictine monk David Steindl-Rast says:

> To my understanding of Jesus, this saying is crucial. For Jesus (not "Jesus"), the Holy Spirit bears witness in his hearers' hearts to the truth and to forgiveness—unconditional forgiveness. All the authentic parables are based on the understanding that Jesus' hearers are able "in the Holy Spirit" to understand "from within" what God is like. We cannot extinguish this Holy Spirit; it is the lifebreath of our lifebreath; but we can, as it were, "stop breathing." That is the sin which even God cannot forgive, because forgiveness is freely offered, not imposed.

p. 9, end of Mark: From the "longer ending" of Mark (16:9–20), which doesn't appear in the earliest and best manuscripts, and is now acknowledged by all reputable scholars to be a later addition, probably from the first half of the second century.

p. 9, Whoever believes and is baptized: Mark 16:16.

p. 9, In all ten directions of the universe: Stephen Mitchell, ed., *The Enlightened Heart: An Anthology of Sacred Poetry*, Harper & Row, 1989, p. 97.

p. 10, "unreachable," as the Upanishads say:

> Self is everywhere, shining forth out of all beings,
> vaster than the vast, subtler than the most subtle,
> unreachable, yet nearer than breath, than heartbeat.
> Eye cannot see it, ear cannot hear it nor tongue
> utter it; only in deep absorption can the mind,
> grown pure and silent, merge with the formless truth.
> He who finds it is free; he has found himself;
> he has solved the great riddle; his heart forever is at peace.
> Whole, he enters the Whole. His personal self
> returns to its radiant, intimate, deathless source.
> As rivers lose name and form when they disappear
> into the sea, the sage leaves behind all traces
> when he disappears into the light. Perceiving the truth,
> he becomes the truth; he passes beyond all suffering,
> beyond death; all the knots of his heart are loosed.
>
> (*The Enlightened Heart*, p. 4)

p. 10, God's true name is I am*:* Exodus 3:14. I am using the word *God* to point to the ultimate, unnamable reality that is the source and essence of all things. *God, Lord,* etc. unfortunately have behind them images of a human (male) potentate. The ancient Jews called this reality YHVH, which probably means "that which causes everything to exist," and which is marvelously unpronounceable. Lao-tzu uses female imagery, but he clearly states that all words are just crude pointers.

> There was something formless and perfect
> before the universe was born.
> It is serene. Empty.
> Solitary. Unchanging.
> Infinite. Eternally present.
> It is the mother of the universe.
> For lack of a better name,
> I call it the Tao.   (chapter 25)

p. 11, a man who had awakened from all dreams: In Buddhism, too, there are the dreamers and the awakened: those who only believe in the Buddha and those who have become Buddhas themselves. One sect, the Pure Land school, is remarkably like traditional Christianity. It teaches absolute dependence on the Buddha and absolute faith in him; those who surrender completely will be reborn in the Western Paradise, the Pure Land, where all is peace and joy.

But the most mature devotees of the Pure Land school have realized that, in the words of the eighteenth-century Japanese Zen Master Hakuin:

> Nirvana is right here, before our eyes;
> this very place is the Lotus Land;
> this very body, the Buddha.

p. 12, a kingdom of God in the future: Brother David Steindl-Rast says:

> Jesus could very well have made both these statements in close juxtaposition: the kingdom of God is coming and at the same time it has come. By "the kingdom of God" Jesus meant "God's saving power made manifest." Thus, the kingdom has come wherever that manifestation takes place—in our hearts, in our relationships, wherever we are given the strength to overcome alienation. (By *alienation* I mean being cut off from others and from our true Self, and I use it as the exact equivalent of *sin*, anything that cuts our wholeness asunder. *Sin* and *sundering* come from the same root.) But the kingdom is still coming until alienation is healed everywhere and in every respect, until wholeness is restored universally. There is a parallel here to Buddhists striving for enlightenment while at the same time affirming that each of us *is* enlightened from the beginning. On the social level, the kingdom has come with every Bodhisattva ["enlightenment-being," the archetype of compassion]; but the Bodhisattva is at the same time the one who for eons and eons awaits what Christians would call the ultimate coming of the kingdom, Christ's coming in glory, a world healed and whole.

It is quite true that the kingdom of God both has come and is coming; but this "is coming" is in the present, not the future.

From the absolute perspective, one is all; when you are healed, the whole universe is healed. Thus, according to the Diamond Sutra, the Bodhisattva who vows to save all beings is still under a fundamental delusion:

> Any Bodhisattva who undertakes the practice of meditation should cherish one thought only: "When I attain perfect wisdom, I will liberate all sentient beings in every realm of the universe, and allow them to pass into the eternal peace of Nirvana." And yet, when vast, uncountable, unthinkable myriads of beings have been liberated, truly no being has been liberated. Why? Because no Bodhisattva who is a true Bodhisattva entertains such concepts as "self" or "others." Thus there are no sentient beings to be liberated and no self to attain perfect wisdom.

Ramana Maharshi clarifies this point:

> People often say that a liberated Master should go out and preach his message to the people. How can anyone be a Master, they argue, as long as there is misery by his side? This is true. But who is a liberated Master? Does he see misery beside him? They want to determine the state of a Master without realizing the state themselves. From the standpoint of the Master their contention amounts to this: A man dreams a dream in which he finds several people. On waking up, he asks, "Have the dream people also woken up?" How ridiculous!
>
> In the same way, a good man says, "It doesn't matter if I never get liberation. Or let me be the last man to get it so that I may help all others to be liberated before I am." Wonderful. Imagine a dreamer saying, "May all these dream people wake up before I do." The dreamer is no more absurd than this amiable philosopher.

p. 12, more interested in what Moses said: A quotation from my friend Rabbi Zalman Schachter.

p. 12, which I have examined at length elsewhere: The Book of Job, North Point Press, 1987.

p. 15, The image of the Master: This small jewel of a poem is by the fifteenth-century Japanese Zen Master Ikkyu.

p. 15, His trust in God is as natural as breathing: For Paul, on the other hand, the moral life is difficult, muscular, and perilous. He has to be constantly vigilant because the flesh is weak; the very language of his consciousness is filled with drama.

For Jesus there is no drama. The more we surrender, the more we are carried along in the current of God's love. We become like the lilies of the field, who do not toil or spin and yet are clothed in a splendor beyond Solomon's; we become impartial and generous like God, who makes the sun rise on the evil and the good, and sends rain to the righteous and the unrighteous. Not that good and evil don't exist. But when we see into the realm beyond good and evil, where everything is pure grace, we are much less likely to be caught up in our own judgments and moral categories, and much more ready to experience every action as easy and natural.

It's sad to see Paul locked in a death-struggle with the demon of sin. Jesus never talks about sin that way, in the authentic passages. Sin and guilt are such terribly inefficient concepts in spiritual practice: mostly dead weight, excrescences of the image of God as a harsh father. It is much simpler to see things done shoddily or harmfully as mistakes, grave mistakes perhaps, but actions arising out of our ignorance, greed, and hatred, and correctable, transformable, with enough sincere effort. The original meaning of *to sin* in Hebrew is "to miss the mark"; it has nothing metaphysical about it. And the sins I commit against others ultimately derive from the sin I commit against myself: I think myself down into a petty, unworthy, miserable creature and lose sight of my original magnificence. As for a sin against God, there is no such thing. Do the clouds sin against the sunlight?

p. 15, for the sick and the despised: Jesus' compassion for the sick is implicit in his healing. His compassion for the poor was undoubtedly just as great, but it is less evident in the authentic passages of the Gospel. He says, "Blessed are the poor" (or "the poor in spirit"); he tells the rich man to sell everything he has and give the money to the poor. But an explicit "social gospel" is relatively scanty. (If there is a core of authenticity in the beautiful passage from Matthew 25 — "For I was hungry and you fed me, I was thirsty and you gave me drink" — it is irrecoverable: the verses speak with an "I" that Jesus never used, and they are imbedded in a parable alien to his all-embracing spirit.)

We see Jesus at work among the poor and the outcast. Perhaps he *says* so little about this ministry because it was such a deep and integral part of the Jewish mind — the mind of the Pharisees as well as of the prophets — that he felt it didn't require special emphasis. Certainly it is more obvious in the Bible and in some of the early Christian writings than in Jesus' explicit teaching. Some examples:

> When you reap the harvest on your land, do not reap to the edges of your field, or gather the gleanings of your harvest. Leave them for the poor and for the stranger [the Gentiles living among you, who because of war, famine, plague, etc. have had to leave their native country and find shelter in Israel]: I am YHVH your God. (Leviticus 23:22)

> For YHVH your God is God of gods and Lord of lords, a great, a mighty, and a terrible God, who favors no one and cannot be bribed, who obtains justice for the fatherless and the widow, and loves the stranger, giving him food and clothing. Therefore you should love the stranger, for you too were strangers in the land of Egypt. (Deuteronomy 10:17ff.)

> If any man among you becomes poor, in any of your towns in the land which YHVH your God gave you, do not harden your heart, or shut your hand against him. But open your hand wide to him, and lend him as much as he needs. Be careful not to have the base thought that the seventh year, the year of remission, is approaching; if you look askance at your needy brother and give him nothing, he will cry to YHVH against you, and you will be guilty of a sin. Give generously to him, and YHVH

your God will bless you in all your work and in everything you do. For there will always be poor in the land; therefore I command you to open your hand wide to your brothers, to everyone who is poor and in need. (Deuteronomy 15:7ff.)

> This is the piety I want:
>   that you loosen the knots of wickedness,
> shatter the heavy yokes,
>   and let the oppressed go free;
> that you share your food with the hungry,
>   and bring the homeless to your house;
> that you clothe the naked when you see them,
>   and never hide from your heart. (Isaiah 58:6f.)

> He keeps his promises forever
>   and does justice to the oppressed;
> he gives food to the hungry
>   and sets the prisoner free;
> he opens the eyes of the blind
>   and lifts up those who have fallen.
> YHVH loves the righteous,
>   and protects the rights of the stranger;
> he defends the orphan and the widow,
>   but he ruins the criminal's plans. (Psalm 146:6ff.)

All the believers had everything in common, and they sold their property and possessions and distributed them to all, according to their need. (Acts 2:44f.)

Religion that is pure and undefiled before our God and Father is this: to care for orphans and widows in their affliction and to keep yourself unstained by the world. (James 1:27)

p. 15, *For this teaching which I give you today:* Deuteronomy 30:11ff.

p. 15, *From another, complementary, viewpoint:* Shunryu Suzuki (1905–1971), Zen Master of the San Francisco Zen Center, once said, "Everything is perfect, but there's a lot of room for improvement."

p. 16, *Tolerant like the sky: Tao Te Ching*, chapter 59.

p. 17, We know so little about his life: See E. P. Sanders's meticulously fair *Jesus and Judaism*, Fortress Press, 1985. This book, especially the excellent chapters "The Sinners" and "The Law," should be required reading for Christian teachers, priests, and ministers.

p. 17, Is it not time: Edward Waldo Emerson and Waldo Emerson Forbes, eds., *Journals of Ralph Waldo Emerson*, vol. 3, Houghton Mifflin Co., 1910, p. 324. For further comments by Emerson, see Appendix 1, pp. 284ff.

p. 18, If Christ was not raised: I Corinthians 15:14.

p. 18, to do justly, to love mercy: Micah 6:8.

p. 19, When you realize where you come from: Tao Te Ching, chapter 16.

p. 20, virginal conception: Catholic scholars distinguish between the virginal conception (the doctrine that Mary conceived Jesus without the participation of a male) and the virgin birth (the doctrine that in giving birth to Jesus, Mary's hymen remained unbroken).

Of the earliest Christian writers, the only two who have heard of the virginal conception are the authors of Matthew 1–2 and Luke 1–2. Mark and John know nothing of this doctrine, though both are aware of the accusation about Jesus's illegitimacy. Paul apparently thinks that Jesus is the son of Joseph and Mary: he refers to Jesus as being "born of the seed of David according to the flesh" (Romans 1:3; cf. II Timothy 2:8 and Acts 2:30, 13:23) and "born of a woman" (Galatians 4:4, with no reference to Mary as a virgin). And the author of the Epistle to the Hebrews says, "Therefore he had to become like his fellow humans in every way" (Hebrews 2:17).

In addition, the original Jews who believed in Jesus as the Messiah, and who were later called Ebionites ("poor ones") or Nazarenes, didn't believe in the virginal conception, as we know from such early heresy hunters as Justin Martyr, Irenaeus, Origen, and Eusebius. The authors of the genealogies in Matthew and Luke probably come from this Jewish-Christian tradition. They seem to be at cross-purposes with the authors of the infancy legends; certainly they are trying to prove that Jesus was a direct descendant of David, through Joseph, though disclaimers seem to have been added by editors at a very early point in the transmission of the text: Matthew 1:16 was apparently altered from "And Jacob begot Joseph, and Joseph begot Jesus" to "And Jacob begot Joseph, the husband of Mary, of whom was begotten Jesus," and Luke 3:23 from "And Jesus . . . was the son of Joseph" to "And Jesus . . . was the son (as it was supposed) of Joseph." The polemics of the medieval rabbis are quick to pounce on this confusion. One of them writes, "If Jesus had no father, how can he be descended from the stock of David? But if the genealogy of Joseph is given to prove that he was of the house of David, Joseph must be his father." Another, the famous Nachmanides, in response to the church's preposterous handy-dandy argument that the Lucan genealogy is actually Mary's, says, "If your Messiah was descended from David on his mother's side, he could not be the heir of the kingdom, because females do not inherit while any male descendants remain."

There is another, contradictory, tradition in which "Jesus," by a kind of rabbinic exegesis, tries to prove that the Messiah is *not* descended from David (Mark 12:35ff.). This passage, along with John 7:40ff., may indicate that Jesus was known not to be of Davidic descent.

About the genesis of the doctrine of the virginal conception, Morton Smith writes, in his fascinating and irritating *Jesus the Magician*:

How is the theory [of the virginal conception] to be explained? Most critics think it was produced to fulfill the prophecy in Isaiah 7:14 which read, in a Greek translation, "Behold, the virgin shall conceive and bear a son." But if the theory was invented to fulfill this text, why is this text not cited in Luke's account of its "fulfillment"? The only New Testament author who knows anything about the fulfillment of Isaiah 7:14 is Matthew (1:23). This is not surprising, because Isaiah 7:14 is the beginning of a prophecy conspicuously unsuited to Jesus' career, and in the original Hebrew it says nothing about a virgin birth [i.e., virginal conception] — the Hebrew has "young woman" instead of "virgin." But Matthew [often takes] Old Testament verses out of context to make them prophecies of gospel stories. In such cases the starting point was commonly the story; the editor's problem was to find a text that could be forced to fit it. Therefore, we can be almost certain that the story of the virgin birth was also given to him by tradition, not invented from the text he twisted to suit it. If so, where did the tradition come from? Why was the story invented? Perhaps because some of Jesus' followers wanted to make him a match for the hellenistic "divine men" who often had divine fathers. Perhaps also because the irregularity of his birth had to be explained. The motives may have coexisted.

(Morton Smith, *Jesus the Magician*, Harper & Row, 1968, pp. 26f.)

As for the doctrine's significance for Christians, Jefferson's friend Joseph Priestley, the great English scientist, in his pamphlet *On the Miraculous Conception of Jesus Christ*, quotes a sermon by a minister named Richard Wright:

Will any Christian deny that Jesus himself preached the Gospel in purity and perfection, that he taught all the essential facts, doctrines and precepts of Christianity? But if it be admitted that he did, it follows, that the miraculous conception is no part of the Gospel, no essential fact of Christianity. It is evidently no part of the Gospel as taught by the apostle and high-priest of our profession, Christ Jesus; for he said not one word on the subject. . . . The circumstances of a person's birth add nothing to the real dignity of his person, or the excellency of his character. A miraculous conception would not make the person conceived more than human. Adam, though without either earthly father or mother, was simply a man. The offspring of a woman can be neither more nor less than a man. Real dignity and excellency of character consist in knowledge, virtue, and goodness. When the excellency of the person of

Christ is brought into view, in the New Testament, it is always referred to his spirit and conduct in real life, never to any peculiar circumstances of his conception and birth; and the dignity to which he is raised, is ever spoken of as the reward of his obedience. His mission is never mentioned as founded on his miraculous conception; but simply on God's having anointed him with the Holy Spirit and with power; nor is that circumstance ever referred to as adding any authority to his mission or doctrine. Jesus is the same precisely, in his person, character, and office, whether the miraculous conception be true or false; i.e., a man approved of God, divinely commissioned, raised up and sent to be the teacher and savior of men.

p. 21, where the Evangelists want us to read black: I am paraphrasing a line from Blake's "The Everlasting Gospel":

> The vision of Christ that thou dost see
> Is my vision's greatest enemy.
> . . . .
> Both [thou and I] read the Bible day and night,
> But thou readst black where I read white.

p. 21, The Illegitimacy of Jesus: Jane Schaberg, *The Illegitimacy of Jesus: A Feminist Theological Interpretation of the Infancy Narratives,* Harper & Row, 1987.

p. 21, Now the birth of Jesus happened in this way: Matthew 1:18ff.

p. 22, Matthew tells us of the rumor: Raymond E. Brown, S.S., *The Virginal Conception and Bodily Resurrection of Jesus,* Paulist Press, 1973, pp. 65f.

p. 22, Abraham begat Isaac: Matthew 1:2ff.

p. 22, Matthew's genealogy of Jesus: Smith, *Jesus the Magician,* p. 26.

p. 23, And when the Sabbath came: Mark 6:2f.

p. 23, According to a later Jewish legal principle: Ethelbert Stauffer, *Jerusalem und Rom im Zeitalter Jesu Christi,* Francke-Verlag, 1957, p. 118. "Son of Mary" would have a pejorative sense in

Samaritan and Mandaean usage as well. "The name Yeshu ben Miriam [Jesus son of Mary] was thought to be such an unbearable insult by the early church that only Mark had the courage to retain it. All the other Evangelists omitted it." (Ethelbert Stauffer, "Jeschu ben Mirjam," in *Neotestamentica et Semitica*, eds. E. E. Ellis and M. Wilcox, Clark, 1969, pp. 119ff.)

> Matthew (12:55) recast the reference to avoid the implication [of illegitimacy], Luke (4:22) replaced "Mary" with "Joseph." Another version of the saying, in John 6:42, also has Joseph. The common explanation, that Mark wrote "son of Mary" because he believed in the virgin birth, is contradicted by the fact that Mark says nothing of the virgin birth, while Matthew and Luke, who both tell stories about it, both refer in this passage to Jesus as the son of his father. Besides, we have already seen Matthew and Luke making other changes in Mark's story to get rid of embarrassing details. Finally, it is incredible that an ancient editor, so sensitive that he wanted to get rid of "the son of Joseph," should have substituted for it "the son of Mary," which was certain to be understood in a pejorative sense. This is proved by the history of the text: a long string of Christian copyists (who surely believed in the virgin birth) changed "the son of Mary" into "the son of the carpenter and of Mary," or just "the son of the carpenter," but not a one changed Luke's "the son of Joseph" or Matthew's "the son of the carpenter" into "the son of Mary." Mark's phrase was offensive; the others were not. These facts make it probable that Jesus was not the son of Joseph; had he been so, "the son of Mary" would never have appeared in a Christian text.
>
> (Smith, *Jesus the Magician*, p. 26)

p. 23, ["Jesus" says:] "I know that you are Abraham's descendants": John 8:37–42, 44.

p. 24, In the midst of this argument: Schaberg, *Illegitimacy of Jesus*, pp. 157f.

p. 24, verse from the Gospel of Thomas: Thomas, 105.

p. 25, The mamzerim *were forbidden marriage:* Schaberg, *Illegitimacy of Jesus*, p. 57.

p. 25, It was inevitable that those: Origen, *Contra Celsum*, trans. Henry Chadwick, Cambridge University Press, 1965, pp. 32f.

p. 27, Nothing can defile a man from the outside: Mark 7:15. This may well be an authentic saying of Jesus. But since it is inextricably embedded in a story that is an early-church polemic, I haven't included it in my version of the Gospel. (See Sanders, *Jesus and Judaism*, pp. 260, 266f.)

p. 27, his wonderfully perceptive late poem: Written, though, in verse that is perilously close to doggerel.

p. 28, Was Jesus born of a virgin pure: Blake, "The Everlasting Gospel" (spelling and punctuation modified).

p. 28, He is despised and rejected of men: Isaiah 53:3f. I have quoted the King James version of this passage because it is so familiar to us from the liturgy and from Handel's *Messiah*. The rest of the passage only *seems* to apply to the crucifixion, but doesn't really, in its details; for example, 53:10: ". . . he will live a long life and see his descendants [i.e., his grandchildren and great-grandchildren]."

p. 28, directly from the lips of Jesus: Mark has preserved two other Aramaic phrases: "*Talitha, koum*," i.e., "*T'litha, koomi*" ("Little girl, get up," 5:41) and "*Ephphatha*," i.e., "*Ethpatakh*" ("Be opened," 7:34). But these may have originated in the healings and exorcisms performed by the Jewish-Christians of the Jerusalem church. Whereas for *abba* we have the testimony not only of Mark 14:36 ("Abba, all things are possible for you"), but also of Romans 8:15 and Galatians 4:6, two of the rare instances in which Paul shows an awareness of traditions about the actual Jesus.

Some scholars think that *abba* is the familiar form—the

equivalent of our "papa" or "daddy"; other scholars disagree. Our knowledge of first-century Jewish Aramaic is too limited to know which opinion is correct.

p. 29, blesses and keeps: Numbers 6:24ff.

p. 29, God as a father:

> And yet, YHVH, you are our father;
>> we are the clay and you are our potter,
>> and we are all the work of your hand.
>>> (Isaiah 64:8)

> "I have become a father to Israel,
>> and Ephraim is my eldest son."
>>> (Jeremiah 31:9)

> He is a father to the fatherless . . .
>> (Psalm 68:5)

> As a father loves [*rahem*] his children,
>> YHVH loves those who revere him.
>>> (Psalm 103:13)

Also Hosea 11:1, Wisdom of Solomon 14:3, and Ecclesiasticus 23:1.

p. 29, God . . . as a mother:

> "As a mother comforts her son,
>> so will I comfort you."
>>> (Isaiah 66:13)

p. 29, Jesus adopted this term for God: Gustaf Dalman, *The Words of Jesus*, trans. D. M. Kay, Clark, 1902, p. 188.

p. 31, four other sons and at least two daughters: Mark 6:3.

p. 31, a later verse in Matthew: Matthew 23:9. The authenticity of this verse is doubtful, but it does seem to express Jesus' attitude.

p. 32, a few ancient manuscripts:

[Manuscripts] D *a b c ff²*, etc., with the notable support of Clement of Alexandria, read "Thou art my [beloved] Son, this day I have begotten thee." Now this reading is quite definitely that cited by Justin and was therefore current in Rome c. 155. Again, on grounds of internal probability it is clearly to be preferred for two reasons. (a) The tendency of scribal alterations would be to make the text of Luke agree with Matthew and Mark, as in [manuscript] B; with this reading, on the contrary, there is a discrepancy between the Gospels. (b) The Lucan reading could readily be quoted in favor of the view, afterwards regarded as heretical, that Christ only became the Son of God at his Baptism. Once, therefore, the assimilation with the other Gospels had been made in any MS, it would be preferred as more orthodox, and would rapidly be taken up into other texts. (Burnett Hillman Streeter, *The Four Gospels: A Study of Origins*, Macmillan, 1924, p. 143)

p. 32, quoted in Acts and Hebrews: Acts 13:33, Hebrews 1:5, 5:5.

p. 32, understood only the baptism of John: Acts 18:25.

p. 32, Did you receive the Holy Spirit: Acts 19:2ff.

p. 33, One who is stronger than I: Mark 1:7f.

p. 33, Then Jesus came from Galilee: Matthew 3:13ff.

p. 33, When all the people were being baptized: Luke 3:21.

p. 33, has John recognize him as the Son of God: According to both Matthew and Luke, shortly before his death John still doesn't know who Jesus is:

> When John was in prison he heard of the works of the Messiah, and he sent his disciples to ask him, "Are you the one who is to come, or shall we look for another?" (Matthew 11:2f.; cf. Luke 7:19)

But the writer of the infancy legend in Luke, forgetting or not knowing this story, imagines that the Baptist is Jesus' cousin, and makes him do a leap of recognition in the womb (Luke 1:41).

p. 34, a man without sin: II Corinthians 5:21, Hebrews 4:15, I Peter 2:22, I John 3:5.

p. 34, He was made sin for us: II Corinthians 5:21.

p. 35, Why do you call me good: Mark 10:18.

p. 37, There once was a man who had two sons: Luke 15:11ff.

p. 37, Later I will examine: See Commentary, pp. 223ff.

p. 39, Even lengthy parables: Erik H. Erikson, "The Galilean Sayings and the Sense of 'I,'" *The Yale Review* 70, spring 1981, p. 355.

p. 40, the image of sunlight passing through a window: This is an image from the relative perspective, the perspective of spiritual practice. From the perspective of the Absolute, it is an untruth. There is no dirt, no window, and no cleaning; nothing but sunlight; in other words, not even sunlight. The two perspectives are expressed in two poems in *The Platform Sutra* of Zen Master Hui-neng (often known as the Sixth Patriarch). The head monk of his monastery had written the following poem:

> The body is the enlightenment-tree,
> the mind is a clear mirror.
> At all times we should wipe it clean,
> and not let the dust collect.

Hui-neng countered with:

> There is no enlightenment-tree,
> and the mirror has no stand.
> From the beginning, not a thing exists,
> so where can the dust collect?

p. 41, Even though we once knew Christ: II Corinthians 5:16. Paul's teaching was based not on the transmission of Jesus' teaching, but on his own visions: "The gospel that I preach is not of human origin; for I neither received it from nor was taught it by any human being, but through a revelation of Jesus Christ" (Galatians 1:11f.).

In his letters we can see evidence of how fiercely opposed to his teaching some of Jesus' original disciples were: they say that Paul "distorts the word of God" (II Corinthians 4:2), they "do not accept" him as an apostle (I Corinthians 9:2), they say that he is "not competent" (II Corinthians 3:5), is "unqualified" to be an apostle (II Corinthians 13:6), some even call him insane (II Corinthians 5:13, 11:21). He counters by saying that those who call his gospel obscure are "on the way to destruction" (II Corinthians 4:3). In a famous and very unpleasant passage (II Corinthians 12:1ff.), he tries to base his authority on a mystical experience he once had.

We have more explicit, though later, evidence of the Jewish-Christian opposition to Paul, in the second-century *Clementine Homilies*, where Peter says:

> How can you be qualified to teach the gospel just because you have had a vision? If you say it is possible, then why did Jesus go to the trouble of spending a whole year with us [the Twelve]? And how can we believe you? If he really appeared to you, why do you teach precisely the opposite of what he taught?

p. 41, cosmic warfare: It is sometimes hard to tell the devils from the angels in Paul's writings, they are all so vindictive. Here, for example, is Jesus looking for all the world like Satan:

> . . . when the Lord Jesus is revealed from heaven with his mighty angels in flaming fire, taking vengeance on those who don't know God and don't obey the gospel of our Lord Jesus, who will pay the penalty of eternal destruction. (II Thessalonians 1:7 ff.)

p. 41, a prince, God's enemy: From Spinoza's Letter LXXVI, to a former pupil of his who had recently converted to Catholicism:

> When you were still in your right mind, you used to worship an infinite God, by whose power all things absolutely occur. Now you dream of a prince, God's enemy, who against God's will entraps and deceives very many men (rarely good ones, to be sure), whom God then hands over to this master of wickedness to be tortured for eternity. God in his justice thus allows

the devil to deceive men and go unpunished; but he by no means allows to remain unpunished the men who have been so wretchedly deceived and entrapped by that same devil.

p. 42, egotism, superstition, and intolerance: And sometimes worse, if we are to believe Luke's account of the repulsive incident in Acts 13:6ff., where Paul, "filled with the Holy Spirit [*sic*]," blinds a "false prophet" named Bar Jesus.

p. 42, that terrace in Dante's Purgatorio: Canto xxvi.

p. 43, his sayings are a marvel: See Chang Chung-yuan, *Original Teachings of Ch'an Buddhism*, Pantheon, 1969, pp. 164ff.

p. 43, Therefore he had to become like his fellow humans: Hebrews 2:17. The author of Hebrews also says that, like the High Priest, the Christ's patience and sympathy with all people come from acknowledging that he, too, is capable of error:

> For every High Priest is taken from among humans and is appointed on behalf of humans in matters concerning God, so that he can offer sacrifices for sins. He is able to be patient in dealing with the ignorant and the erring, since he, too, is susceptible to weakness, and because of this he is obligated to make offerings for his own sins as well as for the people's. (Hebrews 5:1ff.)

p. 43, the relevant verses: There is an additional verse from the Fourth Gospel (John 2:4), which may conceivably transmit an authentic memory of Jesus' attitude toward his mother. When Mary says, at the wedding in Cana, "They have no wine," "Jesus" rudely answers, "What is that to me and to you, woman?"

p. 43, Your mother and your brothers are outside: Mark 3:32.

p. 44, Blessed is the womb that bore you: Luke 11:27.

p. 44, a prophet is not rejected: Mark 6:4. The King James version softens the bitterness of the Greek by translating it "a prophet is not without honor." But the adjective literally means "dishonored" and derives from a verb that means "to dishonor, disgrace, shame, humiliate, treat with contempt."

This saying probably circulated independently; its form in the Oxyrhynchus Papyri is "A prophet is not accepted in his native town, nor can a doctor heal those who know him." This may be a more primitive form. On the other hand, it is unlikely that Mark added "and in his own family and in his own house"; the first of these phrases was difficult enough that Matthew omitted it.

p. 44, as they were traveling along the road: Luke 9:57, 59–62 (parallel at Matthew 8:21f.).

p. 44, Let the dead bury their dead:

> The attitude indicated here is so shocking, not only in Judaism but in the entire Graeco-Roman world, that the saying "Let the dead bury their dead" could hardly be a general proverb. . . . Jesus *consciously* requires disobedience of a commandment understood by all Jews to have been given by God.
>
> (Sanders, *Jesus and Judaism*, p. 254)

p. 45, If anyone comes to me: Luke 14:26 (Matthew 10:37 softens the saying to read "Whoever loves father or mother more than me isn't worthy of me"). I haven't included this detached saying in my version of the Gospel because it lacks a context.

p. 45, Whoever doesn't hate his father and his mother: Thomas, 101.

p. 45, Get rid of your family entanglements: George Bernard Shaw, Preface to *Androcles and the Lion*.

p. 46, For the mature person: Tzu-ssu, *The Central Harmony*, in Stephen Mitchell, ed., *The Enlightened Mind: An Anthology of Sacred Prose*, HarperCollins, 1991, p. 12.

p. 47, I want to give up my job and family: This dialogue and most of the other sayings of Maharshi quoted in this book come from Munagala S. Venkataramiah, *Talks with Sri Ramana Maharshi*, 6th ed., Sri Ramanasramam, 1978.

p. 48, And when his family heard [about all this]: Mark 3:21. The Greek phrase that I have translated as "his family" means literally "those with him," and might also be translated "his friends" or "his relatives." But it is clear that this verse has a sequel in Mark 3:31ff., and therefore that it refers to Jesus' mother and brothers.

p. 48, He is out of his mind: The Greek verb means "to be beside oneself," "to lose one's mind," "to be possessed."

p. 48, two of the best ancient manuscripts: The fifth-century Freer Gospels and the fifth- to sixth-century Bezae Cantabrigiensis; also the fourth-century Gothic translation and three fifth-century manuscripts of the Old Latin translation. It is possible, I suppose, that the alteration was caused by identical slips of the pen (*hoi par' autou,* "those with him," carelessly copied as *peri autou,* "about him"). But the textual commentary to the United Bible Societies' Greek New Testament, which is as definitive as any we are ever likely to have, says, "The original reading *hoi par' autou* apparently proved to be so embarrassing that [the above-mentioned manuscripts] altered it to read, 'When *the scribes and the others* had heard about him . . .'" (Bruce M. Metzger, *A Textual Commentary on the Greek New Testament,* United Bible Societies, 1975, pp. 81f.).

p. 49, physical contortions: According to Morton Smith, "Magicians who want to make demons obey often scream their spells, gesticulate, and match the mad in fury" (*Jesus the Magician,* p. 32).

p. 49, And his mother and his brothers arrived: Mark 3:31ff.

p. 50, It has been urged: C. G. Montefiore, *The Synoptic Gospels,* vol. 1, Macmillan, 1927, p. 95.

p. 51, seemed to him only a few days: Genesis 29:20.

p. 51, ahead of all parting:

Be ahead of all parting, as though it already were
behind you, like the winter that has just gone by.

For among these winters there is one so endlessly winter
that only by wintering through it will your heart survive.

> (Rainer Maria Rilke, *The Sonnets to Orpheus*,
> trans. Stephen Mitchell, Simon & Schuster,
> 1985, p. 97)

p. 52, From there he went to Nazareth: Mark 6:1ff.

p. 52, even his own brothers didn't believe in him: John 7:5.

p. 53, When the young plant is just sprouting: B. V. Narasimha Swami, *Self-Realization: Life and Teachings of Sri Ramana Maharshi*, 8th ed., Sri Ramanasramam, 1976, p. 123.

p. 53, imagined Mary at the foot of the Cross: Since the disciples had scattered after Jesus' arrest, it is unlikely that any of them witnessed his crucifixion. Even according to Mark (followed by Matthew and Luke), there was no one at the foot of the cross, and Jesus' mother is not mentioned among the group of Galilean women followers "watching from far off" (Mark 15:40).

p. 54, There is not one moral virtue: Blake, "The Everlasting Gospel" (spelling and punctuation modified).

p. 54, Jesus himself is said to forgive sins: When Jesus says, "Your sins are forgiven" (Mark 2:5, Luke 7:48), it isn't clear whether he means "I have forgiven your sins" or "God has forgiven your sins." Brother David Steindl-Rast says:

> In the Gospel accounts, it is the *adversaries* of Jesus who accuse him of forgiving sins. Jesus only *reminds* the poor wretches that their sins *are* forgiven. We know this in our inmost heart as soon as we know God as "Abba."

This is a possible and attractive interpretation. On the other hand, the two accounts imply that the adversaries are quite correct in thinking that it is Jesus himself who forgives the sins. And when Mark's Jesus says, "But so that you may know that the Son of Man has authority on earth to forgive sins . . . , I say to you, Rise . . . ," his meaning seems to be, "I, Jesus, have the authority to forgive sins."

p. 55, Forgive us our wrongs: Matthew 6:12.

p. 55, For if you forgive others their offenses: Matthew 6:14.

p. 55, If you don't judge: Luke 6:37f.

p. 55, Peter once asked him: Matthew 18:21f. (parallel at Luke 17:4).

p. 56, Why did the ancient Masters esteem the Tao: Tao Te Ching, chapter 62.

p. 57, They portray Israel: I am using "Israel" here to mean not the northern kingdom of Israel, which was conquered by Assyria in 722 B.C.E., but the Jewish people.

p. 57, In Second Isaiah: Isaiah 54.

p. 57, Jeremiah's image: Jeremiah 3.

p. 57, like an unfaithful wife: We find the same image in Ezekiel (chapters 16 and 23), but the tone is very different: God's pardon in 16:60ff. is grudging, and the details of the betrayal are so violent, so horrified and fascinated, that they seem pornographic. These passages reveal a deeply disturbed sexuality.

p. 57, God is not unfaithful: This image also illuminates a hidden anxiety in traditional Christianity. If you believe in the church as the new Israel, you believe in a God who is unfaithful, who doesn't keep "his" promises. If God gave up on the first Israel and reneged on his promise, what is to prevent him from giving up on the new Israel? In other words, what is to prevent him from giving up on *me*?

p. 57, Go take a whore as your wife: Hosea 1:2.

p. 58, I will marry you to myself forever: Hosea 2:21f.

p. 58, Mary simply disappears from the picture: She surfaces again
only in one passing reference in Acts 1:14.

p. 58, The next morning, as Jesus was teaching in the Temple: John
8:2ff.

p. 59, the strangest history of any text in the Gospels:

> The evidence for the non-Johannine origin of the pericope of
> the adulteress is overwhelming. It is absent from such early
> and diverse manuscripts as $\mathfrak{P}^{66.75}$ ℵ B L N T W X Y Δ Θ Ψ 0141
> 0211 22 33 124 157 209 788 828 1230 1241 1242 1253 2193 *al.*
> Codices A and C are defective in this part of John, but it is
> highly probable that neither contained the pericope, for care-
> ful measurement discloses that there would not have been
> space enough on the missing leaves to include the section
> along with the rest of the text. In the East the passage is absent
> from the oldest form of the Syriac version (syr[c.s] and the best
> manuscripts of syr[p]), as well as from the Sahidic and the sub-
> Achmimic versions and the older Bohairic manuscripts. Some
> Armenian manuscripts and the Old Georgian version omit it.
> In the West the passage is absent from the Gothic version and
> from several Old Latin manuscripts (it[a,l*,q]). No Greek Church
> Father prior to Euthymius Zigabenus (twelfth century) com-
> ments on the passage, and Euthymius declares that the accu-
> rate copies of the Gospel do not contain it.
>
> When one adds to this impressive and diversified list of ex-
> ternal evidence the consideration that the style and vocabu-
> lary of the pericope differ noticeably from the rest of the
> Fourth Gospel (see any critical commentary), and that it in-
> terrupts the sequence of 7:52 and 8:12ff., the case against its
> being of Johannine authorship appears to be conclusive.
>
> At the same time the account has all the earmarks of histor-
> ical veracity. It is obviously a piece of oral tradition which cir-
> culated in certain parts of the Western church and which was
> subsequently incorporated into various manuscripts at var-
> ious places. Most copyists apparently thought that it would in-
> terrupt John's narrative least if it were inserted after 7:52 (D E
> (F) G H K M U Γ Π 28 700 892 *al*). Others placed it after 7:36
> (ms. 225) or after 7:44 (several Georgian mss.) or after 21:25

(1 565 1076 1570 1582 arm^{mss}) or after Luke 21:38 (f^{13}). Significantly enough, in many of the witnesses which contain the passage it is marked with asterisks or obeli, indicating that, though the scribes included the account, they were aware that it lacked satisfactory credentials.

> (Metzger, *Textual Commentary on the Greek New Testament*, pp. 219ff.)

The only natural explanation of the unquestioned facts is that the narrative was current in the third century in a Greek but not a Latin text, though over a narrow range; that towards the end of the fourth century it was introduced in various places, but particularly where it now stands, and was thence taken into the Latin texts; that from the sixth century onwards it was found more and more frequently in the Constantinopolitan texts and all but universally in the Latin texts, and in the course of time was partially introduced into other versions.

> (Brooke Foss Westcott, *The Gospel According to St. John*, vol. 2, John Murray, 1908, p. 381)

p. 59, placed it after Luke 21:38:

The incident appears to belong to the last visit to Jerusalem, so that the position which it occupies in St. Luke is perhaps historically correct.

> (Westcott, Ibid.)

p. 59, has all the earmarks of historical veracity: Metzger, *Textual Commentary on the Greek New Testament*, p. 220.

p. 60, the sins of all the accusing scribes: This tradition goes back as far as Jerome (340?–420).

p. 60, the Son of Man has the authority: Mark 2:10.

p. 61, never actually took place: What we can't be sure about in the life of Jesus, we can be sure about in his words: that forgiveness is always present, for us and in us; that there is nothing we need to do to deserve it; that all we need to do is return. This truth, which Jesus knew intimately, whether or not he was able to embody it before his early death, seems to me the essence of the Christmas legend.

The story of the Annunciation is told from Mary's point of view. But the story of Christmas really belongs to Joseph. We can understand this only if we set aside one of the traditional images of Joseph, as an old man who has married Mary out of kindness, so that he can serve as a protector for her and her child. It is a demeaning image, and it arises from the church's fear of sexuality. It changes Joseph from a husband into an impotent grandfather, a figure who in European folklore is treated with derision and mild contempt. After all, he's a cuckold. So what, if God is the one who cuckolded him. Horns are horns.

Matthew and Luke say nothing about Joseph's age. As a betrothed husband, he would be an adolescent or a young man, and we can imagine him as being twenty-five perhaps. Matthew's Joseph, upon learning that Mary is pregnant, decides to divorce her; but when an angel appears to him announcing the virginal conception, he of course "takes her home to be his wife." This, too, is a demeaning image, since it robs him of his moral decision, and it diverts our attention from what should be the focal point of the legend.

If we are to understand this point, we have to subtract the angel, or realize that the angel is Joseph himself. The story would then begin:

> Now the birth of Jesus happened in this way. Mary, his mother, was engaged to Joseph, but before they came together to live, she was found to be pregnant. And Joseph, being a just man and not wanting to put her to public shame, at first decided to divorce her quietly. But as he was wrestling with this, a voice inside him kept saying, "Joseph, don't be afraid to take Mary as your wife, for what has been begotten in her is of a holy spirit." Finally, he did as the voice told him, and he took Mary home to be his wife. And he didn't have intercourse with her until she had given birth to a son.

And when the time came for Mary to be delivered, she gave birth to her firstborn son and wrapped him in swaddling clothes. And at the end of eight days, he was circumcised, and was named Jesus.

And as the child grew up, he increased in wisdom and stature, and in favor with God and man.

When Mary comes to Joseph and tells him that she is pregnant, Joseph, if he is a man and not a pious stick-figure, will have to struggle with some of the most difficult emotions a man can feel: distrust, rage, hurt, resentment, and a deep wound at the core of his sexual identity. It may take him weeks or months before these emotions lose their bitter momentum. When finally he is able, after great agony and surrender, to forgive her with all his heart, he becomes the embodiment of Jesus' teaching. (This scene has been movingly rendered by William Blake, the most recent of the Hebrew prophets, in Plate 61 of his long poem *Jerusalem*.)

Joseph's forgiveness of Mary, in what could be called the essential Christmas legend, is such a profound symbol, and such a perfect embodiment of the gospel according to Jesus, that it constitutes an undoing, a redoing, a regeneration of the male myth of Adam and Eve, a myth in which the serpent seduces Eve, and man blames her ever afterward for his expulsion from Paradise. (Actually, the moment when Adam blames Eve is the moment when he is expelled.) It is a deluded and slanderous myth, which leaves its traces through all of Judeo-Christian-Islamic culture. An old Gnostic text goes to the heart of the matter when it says, speaking in the voice of the archetypal feminine,

> I am the one called Life [Eve],
> but you have called me Death.
> ("The Thunder, Perfect Mind")

If we focus our attention on Joseph, as Matthew does, and make this a legend of salvation, then Joseph becomes the second Adam. He is given a second chance, as we all are, constantly, a chance to reenact a life drama that we have wretchedly botched at least once before, and to do it right this time. Whether Mary is pregnant by another man or by the Holy Spirit, in Joseph's eyes she has been seduced, as Eve was, and no external angel will ever tell him differently. His first reaction is to retreat into his woundedness and blame her, and hence be cast out of Eden. When he refuses to be seduced himself by the poison of the Accuser when he can finally let go of the offense and of his offended self, and forgive Mary with all his heart, he finds that he is again standing in Eden, the garden of delight, the kingdom of God. Not only does he forgive Mary, but he sees her in her pristine innocence, whatever mistakes she has made. And ultimately, standing in God's place, he realizes that there is nothing to forgive.

This transformation that takes place in Joseph seems to me the subliminal message in the Christmas legend, its point and essence. It flavors the story with an extraordinary sweetness, a sense of human difficulty embraced and overcome. I would even say that Joseph's forgiveness is what retroactively allows the infant Jesus to have been conceived in the Holy Spirit, and allows him to be born in joy and fulfillment, as a son of God.

And if I were to celebrate the birth of that infant, I would gladly sprinkle the story with a few unnecessary angels (borrowed from Luke) singing, "Peace on earth, good will to men." For, as Luke has Jesus say in another context, "Such is the joy among the angels of God over one sinner who returns."

p. 61, When all things are made whole in the Son: I Corinthians 15:28.

THE GOSPEL

1

This is the book of the good news that Jesus of Nazareth proclaimed.

John the Baptizer appeared in the wilderness, proclaiming a baptism of renewal for the forgiveness of sins. And John was clothed in camel's hair, with a belt of animal hide around his waist, and he ate locusts and wild honey. And people from all of Judea went out to him, and many people from Jerusalem, and they were baptized by him in the Jordan River, confessing their sins.

And at that time Jesus came from Nazareth in Galilee, and was baptized in the Jordan by John.

And afterward the Spirit drove him out into the wilderness. And he was in the wilderness for forty days, with the wild animals.

2

And when Jesus heard that John had been arrested, he withdrew to Galilee, and leaving Nazareth, he settled in

Capernaum by the lake. And he began to teach and proclaim the good news of the kingdom of God.

And as he was walking beside the Sea of Galilee, he saw Simon and his brother Andrew casting a fishing net into the lake. And Jesus said to them, "Come, follow me." And immediately they left their nets and followed him.

And walking on a little farther, he saw James the son of Zebedee and John his brother, who were in their boat mending their nets. And he called them, and immediately they left their father Zebedee in the boat with the hired men and followed him.

And they came to Capernaum. And on the Sabbath, Jesus went into the synagogue and taught. And people were astonished at his teaching, for he taught them like someone who has authority, and not like the scribes.

And when they left the synagogue, they went to the house of Simon and Andrew, along with James and John. And Simon's mother-in-law was in bed with a fever. And as soon as they told Jesus about her, he went and took her by the hand and lifted her up, and the fever left her, and she served them.

And that evening, they brought to him everyone who was sick or insane, and the whole village was gathered at the door, and he healed many people.

And early in the morning, while it was still dark, he got up and went out to a remote place and prayed there. And Simon and his companions searched for him, and when they found him, they said to him, "Everyone is looking for you." And he said to them, "Let us go on to the next villages, so that I can proclaim the good news there too."

And he went through all of Galilee, proclaiming the good news in their synagogues and healing many diseases.

And in one of the villages, a leper came and knelt before him and said, "If you wish, you can cleanse me."

And Jesus, moved with compassion, stretched out his hand and touched him and said, "I do wish it; be cleansed."

And immediately the leprosy left him, and he was cleansed.

And Jesus said to him, "Go and show yourself to the priest and offer for your cleansing what Moses commanded."

And the man went out and began to talk about it excitedly, and the news spread, until Jesus could no longer go into a village, but had to stay out in the countryside. And people came to him from every direction.

3

And he went again to the lakeside, and began to teach, and so many people gathered that he had to get into a boat on the lake. And he sat in it, and the whole crowd sat on the shore, up to the water's edge.

And he taught them many things in parables, and said, "What is the kingdom of God like? It is like a man who sows a seed on the earth: he goes about his business, and day by day the seed sprouts and grows, he doesn't know how. The earth bears fruit by itself, first the stalk, then the ear, then the full grain in the ear. And when the grain is ripe, the man goes in with his sickle, because it is harvest time.

"The kingdom of God is like a mustard seed, which is smaller than any other seed; but when it is sown, it grows up and becomes the largest of shrubs, and puts forth large branches, so that the birds of the sky are able to make their nests in its shade.

"The kingdom of God is like yeast, which a woman took and mixed in with fifty pounds of dough, until all of it was leavened.

"The kingdom of God is like a treasure buried in a field, which a man found and buried again; then in his joy he goes and sells everything he has and buys that field.

"Or the kingdom of God is like this: there was a merchant looking for fine pearls, who found one pearl of great price, and he went and sold everything he had and bought it.

"Thus, every scribe who has been trained for the kingdom of God is like a householder who can bring forth out of his treasure room both the new and the old."

And someone asked him, "When will the kingdom of God come?"

And he said, "The kingdom of God will not come if you watch for it. Nor will anyone be able to say, 'It is here' or 'It is there.' For the kingdom of God is within you."

And he said, "When you light a lamp, do you put it under a basket or under a bed? Don't you put it on a lampstand? For there is nothing hidden that can't be made clear, and nothing secret that can't become obvious. Pay attention to what you hear; the measure you give is the measure you receive."

4

Another time, Jesus was walking beside the lake, and a crowd gathered around him, and he taught them. And as he walked on, he saw Levi the son of Alphaeus sitting at the tax booth, and he said to him, "Follow me." And he stood up and followed him.

And many people who held the Law in contempt began to follow Jesus. And the scribes said to him, "Why do you eat with traitors and whores?" And Jesus said to them, "It isn't the healthy who need a doctor, but the sick. My teaching is not meant for those who are already righteous, but for the wicked."

And he went up into the hills and called his disciples and appointed twelve of them to be with him and to be sent out to proclaim the kingdom of God and to heal: Simon, whom he named Peter, James the son of Zebedee and John his brother, whom he named *B'nai-rogez* (which means "sons of thunder"), Andrew, and Philip, and Bartholomew, and Matthew, and Thomas, and James the son of Alphaeus, and Thaddaeus, and Simon the Zealot, and Judas Iscariot.

And he went through all the towns and villages, teaching in their synagogues, and proclaiming the good news of the kingdom of God. And the Twelve went with him, and also certain women whom he had cured of diseases and infirmities: Mary of Magdala, who had been insane, and Joanna the wife of Herod's steward Kooza, and Susannah, and many others, who provided for them out of their own resources. And his fame spread throughout the surrounding region of Galilee, and people brought the sick on stretchers to wherever they heard he was staying, and whenever he came to a town or village, they would lay down the sick in the marketplace. And they brought him those who were suffering from many kinds of diseases and torments, and demoniacs, and epileptics, and paralytics, and he healed them.

And after Jesus returned to Capernaum, people heard that he was at home; and so many gathered in the house that there was no room, not even in front of the door.

And as he was teaching, some people brought a paralytic to him, carried by four men. And when they couldn't get near him because of the crowd, they made a hole in the roof over the place where Jesus was, and they lowered the mat, with the paralytic lying on it, through the hole.

And when Jesus saw how deeply they trusted him, he said to the paralytic, "Stand up, child; take your mat and go home."

And immediately the man stood up and took the mat and walked out of the house in front of everyone. And they were all amazed, and glorified God and said, "We have never seen anything like this!"

5

And large crowds followed him from Galilee and the Decapolis and Jerusalem and Judea and beyond the Jordan. And seeing the crowds, he went up onto a hill, and when he had sat down, his disciples gathered around him. And he began to teach them, and said,

"Blessed are the poor in spirit, for theirs is the kingdom of God.

"Blessed are those who grieve, for they will be comforted.

"Blessed are those who hunger and thirst for righteousness, for they will be filled.

"Blessed are the merciful, for they will receive mercy.

"Blessed are the pure in heart, for they will see God.

"Blessed are the peacemakers, for they will be called sons of God.

"No one lights a lamp and then puts it under a basket, but on a lampstand, and it gives light to everyone in the house. In the same way, let your light shine before men, so that they may see your good works and glorify your Father in heaven.

"Don't think that my purpose is to destroy the Law; my purpose is not to destroy the Law but to fulfill it. For I tell you that unless your righteousness is deeper than the righteousness of the scribes, you will never enter the kingdom of God.

"You have heard that it was said to our forefathers, *You shall not murder* and *Whoever murders is liable to judgment*. But I tell you that anyone who hates his brother will be liable to judgment.

"You have heard that it was said, *You shall not commit adultery*. But I tell you that anyone who harbors lust for a woman has already committed adultery with her in his heart.

"You have heard that it was said, *You shall not perjure yourselves*. But I tell you, don't take any oaths at all. Let your 'Yes' mean 'Yes' and your 'No' mean 'No.'

"You have heard that it was said, *An eye for an eye and a tooth for a tooth*. But I tell you, don't resist a wicked man. If anyone hits you on one cheek, turn the other cheek to him also. And if anyone wants to sue you and take your shirt, let him have your coat as well. And if a soldier forces you into service for one mile, go two miles with him. Give to everyone who asks, and don't refuse anyone who wants to borrow from you.

"You have heard that it was said, *You shall love your neighbor*. But I tell you, love your enemies, do good to those who hate you, bless those who curse you, and pray for those who mistreat you, so that you may be sons of your Father in heaven; for he makes his sun rise on the wicked and on the good, and sends rain to the righteous and to the unrighteous.

"For if you love only those who love you, what credit is that to you: don't even the tax-gatherers do the same? And if you do good only to those who do good to you: don't even the Gentiles do the same? But love your enemies, and give, expecting nothing in return; and your reward will be great, and you will be sons of the Most High, for he is kind even to the ungrateful and the wicked. Therefore be merciful, just as your Father is merciful.

"Be careful not to do your righteous acts in public, in order to be seen. When you give charity, don't blow a trumpet to announce it, as the hypocrites do in the synagogues and in the streets, so that people will praise them. Truly I tell you, they have their reward. But when you give charity, don't let your left hand know what your right hand is doing, and keep your charity a secret; and your Father, who sees what is secret, will reward you.

"And when you pray, don't be like the hypocrites, who love to stand and pray in the synagogues and the street corners, so that people will see them. But when you pray, go into your inner room and shut the door and pray in secret to your Father; and your Father, who sees what is secret, will reward you.

"And in your prayers, don't talk on and on, as the Gentiles do; for they think that unless they use many words they won't be heard. Don't be like them, for your Father knows what you need even before you ask him. But pray like this:

Our Father in heaven,
   hallowed be your name.
May your kingdom come,
   may your will be done
   on earth as it is in heaven.
Give us this day our daily bread,
   and forgive us our wrongs
   as we forgive those who have wronged us.
And do not lead us into temptation,
   but deliver us from evil.

For if you forgive others their offenses, your heavenly Father will forgive you.

"The eye is the lamp of the body. So if your eye is clear, your whole body is luminous; but if your eye isn't clear, your whole body is dark. And if the light in you is darkness, how great that darkness is.

"Can a blind man lead a blind man? Won't they both fall into a ditch? A disciple is not above his teacher, but every disciple who is fully taught will be like his teacher."

6

"Ask, and it will be given to you; seek, and you will find; knock, and the door will be opened to you. For everyone who asks, receives; and he who seeks, finds; and to him who knocks, the door will be opened.

"What man among you, when his son asks him for a loaf of bread, will give him a stone; or when he asks for a fish, will give him a snake? If you, then, who are imperfect, know how to give good gifts to your children, how much more will your Father, who is perfect, give good things to those who ask him.

"Therefore I tell you, don't be anxious about what you will eat or what you will wear. Isn't your life more than its food, and your body more than its clothing? Look at the birds of the sky: they neither sow nor reap nor gather into barns, yet God feeds them. Which of you by thinking can add a day to his life? And why do you worry about clothing? Consider the lilies of the field, how they grow: they neither toil nor spin. And yet I tell you that not even Solomon in all his glory was robed like one of these. Therefore, if God so clothes the grass, which grows in the field today, and tomorrow is thrown into the oven, won't he all the more clothe you? So don't worry about these things and say, 'What will we eat?' or 'What will we wear?' For that is what the Gentiles seek; and your Father knows that you need these things. But first seek the kingdom of God; and these things will be given to you as well.

"Aren't two sparrows sold for a penny? Yet not one of them falls to the ground apart from your Father. As for you, every hair on your head is numbered. So don't be afraid: you are worth more than many sparrows.

"Don't judge, and you will not be judged. For in the same way that you judge people, you yourself will be judged.

"Why do you see the splinter that is in your brother's eye, but don't notice the log that is in your own eye? First take the log out of your own eye, and then you will see clearly enough to take the splinter out of your brother's eye.

"So if you don't judge, you will not be judged; if you don't condemn, you will not be condemned; if you forgive, you will be forgiven; if you give, things will be given to you: good measure will be poured into your lap, pressed down, shaken together, and overflowing. For the measure by which you give is the measure by which you will receive.

"Therefore, whatever you want others to do to you, do to them. This is the essence of the Law and the prophets.

"Enter by the narrow gate. For the gate is wide and the way is easy that leads to suffering, and those who go through it are many. But the gate is narrow and the way is hard that leads to true life, and those who find it are few.

"Everyone who hears what I say and does it is like a man who built his house upon rock; and the rain fell and the floods came and the winds blew and beat against that house, and it didn't fall, because it was founded on rock. And everyone who hears what I say and doesn't do it is like a man who built his house upon sand; and the rain fell and the floods came and the winds blew and beat against that house, and it fell; and great was its fall."

7

And when Jesus came down from the hill, he went to the lakeside with his disciples, and large crowds from Galilee followed; and large crowds, hearing of his works, came to him from Judea and Jerusalem as well, and from Idumea and beyond the Jordan and the region of Tyre and Sidon. And he told the disciples to have a boat ready for him, so that he wouldn't be crushed by the crowd, for he had healed many people, and the crippled and sick were all pressing in on him to touch him.

Then he went into the house; and such a large crowd gathered around them that they didn't even have time to eat.

And when his family heard about all this, they went to seize him, for they said, "He is out of his mind."

And a mute demoniac was brought to Jesus, and he healed him, and the man began to speak. And all the people were amazed.

But certain scribes who had come down from Jerusalem said, "He is possessed by Beelzebul" and "He casts out demons by using the prince of demons."

And his mother and his brothers arrived, and standing outside, they sent in a message asking for him.

And people in the crowd sitting around him said to him, "Your mother and your brothers are outside and want to see you."

And Jesus said, "Who are my mother and my brothers?" And looking at those who sat in a circle around him, he said, "*These* are my mother and my brothers. Whoever does the will of God is my brother, and sister, and mother."

Once, when Jesus had returned by boat from the other side of the lake, a large crowd gathered around him at the shore. And one of the leaders of the synagogue came to him and prostrated himself at his feet and said, "My little girl is near death; come, I beg of you, lay your hands on her and save her life."

And Jesus went with him. And a large crowd followed and pressed in on him.

And there was a woman in the crowd who had been bleeding for a dozen years, and she had been treated by many doctors, and had spent all her money, and hadn't gotten better but worse. And she had heard about Jesus, and she came up behind him in the crowd and touched his robe, for she thought, "If I touch even his clothes, I will be healed." And immediately the bleeding dried up, and she knew in her body that she was cured of the disease.

And immediately Jesus felt in himself that power had gone forth from him, and he turned around in the crowd and said, "Who touched my clothes?"

And his disciples said to him, "You see the crowd pressing in on you; why do you ask, 'Who touched me?'"

And he looked around to see who had done it.

And the woman, frightened and trembling, knowing what had happened to her, came and prostrated herself before him and told him the whole truth. And Jesus said to her, "Daughter, your trust has healed you. Go in peace, and be cured of your disease."

Before he had finished speaking, some people came to

the leader of the synagogue and said, "Your daughter is dead: why bother the rabbi any further?"

But Jesus overheard this, and said to him, "Don't be afraid; only trust." And he wouldn't let anyone go with him except Peter and James and John the brother of James.

And when they arrived at the leader's house, he found a great commotion, and loud sobbing and wailing. And he went in and said to them, "Why all this commotion? The child is not dead but sleeping." And they laughed at him.

But he ordered them all out, and took the child's father and mother and his three disciples, and went in to where the child was. And he took her hand and said, "*T'litha, koomi*" (which means, "Child, get up"). And immediately the girl got up and began to walk. And they were filled with great astonishment. And he told them to give her something to eat.

From there he went to Nazareth, his native town, and his disciples followed him.

And when the Sabbath came, he began to teach in the synagogue, and many people who heard him were bewildered, and said, "Where does this fellow get such stuff?" and "What makes *him* so wise?" and "How can he be a miracle-worker? Isn't this the carpenter, Mary's bastard, the brother of James and Joseph and Judas and Simon, and aren't his sisters here with us?" And they were prevented from believing in him.

And Jesus said, "A prophet is not rejected except in his own town and in his own family and in his own house."

And he was unable to do any miracle there, because of their disbelief.

8

And from there Jesus set out and went to the region around
Tyre. And he went into a house, and didn't want anyone
to know that he was there, but he couldn't remain hidden.
For soon a Gentile woman, a Syrophoenician by race,
heard of him, and came and prostrated herself at his feet
and said, "Take pity on me, sir; my daughter is possessed
by a demon."

And he said to her, "It is not right to take the children's
food and throw it to the dogs."

And she said, "True, sir; yet even the dogs under the
table eat the children's scraps."

And Jesus answered, "Well said. Now go home; the
demon has left your daughter."

And when she went home, she found the child lying in
bed, and the derangement was gone.

And Jesus returned from the region of Tyre, and went by
way of Sidon to the Sea of Galilee, through the region
of the Decapolis.

And they brought him a man who was deaf and could
hardly speak, and they begged him to lay his hands on
him. And he took him aside, away from the crowd, and
put his fingers into the man's ears, and spat and touched
the man's tongue; and looking up into the sky, Jesus
sighed, and said to him, "*Ethpatakh!*" (which means, "Be
opened!"). And immediately his ears were opened, his
tongue was released, and he spoke clearly. And the people
were exceedingly astonished.

And a woman in the crowd called out to him, "Blessed is the womb that bore you and the breasts that you sucked."

And Jesus said, "No: blessed rather are those who hear the word of God and obey it."

Another time, in Bethsaida, they brought a blind man to Jesus and begged him to touch him. And he took the blind man by the hand and led him out of the village; and he spat into his eyes, and laid his hands on them, and asked him, "Can you see anything?"

And he looked up and said, "I see men, like trees walking."

And Jesus again laid his hands on his eyes, and the man looked, and his sight was restored, and he could see everything distinctly.

Still another time, a man in the crowd said to him, "Rabbi, I brought you my son; he is possessed by a mute spirit, and when it attacks him, it throws him around, and he foams and grinds his teeth and gets stiff."

And they brought the boy to him; and immediately he was thrown down violently, and he thrashed around, foaming at the mouth. And Jesus asked the father, "How long has this been happening to him?"

And he said, "Since he was a child. It has tried to kill him many times, and thrown him into the fire or the water. But if it is possible for you to do anything, take pity on us and help us."

And Jesus said to him, " '*If* it is possible'! Anything is possible when you believe it is."

And the boy's father cried out, "I believe; help my unbelief."

And Jesus put his hands on the boy and spoke to him. And the boy cried out and went into convulsions, and then became like a corpse, so that most of the people were saying he had died. But Jesus took him by the hand and lifted him, and he stood up.

Once, when they were in Capernaum, the disciples asked Jesus, "Who is the greatest in the kingdom of God?"

And he called a child over, and put him in front of them; and taking him in his arms, he said, "Truly I tell you, unless you return and become like children, you can't enter the kingdom of God."

Peter once asked him, "Sir, how often should I forgive my brother if he keeps wronging me? Up to seven times?"

And Jesus said to him, "Not just seven: seventy times seven."

9

Once a certain scribe stood up and said, "Rabbi, what must I do to gain eternal life?"

And Jesus said to him, "What is written in the Law?"

And the scribe said, "*You shall love the Lord your God with all your heart and with all your soul and with all your strength and with all your mind,* and *You shall love your neighbor as yourself.*"

And Jesus said, "You have answered correctly. Do this and you will live."

And the scribe said, "But who is my neighbor?"

And Jesus said, "A certain man, while traveling from

Jerusalem to Jericho, was set upon by robbers, who stripped him and beat him and left him on the road, half dead. And a priest happened to be going down that road, and when he saw him, he passed by on the other side. And a Levite, too, came to that place and saw him and passed by on the other side. But a Samaritan who was traveling that way came upon the man, and when he saw him, he was moved with compassion, and he went over to him and bound up his wounds, pouring oil and wine on them, and put him on his own donkey and brought him to an inn and took care of him. And on the next day he took out two silver coins and gave them to the innkeeper and said, 'Take care of him; and if it costs more than this, I will reimburse you when I come back.'

"Which of these three, do you think, turned out to be a neighbor to that man?"

And the scribe said, "The one who treated him with mercy."

And Jesus said, "Go then, and do as he did."

Another time, the tax-gatherers and prostitutes were all crowding around to listen to him. And the scribes grumbled, and said, "This fellow welcomes criminals and eats with them."

And Jesus told them this parable. "What do you think: If a man has a hundred sheep and one of them strays, doesn't he leave the ninety-nine on the hills and go looking for the one that strayed? And when he finds it, he is filled with joy, and he puts it on his shoulders and goes home and gathers his friends and neighbors and says to them, 'Rejoice with me: I found my sheep that was lost.'

"Or if a woman has ten silver coins and loses one of them, doesn't she light a lamp and sweep the house and keep searching until she finds it? And when she finds it, she gathers her friends and neighbors and says, 'Rejoice with me: I found the coin that I lost.' In just the same way, I tell you, God rejoices over one sinner who returns."

And he said, "There once was a man who had two sons. And the younger one said to him, 'Father, let me have my share of the estate.' So he divided his property between them. And not many days afterward, having turned his share into money, the younger son left and traveled to a distant country, and there he squandered his inheritance in riotous living. And after he had spent it all, a severe famine arose in that country; and he was destitute. And he went and hired himself out to a citizen of that country, who sent him to his farm to feed the pigs. And he longed to fill his belly with the husks that the pigs were eating; and no one would give him any food. And when he came to himself, he said, 'How many of my father's hired men have more than enough to eat, while I am dying of hunger. I will get up and go to my father, and say to him, "Father, I have sinned against God and against you, and I am no longer worthy to be called your son. Let me be like one of your hired men."' And he got up, and went to his father. And while he was still a long way off, his father saw him, and was moved with compassion, and ran to him, and threw his arms around him, and kissed him. And the son said to him, 'Father, I have sinned against God and against you, and I am no longer worthy to be called your son.' But the father said to his servants, 'Quick, bring out the best robe we have and put it on him; and put a ring on his hand,

and sandals on his feet. And bring the fatted calf, and kill it; and let us eat and make merry. For this son of mine was dead, and he has come back to life; he was lost, and is found.' And they began to make merry.

"Now the older son had been out in the fields; and on his way home, as he got closer to the house, he heard music and dancing, and he called over one of the servants and asked what was happening. And the servant said, 'Your brother has come, and your father has killed the fatted calf, because he has him back safe and sound.' And he was angry and would not go in. And his father came out and tried to soothe him; but he said, 'Look: all these years I have been serving you, and never have I disobeyed your command. Yet you never even gave me a goat, so that I could feast and make merry with my friends. But now that this son of yours comes back, after eating up your money on whores, you kill the fatted calf for him!' And the father said to him, 'Child, you are always with me, and everything I have is yours. But it was proper to make merry and rejoice, for your brother was dead, and he has come back to life; he was lost, and is found.' "

10

And when Jesus had finished saying these things, he left Galilee and entered the territory of Judea. And large crowds gathered around him, and he healed and taught.

And some people were bringing children to him, for him to bless; but the disciples rebuked them. And when Jesus saw this, he was indignant, and said to them, "Let the children come to me, don't try to stop them; for the kingdom of God belongs to such as these. Truly I tell you, whoever doesn't accept the kingdom of God like a child cannot enter it." And he took them in his arms, and put his hands on them, and blessed them.

And one day, as he was setting out, a man ran up and fell on his knees before him, and said, "Good Rabbi, what must I do to gain eternal life?"

And Jesus said to him, "Why do you call me good? No one is good except God alone. You know the commandments: *Do not murder, Do not commit adultery, Do not steal, Do not bear false witness, Do not defraud, Honor your father and mother.*"

And the man said, "Rabbi, all these I have kept since I was a boy."

And Jesus, looking at him, loved him, and said, "There is one thing that you lack: go, sell everything you have and give it to the poor, and you will have treasure in heaven; then come and follow me."

But when he heard this, his face clouded over, and he went away sick at heart, for he was a man who had large estates.

And Jesus looked around at his disciples and said, "Children, how hard it is for the rich to enter the kingdom of God. It is easier for a camel to go through the eye of a needle than for a rich man to enter the kingdom of God."

And as they were traveling along the road, he said to a certain man, "Follow me."

And the man said, "Let me first go and bury my father."

But Jesus said to him, "Let the dead bury their dead."

Another man said to Jesus, "I will follow you, sir, but let me first say good-bye to my family."

And Jesus said to him, "No one who puts his hand to the plow and then looks back is ready for the kingdom of God."

11

And as they came near Jerusalem, to Bethany and Bethphage and the Mount of Olives, the large crowds coming for the festival spread their cloaks in front of him on the road, and some people spread brushwood that they had cut in the fields. And those who walked in front of him and those who followed shouted, "Blessed is he who comes in the name of the Lord; praise God in the highest heavens!"

And when he entered Jerusalem, the whole city was stirred up, wondering who he was. And the crowds said, "This is the prophet Jesus, from Nazareth in Galilee."

And he entered the Temple and looked around at everything; but since it was already late, he went out to Bethany with the Twelve.

And every day Jesus would go to the Temple to teach, and at night he would stay on the Mount of Olives. And early in the morning he would go back into the Temple, and all the people gathered around him, and he sat and taught them. And they listened to him with delight.

One day, as he was teaching in the Temple, some scribes said to him, "Rabbi, is it lawful to pay the tax to Caesar, or not?"

And Jesus said, "Bring me a coin."

And they brought one. And he said, "Whose image is on it?"

And they said, "Caesar's."

And Jesus said, "Give to Caesar the things that are Caesar's, and to God the things that are God's."

Later, a certain scribe who had been listening to Jesus and had observed how well he answered people's questions asked him, "Which commandment is the greatest of all?"

And Jesus answered, "*Hear, O Israel: the Lord our God is one; and you shall love the Lord your God with all your heart and with all your soul and with all your mind and with all your strength.* This is the first and greatest commandment. And there is a second one that is like it: *You shall love your neighbor as yourself.* On these two commandments all the Law and the prophets depend."

And the scribe said to him, "Excellent, Rabbi! You have said the truth, that God is one and there is no other beside him, and to love him with all your heart and all your understanding and all your strength, and to love your neighbor as yourself, is worth far more than all burnt offerings and sacrifices."

And Jesus, seeing that he had spoken wisely, said to him, "You are not far from the kingdom of God."

12

The next morning, as Jesus was teaching in the Temple, the scribes brought a woman who had been caught in adultery, and they stood her in the middle. And they said to him, "Rabbi, this woman was caught in adultery, in the very act. Moses in the Law commanded us to stone such women to death; what do *you* say?"

But Jesus stooped down and with his finger wrote on the ground.

And as they continued to question him, he stood up and said to them, "Let whoever of you is sinless be the first to throw a stone at her." And again he stooped down and wrote on the ground.

And when they heard this, they went out one by one, the older ones first. And Jesus was left alone, with the woman still standing there.

And Jesus stood up, and said to her, "Woman, where are they? Has no one condemned you?"

And she said, "No one, sir."

And Jesus said, "I don't condemn you either. Go now, and sin no more."

13

And the day before the Passover and the festival of Unleavened Bread, in the evening, he came into the city with the Twelve, and they ate supper. And after they had sung a psalm, they went out to the Mount of Olives, across the Kidron valley, to a garden called Gethsemane.

And Jesus said, "Sit here, while I pray." And going off by himself, he prostrated himself on the ground and prayed. And he said, "Abba, all things are possible for you. Take this cup from me. Nevertheless, not what I want, but what you want."

And when he got up from his prayer and went to the disciples, he found them asleep. And he said to them, "Why are you sleeping? Couldn't you stay awake for even one hour?" And they didn't know what to answer.

And suddenly Judas came, one of the Twelve, with a battalion of Roman soldiers and some officers from the chief priests, carrying swords and clubs and lanterns and torches. And he went up to Jesus and said, "Rabbi!" and kissed him. And they seized Jesus and bound him, and took him away.

And all the disciples abandoned him, and fled.

14

And they took Jesus to the High Priest.

And Peter followed at a distance, into the courtyard of the High Priest. And the slaves and attendants had made a charcoal fire, because it was a cold night; and they were standing around the fire, warming themselves. And Peter stood with them and warmed himself.

And one of the slave-girls of the High Priest came. And when she saw Peter, she looked at him closely and said, "You were there too, with that fellow from Nazareth, that Jesus." But he denied it, saying, "I don't know what you're talking about."

And after a while, someone else said to Peter, "You have a Galilean accent; you must be one of them." And he said, "God curse me if I know the man!" And at that moment the cock crowed. And Peter went out and burst into tears.

And early the next morning, the chief priests, with the elders and scribes, bound Jesus and took him away and handed him over to Pilate. And Pilate sentenced Jesus to death, and flogged him, and handed him over to his soldiers to be crucified.

And they took him out to crucify him, and seized a man named Simon of Cyrene, who was passing by on his way in from the country, and made him carry the cross.

And they brought him to the place called Golgotha (which means "the place of the skull"). And some women offered him drugged wine, but he wouldn't take it.

And at about nine o'clock they crucified him.

And above his head the charge against him was written: THE KING OF THE JEWS. And with him they crucified two Zealots, one on his right and one on his left.

And at about three o'clock in the afternoon, Jesus uttered a loud cry, and died.

COMMENTARY

Baptism

This is the book of the good news that Jesus of Nazareth proclaimed.

John the Baptizer appeared in the wilderness, proclaiming a baptism of renewal for the forgiveness of sins. And John was clothed in camel's hair, with a belt of animal hide around his waist, and he ate locusts and wild honey. And people from all of Judea went out to him, and many people from Jerusalem, and they were baptized by him in the Jordan River, confessing their sins.

And at that time Jesus came from Nazareth in Galilee, and was baptized in the Jordan by John.

And afterward the Spirit drove him out into the wilderness. And he was in the wilderness for forty days, with the wild animals.

baptism: According to Josephus:

> John was a good man and had exhorted the Jews to lead righteous lives, to practice justice toward their fellows and piety toward God, and so doing to join in baptism. In his view this was a necessary preliminary if baptism was to be acceptable to God. They must not employ it to gain pardon for whatever sins they committed, but as a consecration of the body implying that the soul was already thoroughly cleansed by right behavior.
> (*Jewish Antiquities*, in *Works*, vol. 9, trans. Louis H. Feldman, Harvard University Press, 1965, pp. 81f.)

Jesus: The Hebrew/Aramaic is Yeshu, a shortened form of Ye-hoshua (Joshua).

Nazareth: The Gospel of Mark provides no information about Jesus' birthplace; it just says that "Jesus came from Nazareth in Galilee." The legend that he was born in Bethlehem occurs only in the infancy narratives in Matthew and Luke. Both authors thought that since Jesus was the Messiah, and since it had been prophesied that the Messiah would be born in Bethlehem (Micah 5:2), Jesus must have been born in Bethlehem. But since it was well known that Jesus came from Nazareth, they created mutually contradictory explanations. According to Matthew, Joseph and Mary were living in Bethlehem when Jesus was conceived; after his birth, an angel in a dream warned Joseph of Herod's (unhistorical) massacre of the children, and they fled to Egypt; when they returned to Israel after Herod's death, another dream angel warned Joseph to move to Nazareth, and that explains why Jesus grew up there. But according to Luke, Joseph and Mary were living in Nazareth; just before Mary was due to give birth, they had to travel to Bethlehem, Joseph's ancestral town, for the (unhistorical) census called for by the emperor Augustus, and that explains why Jesus was born there; shortly after his circumcision, they returned to Nazareth.

baptized in the Jordan by John: Mark or his source, followed by Matthew and Luke, heavily mythologizes this incident: sky opening, spirit descending in the form of a dove, heavenly voice acknowledging Jesus as the divine Son. Morton Smith (*Jesus the Magician*, pp. 96ff.) adduces some astonishing parallels from ancient magical practices.

Visions, revelations, prophecies, ecstasies, experiences of being caught up, like Paul, into the third or seventh heaven and seeing things unspeakable—these occur east and west, north and south, in every shamanic and religious tradition, given the proper conditions of sensory deprivation or religious fervor or concentration. But any good spiritual teacher will discourage us from taking them too seriously, and will teach us to let them come and go like any other experience. Why? In any vision there is still a subject and an object; we are here, the vision is there. We may see the Mother of God or

God the Father on his imperial throne; but after the vision fades, if we haven't seen to the source of all visions, we take up our lives again untransformed. The problem with most mystical experiences is their residue of fascination. People who have them are tempted to think that God is more present there than in other aspects of their life. The experiences are like medicine that cures a disease but has strong and harmful side effects. Usually the cure itself needs to be cured.

The result of genuine spiritual training is that we can allow life to come and go as it wishes. In other words, we can let God's will be done with our wholehearted assent. Eventually, the ordinary becomes the greatest miracle of all. As the eighth-century Zen adept Layman P'ang said:

> My daily affairs are quite ordinary;
> but I'm in total harmony with them.
> I don't hold on to anything, don't reject anything;
> nowhere an obstacle or conflict.
> Who cares about wealth and honor?
> Even the poorest thing shines.
> My miraculous power and spiritual activity:
> drawing water and carrying wood.
>
> (*The Enlightened Heart*, p. 35)

sources: cf. *Mark 1:1; Mark 1:4–6; Mark 1:9; Mark 1:12f.*

He Begins to Teach

And when Jesus heard that John had been arrested, he withdrew to Galilee, and leaving Nazareth, he settled in Capernaum by the lake. And he began to teach and proclaim the good news of the kingdom of God.

And he began to teach: According to Luke 3:23, "Jesus, when he began [to teach], was about thirty years old."

the good news:

> What is "the good news"? That true life, eternal life, has been found—it is not something promised, it is already here, it is *within you:* as life lived in love, in love without subtraction or exclusion, without distance. Everyone is the child of God—Jesus definitely claims nothing for himself alone—and as a child of God everyone is equal to everyone else.
>
> (Friedrich Nietzsche, *The Antichristian.* For further insights of Nietzsche's, see Appendix 1, pp. 291f.)

the kingdom of God: Mark adds a verse here, which could be translated "And he said, 'The time is fulfilled, the kingdom of God has arrived. Return [to God], and trust the good news.'"

In the Gospel of Thomas, there are two dialogues on this subject that might well be authentic:

> The disciples said to him, "When will the kingdom come?" Jesus said, "It will not come if you look for it. Nor can you say, 'It is here' or 'It is there.' For the kingdom of the Father is already spread out over the earth, but people don't see it." (Thomas, 113)

> The disciples said to him, "When will the repose of the dead happen, and when will the new world come?" Jesus said, "What you are waiting for has already come, but you don't recognize it." (Thomas, 51)

sources: Matthew 4:12f.; Mark 1:14

The First Disciples

These two incidents are what the German scholar Rudolf Bult-mann called "ideal scenes": incidents which the Evangelist or a previous editor created as examples of actual events. Here, although the scenes are obviously stylized, they give a sense of the great personal magnetism that Jesus must have had.

And as he was walking beside the Sea of Galilee, he saw Simon and his brother Andrew casting a fishing net into the lake. And Jesus said to them, "Come, follow me." And immediately they left their nets and followed him.

And walking on a little farther, he saw James the son of Zebedee and John his brother, who were in their boat mending their nets. And he called them, and immediately they left their father Zebedee in the boat with the hired men and followed him.

Follow me: Mark adds a phrase that was circulating in the early church: "and I will make you fishers of men." But Jesus is calling Simon and Andrew to be disciples, not apostles, and, as D. E. Nineham comments in *The Gospel of St. Mark* (Penguin Books, 1963, p. 72), these words "make much more obvious sense in the light of later Christian practice and usage."

And immediately they left their nets and followed him: John's Gospel presents a slightly more realistic account:

And the two disciples [of John the Baptist] followed Jesus. And Jesus turned and saw them following him and said, "What are you seeking?" They said to him, "Rabbi" (which, being translated, means Teacher), "where are you staying?" He said to them, "Come and see." So they went and saw where he was staying, and they stayed with him that day. (John 1:37ff.)

source: Mark 1:15–20

At Capernaum

The last editorial comment here—"he taught them like some-one who has authority, and not like the scribes"—gives us a glimpse of the powerful impression Jesus made on the common people, and probably contains some authentic memory of him.

And they came to Capernaum. And on the Sabbath, Jesus went into the synagogue and taught. And people were astonished at his teaching, for he taught them like someone who has authority, and not like the scribes.

scribes: The class made up of Bible teachers, lawyers, and nota-ries.

In a larger sense, the scribes are those who have made them-selves a cozy den in the religious doctrine of their time. In cer-tain ways they are admirable, and if their lives are decent and generous they deserve much praise. But they are not good teachers of spiritual truth, because they only *believe* in—they haven't experienced—God. They don't realize that all holy texts are provisional, and that the true word of God is the word that has become flesh.

When Jesus spoke, he didn't need to quote scripture; his own heart was scripture. That is why he could speak with au-thority.

It is equally true, from a complementary perspective, that everything Jesus said was a commentary on Deuteronomy 6:5 ("Love God with all your heart"), and that everything he did was a commentary on Leviticus 19:18 ("Love your neighbor as yourself").

On Scripture: Two Dialogues, Two Monologues

1

In December of 1973, six months after I had begun living and practicing with Zen Master Seung Sahn, I went to him and said, "Isn't it about time I began to learn Sanskrit and Chinese?"

"Why?"

"Well," I said, "the Buddha's most profound words are in the Sanskrit and Chinese sutras. Shouldn't I get as close to them as I can?"

He gave me a look that almost knocked me off my feet. It was one of his withering looks, not for the faint of heart, a mixture of hilarity and disbelief: how had I been his student this long and *still* not have understood?

Then he said, very slowly, as if to a retarded child, "The ultimate teaching is beyond words. So what good will it do you to get close to the Buddha's words?"

I gulped. A short, uncomfortable silence. Then he said, "There is only one thing now that is important."

I didn't dare ask him what that one thing was.

But I knew.

2

According to Jeremiah (31:33ff.), God says of the End of Days (which is always occurring, if we let it), "I have put my truth in your innermost mind, and I have written it in your heart. No longer does a man need to teach his brother about God. For all of you know Me, from the most ignorant to the most learned, from the poorest to the most powerful."

3

The Buddha said, "A man walking along a highroad sees a great river, its near bank dangerous and frightening, its far bank safe. He collects sticks and foliage, makes a raft, paddles across the river, and reaches the other shore. Now suppose that, after he reaches the other shore, he takes the raft and puts it on his head and walks with it on his head wherever he goes. Would he be using the raft in an appropriate way? No; a reasonable man will realize that the raft has been very useful to him in crossing the river and arriving safely on the other shore, but that once he has arrived, it is proper to leave the raft behind and walk on without it. This is using the raft appropriately.

"In the same way, all truths should be used to cross over; they should not be held on to once you have arrived. You should let go of even the most profound insight or the most wholesome teaching; all the more so, unwholesome teachings."

4

The great Zen Master Kuei-shan asked his student Yang-shan (who was to become an equally great teacher), "In the forty volumes of the Nirvana Sutra, how many words come from the Buddha and how many from demons?"

Yang-shan said, "They are *all* demons' words."

Kuei-shan said, "From now on, no one will be able to pull the wool over your eyes!"

source: Mark 1:21f.

First Healings

Further "ideal scenes": stylized examples of actual, typical events.

And when they left the synagogue, they went to the house of Simon and Andrew, along with James and John. And Simon's mother-in-law was in bed with a fever. And as soon as they told Jesus about her, he went and took her by the hand and lifted her up, and the fever left her, and she served them.

And that evening, they brought to him everyone who was sick or insane, and the whole village was gathered at the door, and he healed many people.

And early in the morning, while it was still dark, he got up and went out to a remote place and prayed there. And Simon and his companions searched for him, and when they found him, they said to him, "Everyone is looking for you." And he said to them, "Let us go on to the next villages, so that I can proclaim the good news there too."

And he went through all of Galilee, proclaiming the good news in their synagogues and healing many diseases.

he healed many people: For comments on Jesus' healings by a gifted present-day healer, see Appendix 2, pp. 295ff.

sick or insane:

> Almost nobody thinks the preserved stories are accurate in all details, but few scholars would deny that at least some of them probably derive from reports of "cures" that actually occurred in Jesus' presence and were understood by the patients, the observers, and Jesus himself as miracles performed by him.

> Such cures made Jesus famous. To understand their importance, we must remember that ancient Palestine had no hospitals or insane asylums. The sick and insane had to be cared for by their families, in their homes. The burden of caring for them was often severe and sometimes, especially in cases of violent insanity, more than the family could bear—the afflicted were turned out of doors and left to wander like animals. This practice continued to the present century; I shall never forget my first experience in the "old city" of Jerusalem in 1940. The first thing I saw as I came through the Jaffa Gate was a lunatic, a filthy creature wearing an old burlap bag with neck and armholes cut through the bottom and sides. He was having a fit. It seemed to involve a conversation with some imaginary being in the air in front of him. He was pouring out a flood of gibberish while raising his hands as if in supplication. Soon he began to make gestures, as if trying to protect himself from blows, and howled as if being beaten. Frothing at the mouth, he fell to the ground on his face, lay there moaning and writhing, vomited, and had an attack of diarrhea. Afterwards he was calmer, but lay in his puddles of filth, whimpering gently. I stood where I had stopped when I first saw him, some fifty feet away, rooted to the spot, but nobody else paid any attention. There were lots of people in the street, but those who came up

to him merely skirted the mess and walked by. He was lying on the sidewalk in front of a drugstore. After a few minutes a clerk came out with a box of sawdust, poured it on the puddles, and treated the patient with a couple of kicks in the small of the back. This brought him to his senses and he got up and staggered off, still whimpering, rubbing his mouth with one hand and his back with the other. When I came to live in the "old city" I found that he and half a dozen like him were familiar figures.

Such was ancient psychotherapy. Those not willing to put their insane relatives into the street had to endure them at home. Also, since rational medicine (except for surgery) was rudimentary, lingering and debilitating diseases must have been common, and the victims of these, too, had to be cared for at home. Accordingly, many people eagerly sought cures, not only for themselves, but also for their relatives. Doctors were inefficient, rare, and expensive. When a healer appeared—a man who could perform miraculous cures, and who did so for nothing!—he was sure to be mobbed. In the crowds that swarmed around him desperate for cures, cures were sure to occur. With each cure, the reputation of his powers, the expectations and speculations of the crowd, and the legends and rumors about him would grow.

(Morton Smith, *Jesus the Magician*,
Harper & Row, 1968, pp. 8f.)

source: *Mark 1:29–39*

He Heals a Leper

And in one of the villages, a leper came and knelt before him and said, "If you wish, you can cleanse me."

And Jesus, moved with compassion, stretched out his hand and touched him and said, "I do wish it; be cleansed."

And immediately the leprosy left him, and he was cleansed.

And Jesus said to him, "Go and show yourself to the priest and offer for your cleansing what Moses commanded."

And the man went out and began to talk about it excitedly, and the news spread, until Jesus could no longer go into a village, but had to stay out in the countryside. And people came to him from every direction.

what Moses commanded: Leviticus 14:1ff. This sentence, which goes against the grain of the Gospels' portrayal of Jesus as being in conflict with the Law, may indicate that the account is historically accurate.

sources: Luke 5:12, Mark 1:40; Mark 1:40–42; Mark 1:44f.

The Kingdom of God (1)

Another "ideal scene." The parables originally circulated as independent sayings, as did all the words of Jesus; only much later were they placed in their current settings by the Evangelists or by previous editors.

The subject of this first parable is the birth of spiritual awareness, its mystery and wonder. Just as a seed, under the proper conditions of sunlight and water, sprouts in the ground, so God's grace bursts into awareness, suddenly, effortlessly, and beyond our control. And just as the plant ripens by itself, so the awareness, if we provide it with the proper nourishment, ripens into gratitude, compassion, and transparency.

And he went again to the lakeside, and began to teach, and so many people gathered that he had to get into a boat on the lake. And he sat in it, and the whole crowd sat on the shore, up to the water's edge.

And he taught them many things in parables, and said, "What is the kingdom of God like? It is like a man who sows a seed on the earth: he goes about his business, and day by day the seed sprouts and grows, he doesn't know how. The earth bears fruit by itself, first the stalk, then the ear, then the full grain in the ear. And when the grain is ripe, the man goes in with his sickle, because it is harvest time."

he doesn't know how:

> In spite of all the farmer's work and worry,
> he can't reach down to where the seed is slowly
> transmuted into summer. The earth *bestows*.
>> (Rainer Maria Rilke, *The Sonnets to Orpheus*,
>> trans. Stephen Mitchell, Simon & Schuster,
>> 1985, p. 41)

sources: Mark 4:1; Mark 4:2,30,26f.; Mark 4:28

The Kingdom of God (2)

These five parables tell about the discovery and growth of the kingdom of God. But aren't discovery and growth contradictory metaphors? If the kingdom of God is discovered all at once, like a treasure, how can it grow slowly and invisibly, like a plant?

Here Jesus is talking about two different aspects of the experience. When we first discover the kingdom, we are overwhelmed by wonder and joy, and we realize that nothing in the world of birth and death has ultimate value, and that therefore everything does. From the first moment, the kingdom is fully present, like a treasure, like a pearl.

But in terms of its effect, the kingdom of God is something that grows gradually. When we discover it, we are still clogged up with many kinds of selfish concerns, which divert our attention from it and obstruct its power in our life. Gradually, as our transparency grows, its power grows. Not that the light isn't fully present, from the beginning; it's just that we can't yet allow it to shine through.

"The kingdom of God is like a mustard seed, which is smaller than any other seed; but when it is sown, it grows up and becomes the largest of shrubs, and puts forth large branches, so that the birds of the sky are able to make their nests in its shade.

"The kingdom of God is like yeast, which a woman took and mixed in with fifty pounds of dough, until all of it was leavened.

"The kingdom of God is like a treasure buried in a field, which a man found and buried again; then in his joy he goes and sells everything he has and buys that field.

"Or the kingdom of God is like this: there was a merchant looking for fine pearls, who found one pearl of great price, and he went and sold everything he had and bought it.

"Thus, every scribe who has been trained for the kingdom of God is like a householder who can bring forth out of his treasure room both the new and the old."

like a mustard seed: The mustard plant can grow to a height of four feet or more. The point of this parable is the contrast between the smallness of the seed and the largeness of the shrub. This small seed is in every human being, even if we aren't conscious of it, even if we can't feel a glimmer of radiance inside us. But once we turn our attention toward it, it begins to grow. Jesus calls it the kingdom of God; another name for it is the tree of life. When it is fully grown, it gives shelter to all the despised and wounded creatures inside our heart, and to all creatures on earth.

Meister Eckhart said, "The seed of God is in us. If you are an intelligent and hard-working farmer, it will thrive and grow up into God, whose seed it is, and its fruits will be God-fruits. Pear seeds grow into pear trees, nut seeds grow into nut trees, and God seeds grow into God."

In Meister Eckhart's metaphor, as in Rilke's, there is no conflict between those absurd categories "faith" and "works."

In one sense, the farmer can't do anything; he can't cause the sun to shine or the rain to fall, and he "can't reach down to where the seed is slowly / transmuted into summer." In another sense, *everything* is up to him; if he doesn't prepare the soil and plant the crops, God can make nothing happen. Everything is grace; but unless we prepare for grace, we will never know it has come.

like yeast: It spreads everywhere, into every last part of the loaf, the life.

like a treasure: Could Jesus have meant to propose a dishonest man as a symbol for someone who finds the kingdom of God? (The man reburies the treasure and buys the field under false pretenses; under normal circumstances in Jewish law the owner would have been entitled to half the treasure.) Perhaps the parable originally had a simpler form, more or less as follows: "The kingdom of God is like a treasure buried in a field, which a man found and dug up and rejoiced." It could be that in Matthew's version it has absorbed the concluding phrases of the parable of the Pearl.

In any event, the point of the parable is the finding, and Jesus wants his hearers to share the man's joy, not to analyze his morality. Reburying the treasure and buying the field have nothing to do with the spiritual truth Jesus is teaching here. In reality, you can find the treasure only on your own land.

The best commentary on this parable is a story about two eighth-century Chinese Zen Masters:

> When Hui-hai was a young monk and first came to the great Master Ma-tzu, the Master asked him, "What have you come here for?"
>
> Hui-hai said, "I have come seeking the Buddha's teaching."
>
> "What a fool you are!" Ma-tzu said. "You have the greatest treasure in the world inside you, and yet you go around asking other people for help. What good is this? I have nothing to give you."

Hui-hai bowed and said, "Please, Master, tell me what this treasure is."

Ma-tzu said, "Where is your question coming from? *This* is your treasure. It is precisely what is asking the question at this very moment. Everything is stored in this precious treasure-house of yours. It is there at your disposal, you can use it as you wish, nothing is lacking. You are the master of everything. Why then are you running away from yourself and seeking for things outside?"

Upon hearing these words, Hui-hai realized his own mind. Beside himself with joy, he bowed deeply to the Master.

Much later, when he himself was a great Master (known, interestingly enough, as the Great Pearl), Hui-hai gave the following speech:

Friends and brothers, it is all right for you to be monks, but it is much better to be men unattached to all things. Why should you run around making karma that will hem you in like a criminal's chains? Trying to empty your minds, straining to attain enlightenment, blabbering about your understanding of the Buddha-Dharma—all this is a waste of energy. Once, the great Ma-tzu said to me, "Your own treasure house already contains everything you need. Why don't you use it freely, instead of chasing after something outside yourself?" From that day on, I stopped looking elsewhere. Just make use of your own treasure house according to your needs, and you will be happy men. There isn't a single thing that can be grasped or rejected. When you stop thinking that things have a past or future, and that they come or go, then in the whole universe there won't be a single atom that is not your own treasure. All you have to do is look into your own mind; then the marvelous reality will manifest itself at all times. Don't search for the truth with your intellect. Don't search at all. The nature of the mind is intrinsically pure. Thus the Flower Garland Sutra says: "All things have neither a beginning nor an end." For those who are able to interpret these words correctly, the Buddhas are always present. Furthermore, the Vimalakirti Sutra says: "Reality is perceived through your own body." If you don't run after sounds and sights, or let appearances give rise to conceptual thinking, you will become men unattached to all things. That's enough for now. Take good care of yourselves.

who found one pearl of great price, and he went and sold everything he had: Wholeheartedness is the one requirement. We have to give ourselves completely, and let go of everything in our life, especially of life itself. This "everything" turns out to be infinitely less than the nothing that we receive.

Ramana Maharshi said:

Reality is simply the loss of the ego. Destroy the ego by seeking its identity. It will automatically vanish and reality will shine forth by itself. This is the direct method.

There is no greater mystery than this, that we keep seeking reality though in fact we *are* reality. We think that there is something hiding reality and that this must be destroyed before reality is gained. How ridiculous! A day will dawn when you will laugh at all your past efforts. That which will be on the day you laugh is also here and now.

every scribe: Scholars who consider this verse to be a later addition explain "scribe" here as "Christian scribe." But it would be typical of Jesus that in spite of opposition from the scribes, he could state here that they too are capable of entering the kingdom of God. In his generosity toward his opponents, he is practicing his own precept of loving your enemies (unlike the bitter, vituperative "Jesus" of Matthew 23 or John 8).

the new and the old: When it comes out of the treasure room, the new has the resonance of the old, and the old has the lustre of the new.

sources: Mark 4:31f.; Matthew 13:33; Matthew 13:44–46; Matthew 13:52

The Kingdom of God (3)

The most transparent words in the Gospel, and the essence of the good news.

And someone asked him, "When will the kingdom of God come?"
And he said, "The kingdom of God will not come if you watch for it.
Nor will anyone be able to say, 'It is here' or 'It is there.' For the kingdom of God is within you."

someone asked him: Luke reads, "The Pharisees asked him."

> The Pharisees as auditors have been introduced by Luke, who found the saying with no hearers mentioned, just as in certain cases he seems to have constructed the situation from the saying itself. The saying might suggest "disciples" or "the people" or "a certain man," but "Pharisees" seems hardly possible.
> (Burton Scott Easton, "Luke 17:20–21. An Exegetical Study," *American Journal of Theology* 16, p. 279)

When will the kingdom of God come: My friend the Zen teacher John Tarrant comments, "Ordinary mind is the Tao. If you turn toward it, you turn away from it."

if you watch for it: Literally, "with observation," that is, "with outward signs that can be perceived."

> My experience tells me that the Kingdom of God is within us, and that we can realize it not by saying "Lord, Lord," but by doing His will and His work. If, therefore, we wait for the Kingdom to come as something coming from outside, we shall be sadly mistaken.
>
> (Mohandas K. Gandhi, *The Collected Works of Mahatma Gandhi*, vol. 37, The Publications Division, Ministry of Information and Broadcasting, Government of India, 1970, p. 261)

There is an important passage from the Gospel of Thomas that helps to explain the present saying:

> Jesus said, "If your teachers say to you, 'Look, the kingdom is in heaven,' then the birds will get there before you. But the kingdom is within you, and it is outside you. If you know yourselves, then you will be known; and you will know that you are the sons of the living Father." (Thomas, 3)

within: The Greek preposition *entos* is, in many modern versions, translated "among." But its regular meaning is "within"; it is used in Matthew 23:26 to mean "the inside" (of a cup); and in the Septuagint, which Luke knew well, it always refers to the inward parts of a person ("my heart within me," Psalms 39:4 and 109:22; "everything within me," Psalm 103:1).

(i) *entos* is properly a strengthened form of *en* used where it is important to exclude any of the possible meanings of that preposition other than "inside." . . . (ii) When Luke means "among," he says *en mesoi*, an expression which occurs about a dozen times in the Third Gospel and the Acts. If he meant "among" here, why did he vary his usage? (iii) If appeal be made to an underlying Aramaic, the prepositions in that language meaning respectively "among" and "within" are distinct, and there is no reason why a competent translator should confuse them. (iv) "Among" does not give a logical sense. A thing which is "among you" is localized in space, more or less. On the other hand you cannot say "Lo here, or there!" of that which is "within," and the Kingdom of God is said not to be localized in space, *because* it is *entos humōn*. This might be understood as the counterpart of the "Q" saying discussed above: the Day of the Son of Man is not localized in space (or time) because it is instantaneous and ubiquitous; the Kingdom of God is not localized because it is "within you." In other words, the ultimate reality, though it is revealed in history, essentially belongs to the spiritual order, where the categories of space and time are not applicable. There is however another possible meaning. In the *Harvard Theological Review*, vol. xli, no. 1 (1948), C. H. Roberts argued persuasively on the basis of evidence from papyri and elsewhere, that *entos humōn* means "in your hands," "within your power." That is, the Kingdom of God is not something for which you have to watch anxiously (*ou meta paratērēseōs*), but is an available possibility here and now, for those who are willing to "receive it as a little child."   (C. H. Dodd, *The Parables of the Kingdom*, Charles Scribner's Sons, 1961, pp. 62f.)

For the kingdom of God is within you: Where is this "within"? It can't be observed by a surgeon, just as heaven can't be found by an astronaut.

Ramana Maharshi comments:

The ultimate truth is so simple. It is nothing more than being in the pristine state. This is all that needs to be said.

All religions have come into existence because people want something elaborate and attractive and puzzling. Each religion is complex, and each sect in each religion has its adherents and antagonists. For example, an ordinary Christian won't be satisfied unless he is told that God is somewhere in the far-off heavens, not to be reached by us unaided; Christ alone knew Him and Christ alone can guide us; worship Christ and be saved. If he is told the simple truth, that "the kingdom of heaven is within you," he is not satisfied, and will read complex and far-fetched meanings into it.

Only mature minds can grasp the simple truth in all its nakedness.

source: Luke 17:20f.

The Inner Light (1)

Light, seed, treasure: all these are metaphors for the kingdom of God within us, the vivid, loving, ruthless intelligence that makes itself felt in the heart.

And he said, "When you light a lamp, do you put it under a basket or under a bed? Don't you put it on a lampstand? For there is nothing hidden that can't be made clear, and nothing secret that can't become obvious. Pay attention to what you hear; the measure you give is the measure you receive."

There is nothing hidden that can't be made clear: "Recognize what is in your sight," Jesus says in the Gospel of Thomas, "and what is hidden will become clear to you"(Thomas, 5).

sources: *Mark 4:21–24, Luke 8:17*

With the Wicked

Two "ideal scenes."

Another time, Jesus was walking beside the lake, and a crowd gathered around him, and he taught them. And as he walked on, he saw Levi the son of Alphaeus sitting at the tax booth, and he said to him, "Follow me." And he stood up and followed him.

And many people who held the Law in contempt began to follow Jesus. And the scribes said to him, "Why do you eat with traitors and whores?" And Jesus said to them, "It isn't the healthy who need a doctor, but the sick. My teaching is not meant for those who are already righteous, but for the wicked."

people who held the Law in contempt: Literally, "tax-collectors and sinners." In a present-day context, neither word has much of a sting to it: our tax-collectors are law-abiding citizens, and a "sin" can mean something as trivial as not going to church on

Sunday. But in Jesus' time, the words referred to hardened criminals, whose sins would have shocked and disgusted any decent person.

> The word "sinners" in English versions of the Bible translated the Greek word *hamartōloi*. Behind *hamartōloi* stands, almost beyond question, the Hebrew word *resha'im* (or the Aramaic equivalent) . . . It is best translated "the wicked," and it refers to those who sinned wilfully and heinously and who did not repent. . . . "Tax-collectors" were traitors. More precisely, they were quislings, collaborating with Rome. The wicked equally betrayed the God who redeemed Israel and gave them his law. There was no neat distinction between "religious" and "political" betrayal in first-century Judaism.
>
> (E. P. Sanders, *Jesus and Judaism*, Fortress Press, 1985, pp. 177ff.)

We might even say that Jesus' particular mission was to the first-century equivalent of the Mafia:

> Those Jews who collaborated with the Roman tax-farmers by acting for them as tax-gatherers were regarded as criminals, and specifically as robbers. This was because many of the taxes were regarded as unjust . . . and the methods of tax-collecting were often cruelly oppressive. Philo describes the tortures used by tax-collectors in Egypt. . . . Since the tax-farmers had bought the tax-concession, they were allowed to exact as much as they could extort from the people. Their violence and menaces forced many citizens into outlawry, both in Palestine and Egypt.
>
> (Hyam Maccoby, *Early Rabbinic Writings*, Cambridge University Press, 1988, pp. 142f.)

the scribes: Mark says, "the scribes of the Pharisees."

> Almost all Gospel references to the Pharisees can be shown to derive from the 70s, 80s and 90s, the last years in which the Gospels were being edited.
>
> (Smith, *Jesus the Magician*; see the convincing evidence on pp. 29, 153ff.)

Why do you eat with traitors and whores: Whitman, in "Song of Myself," wonderfully conveys Jesus' spirit of inclusiveness:

This is the meal pleasantly set. . . . this is the meat and drink
    for natural hunger,
It is for the wicked just the same as the righteous. . . . I make
    appointments with all,
I will not have a single person slighted or left away,
The keptwoman and sponger and thief are hereby invited
    . . . . the heavy-lipped slave is invited . . . . the venerealee
    is invited,
There shall be no difference between them and the rest.

It is essential to understand that what is at issue here is *associating* with the wicked, not *forgiveness* of the wicked. The traditional Christian view falsifies the issue, as Professor Sanders forcefully points out:

The position is basically this: *We* (the Christians, or the true Christians) believe in grace and forgiveness. Those religious qualities *characterize* Christianity, and thus could not have been present in the religion from which Christianity came. Otherwise, why the split? But the Jews, or at least their leaders, the Pharisees, did not believe in repentance and forgiveness. They not only would not extend forgiveness to their own errant sheep, they would kill anyone who proposed to do so.

The position is so incredible that I wish it were necessary only to state it in order to demonstrate its ridiculousness. But thousands believe it, and I shall try to show what is wrong with it. Let us focus first on the *novelty* of an offer of forgiveness. The tax collectors and sinners, [the scholar Norman] Perrin assures us, "responded in glad acceptance" to Jesus' saying that they would be forgiven. But was this news? Did they not know that if they renounced those aspects of their lives which were an affront to God's law, they would have been accepted with open arms? Is it a serious proposal that tax collectors and the wicked longed for forgiveness, but could not find it within ordinary Judaism? That they thought that only in the messianic age could they find forgiveness, and thus responded to Jesus "in glad acceptance"? Perrin, citing only irrelevant evidence, asserts that the "sinners" "were widely regarded as beyond hope of penitence or forgiveness," and thus he denies one of the things about Judaism which everyone should know: there was a universal view that forgiveness is *always* available to those who return to the way of the Lord.

(*Jesus and Judaism*, p. 202)

The point of the passage is that the scribes were shocked at Jesus' association with the wicked; being ordinary pious people, they thought that it was dangerous and futile to mix with such characters. Their attitude was exactly the same as the attitude of Paul and the early church—for example, "Have nothing to do with any fellow-Christian who is a fornicator or a greedy man" (I Corinthians 5:11); "Do not mix with unbelievers" (II Corinthians 6:14). Even someone as openhearted as the nineteenth-century Indian saint Ramakrishna advised his disciples, as a practical matter (since they either hadn't yet had a genuine spiritual experience, or were in the first, vulnerable stages of opening), to avoid contact with the wicked:

> It is said in the scriptures that water is a form of God. But some water is fit to be used for worship, some water for washing the face, and some only for washing plates or dirty linen. This last sort cannot be used for drinking or for worship. In the same way, God undoubtedly dwells in the hearts of all—holy and unholy, righteous and unrighteous; but a man should not have dealings with the unholy, the wicked, the impure. He must not be intimate with them. With some of them he may exchange words, but with others he shouldn't go even that far. He should keep aloof from such people.
>
> (Swami Nikhilananda, trans., *The Gospel of Sri Ramakrishna* (abridged edition), Ramakrishna-Vivekananda Center, 1942, pp. 132f.)

We find an even more mature statement in the Sufi saint Dhu'l-Nun al-Misri (796–861):

> God says to his saints, "If you meet someone who is sick through separation from me, heal him; or if he is a fugitive from me, seek him out; or if he is afraid of me, reassure him; or if he desires union with me, show him favor; or if he seeks to approach me, encourage him. If he despairs of my grace, help

him; or if he hopes for my lovingkindness, give him good news; or if he has right thoughts of me, welcome him; or if he shows love to me, be kind to him; or if he seeks to know my attributes, give him guidance; or if he does evil in spite of my lovingkindness, remonstrate with him; or if he is forgetful of it, remind him. If anyone who is injured asks help of you, give it to him; and if anyone joins you in my name, show friendship: if he goes astray, search for him, but if he wants to make you sin, put him away from you." (Margaret Smith, trans., *Readings from the Mystics of Islam*, Luzac & Co., 1950, p. 24)

The most useful commentary on this aspect of Jesus' teaching is from the great twenty-seventh chapter of the Tao Te Ching:

> The Master is available to all people
> and doesn't reject anyone.
> He is ready to use all situations
> and doesn't waste anything.
> This is called embodying the light.
>
> What is a good man but a bad man's teacher?
> What is a bad man but a good man's job?
> If you don't understand this, you will get lost,
> however intelligent you are.
> It is the great secret.

This is not a question of conscience, but of vision. Because the Master's vision comes from beyond good and bad, he can love the essential humanity in all people, and he can see the good within the bad. He doesn't *do* anything to help others; in simply being himself he is helping them in the best possible way.

Jesus' attitude, and Lao-tzu's, is rare. It takes great maturity to stay centered when everyone around you is lost in selfishness. It also takes great compassion. "To pull someone out of the mud," the Hasidic Master Israel Baal Shem Tov said, "you must step into the mud yourself."

It isn't the healthy who need a doctor, but the sick: Similar statements appear in Pausanias and Diogenes Laertius; it may have been a proverb, and for this reason several good scholars have doubted its authenticity. Whether or not Jesus actually said it, it seems like an appropriate statement of how he conceived his principal mission: as being in service of the extreme cases, those in greatest moral need. (And since there is a great difference between not being sick and being in robust health, we can say that his teaching is also for those who are just relatively healthy.)

My teaching is not meant for those who are already righteous: Literally, "I came not to call the righteous, but sinners." The authenticity of this statement, too, has been doubted by Professor Sanders and other good scholars, and correctly so.

> All [I-sayings] come under suspicion of being the products of Christian reflection on the historical appearance of Jesus. They are summaries of his total impact and significance for Christian faith. (Arland J. Hultgren, *Jesus and His Adversaries*, Augsburg Publishing House, 1979, p. 110)

I have included it anyway, because it, too, seems to me like an appropriate summary of his mission.

Those who are *fully* righteous—that is, transparent—don't need to be taught.

> A monk said to the great T'ang dynasty Zen Master Ma-tzu, "Suppose you met a man who was unattached to all things—what would you teach him?"
>
> Ma-tzu said, "I would just let him experience the great Tao."

Of all the people who appear in the Gospel, Jesus would probably have considered only John the Baptist as being fully righteous. Two others seem to be approaching that state: the scribe who was "not far from the kingdom of God" and the rich man whom Jesus "loved."

for the wicked: Jesus would have agreed with the twentieth-century Jewish mystic Rav Kook: "It is our right to hate an evil man for his actions, but because his deepest self is the image of God, it is our duty to honor him with love."

It is not that there is no distinction between pure and impure. But we are all born between urine and feces, and even in the most degraded among us, the innocence we once came from is still somewhere alive. Beneath all our pain and delusions and unsatisfied desires, it shines with its pristine light, as it did in the beginning. As an old Chinese poet describes the lotus:

> How spotlessly it arises from its slimy bed!
> How modestly it rests on the surface of the clear pool!

When we look with the eye of nonjudgment—that is, with the eye of love—our vision includes all of humanity.

———

A few additional words on this subject. We can be sure that Jesus felt he had a particular mission to the wicked, and it is very probable that he was misunderstood and bitterly criticized for this. Thus he says in Matthew 11:18 (which sounds like an accurate historical reminiscence): "For John [the Baptist] was an ascetic, and they said, 'He has a demon'; I am not an ascetic, and they say, 'Look, a glutton and a wine-drinker, a friend of tax-gatherers and whores!'"

Nowhere in the Gospels, though, do we hear what it was that Jesus said to the wicked. Perhaps he told them parables like the Lost Sheep or the first part of the Prodigal Son. Or perhaps, like Lao-tzu's Master, "he acted without doing anything, and taught without saying a word," simply being himself and letting these lost people gradually absorb his radiance.

There remains the question of repentance. In his mission to the wicked, Jesus is following one of the milder moods of the prophetic tradition:

> "If a wicked man repents of all the sins he has committed and keeps all My laws and acts justly and righteously, he will live and not die. None of his offenses will be remembered against him; because of his righteous actions he will live. Do I desire

the death of a wicked man?" says the Lord YHVH. "Don't I want him to repent of his wickedness and live?" (Ezekiel 18:21ff.)

So at some point he almost certainly would have taught the wicked about repentance and restitution. But the only mention of restitution in the Gospel accounts is in Luke's story of Zacchaeus, the rich superintendent of taxes, and even there Jesus doesn't teach it; it arises spontaneously:

> And people began to grumble, and said, "He has gone in to stay with a sinful man."
>
> And Zacchaeus stood and said to the Lord, "Look, Lord, I promise to give half of my possessions to the poor; and if I have cheated anyone, I will pay him back four times over." (Luke 19:7f.)

Professor Sanders comments:

> This story was created by Luke (or possibly a pre-Lucan editor) to emphasize repentance and *reform*. It emphasizes these qualities so effectively that their scarcity elsewhere becomes striking. Jesus doubtless believed in reconciliation between the wicked and God, but the absence of passages which call for repentance and restitution shows at least that he did not aim at restoring the wicked to *the* community. If Jesus, by eating with tax collectors, led them to repent, repay those whom they had robbed, and leave off practicing their profession, he would have been a national hero. (*Jesus and Judaism*, p. 203)

Whatever Jesus may have taught, restitution is an essential element in making things right and returning to God. It receives its proper emphasis in the excellent twelve-step program of Alcoholics Anonymous, in which the eighth step is "To make a list of all persons we have harmed and to become willing to make amends to them all," and the ninth step is "To make direct amends to such people wherever possible, except when to do so would injure them or others."

The point is not that there are any preconditions which must be satisfied before God will forgive us; God's forgiveness is always present. It is rather that the desire to make restitution is the necessary result of true repentance. If we don't feel a deeply uncomfortable need to clean up the messes we have made, we can be sure that our repentance isn't genuine.

source: Mark 2:13–17

The Twelve

And he went up into the hills and called his disciples and appointed twelve of them to be with him and to be sent out to proclaim the kingdom of God and to heal: Simon, whom he named Peter, James the son of Zebedee and John his brother, whom he named B'nai-rogez (which means "sons of thunder"), Andrew, and Philip, and Bartholomew, and Matthew, and Thomas, and James the son of Alphaeus, and Thaddaeus, and Simon the Zealot, and Judas Iscariot.

And he went through all the towns and villages, teaching in their synagogues, and proclaiming the good news of the kingdom of God. And the Twelve went with him, and also certain women whom he had cured of diseases and infirmities: Mary of Magdala, who had been insane, and Joanna the wife of Herod's steward Kooza, and Susannah, and many others, who provided for them out of their own resources. And his fame spread throughout the surrounding region of Galilee, and people brought the sick on stretchers to wherever they heard he was staying, and whenever he came to a town or village, they would lay down the sick in the marketplace. And they brought him those who were suffering from many kinds of diseases and torments, and demoniacs, and epileptics, and paralytics, and he healed them.

appointed twelve of them:

> Apart from what we learn from the symbolic nature of the number twelve, we do not know Jesus' purpose in calling

them. Mark 3:14 says that it was for them "to be with him," and that has recently been taken to be a plain statement of fact. But Mark cannot have known what was in Jesus' mind.

(Sanders, Jesus and Judaism, p. 103)

Zealot: The patriotic, revolutionary, and terrorist movement, whose purpose was to free Israel from Roman domination and return it to the sovereignty of "God."

B'nai-rogez: Mark's meaningless *boanerges* is usually explained as a corrupt transliteration of a Hebrew or Aramaic name. "B'nai-rogez" (literally, "the sons of anger," i.e., "the angry ones"), a conjecture of the Aramaic scholar Gustaf Dalman, is problematic, but there is no better guess.

and also certain women: This information appears only in Luke; but it seems to be confirmed by a reference in Mark (15:41) to the women who supposedly watched the crucifixion from a distance: "[women] who had followed him and taken care of him when he was in Galilee."

sources: Mark 3:13–19; Matthew 4:23, Luke 8:1; Luke 8:2f.; Mark 1:28, 6:55f.; Matthew 4:24; Matthew 9:36

He Heals a Paralytic

And after Jesus returned to Capernaum, people heard that he was at home; and so many gathered in the house that there was no room, not even in front of the door.

And as he was teaching, some people brought a paralytic to him, carried by four men. And when they couldn't get near him because of the crowd, they made a hole in the roof over the place where Jesus was, and they lowered the mat, with the paralytic lying on it, through the hole.

And when Jesus saw how deeply they trusted him, he said to the paralytic, "Stand up, child; take your mat and go home."

And immediately the man stood up and took the mat and walked out of the house in front of everyone. And they were all amazed, and glorified God and said, "We have never seen anything like this!"

sources: *Mark 2:1–5,11; Mark 2:12*

The Beatitudes

The Sermon on the Mount never took place in actuality, but is a collection of Jesus' teachings compiled by Matthew. According to Luke, in his shorter collection, the "sermon" was given on a plain.

And large crowds followed him from Galilee and the Decapolis and Jerusalem and Judea and beyond the Jordan. And seeing the crowds, he went up onto a hill, and when he had sat down, his disciples gathered around him. And he began to teach them, and said,

"Blessed are the poor in spirit, for theirs is the kingdom of God.

"Blessed are those who grieve, for they will be comforted.

"Blessed are those who hunger and thirst for righteousness, for they will be filled.

"Blessed are the merciful, for they will receive mercy.

"Blessed are the pure in heart, for they will see God.

"Blessed are the peacemakers, for they will be called sons of God."

poor in spirit: For the most profound clarification of this verse, see Meister Eckhart's sermon on it, in which he defines a person who is poor in spirit as "one who wants nothing and knows nothing and has nothing." (A translation of the complete sermon appears in *The Enlightened Mind*.)

Blessed are those who grieve: Ramakrishna said, "People weep rivers of tears because they don't have a child or can't get money. But who sheds even one teardrop because he has not seen God?"

That is the most fruitful grief. But all grief, if experienced attentively enough, can be fruitful. Rilke, talking about a moment of ultimate, jubilant affirmation, says:

> How dear you will be to me then, you nights
> of anguish. Why didn't I kneel more deeply to accept you,
> inconsolable sisters, and, surrendering, lose myself
> in your loosened hair. How we squander our hours of pain.
> How we gaze beyond them into the bitter duration
> to see if they have an end. Though they are really
> seasons of us, our winter-
> enduring foliage, ponds, meadows, our inborn landscape,
> where birds and reed-dwelling creatures are at home.
>
> ("Original Version of the Tenth Elegy," *The Selected Poetry of Rainer Maria Rilke*, ed. and trans. Stephen Mitchell, Random House, 1982, p. 217)

This beatitude and the next one concern people who are still searching for the kingdom of God, not people who have already found it.

Blessed are those who hunger and thirst for righteousness: The exemplar of this spiritual state is Job. The greater the hunger, the greater the fulfillment.

The Jewish-Alexandrian philosopher Philo (c. 20 B.C.E.– c. 50 C.E.) said,

> When the righteous man searches for the nature of all things, he makes his own admirable discovery: that everything is God's grace. Every being in the world, and the world itself, manifests the blessings and generosity of God.

Blessed are the merciful: "Whoever has mercy on others will obtain mercy from God" (Talmud). Here, as everywhere, God is a mirror of the soul, and we receive what we give.

Blessed are the pure in heart: Synonymous with the "poor in spirit." As in the first beatitude, it would be more accurate to use the present tense here: "Blessed are the pure in heart, for they already see God." Seeing God means that they have died to self, since "no one can see God and live" (Exodus 33:20). Not that selfish concerns don't arise for them; but they aren't attached to these concerns; they have no self for selfishness to stick to; hence they can be carried along in the clear current of what is.

see God: Paul, in his hope and desperation, confused the death of the body with the death of self, and mistook his own spiritual unclarity for the human condition. "For now we see dim images in a mirror, but then" — the great "then" — "we will see face to face" (I Corinthians 13:12). Those who have entered the kingdom of God don't need to leave their bodies in order to see God face to face.

Blessed are the peacemakers: *Shalom*, the word for "peace" in Hebrew, comes from a root that means "wholeness." When we make peace in our own heart, we make peace for the whole world.

> The wisdom from above is in the first place pure, then peaceloving, considerate, openhearted, filled with compassion and acts of kindness, impartial, and sincere. Peace is the soil in which righteousness is sown, and the peacemakers will reap its harvest. (James 3:17f.)

sons of God: See pp. 69f.

sources: Matthew 4:25–5:4; Matthew 5:6–9

The Inner Light (2)

Before we can share the light, we have to find it. When we embody it, we can't help sharing it, because it has no limits. In these verses, Jesus' instinctive generosity makes itself deeply felt.

"No one lights a lamp and then puts it under a basket, but on a lampstand, and it gives light to everyone in the house. In the same way, let your light shine before men, so that they may see your good works and glorify your Father in heaven."

No one lights a lamp: Matthew's version of a metaphor that I have already included in Mark's version. Like every spiritual teacher, Jesus must have repeated his essential teachings many times, emphasizing different aspects on different occasions. (When someone once complained to my old Zen Master, "You always say the same thing," he said, "That's because you never hear it.")

The lamp this metaphor points to isn't a lamp we can light. It is already lit; it was shining before the universe began.

Of this light, which our Judeo-Christian-Islamic culture calls God and Buddhists call Mind, the ninth-century Zen Master Huang-po said:

This pure Mind, which is the source of all things, shines forever with the radiance of its own perfection. But most people are not aware of it, and think that Mind is just the faculty that sees, hears, feels, and knows. Blinded by their own sight, hearing, feeling, and knowing, they don't perceive the radiance of the source. If they could eliminate all conceptual thinking, this source would appear, like the sun rising through the empty sky and illuminating the whole universe.

it gives light to everyone in the house: Even if they can't see it; even if they are in the attic or the cellar.

let your light shine before men: Ramana Maharshi said:

> If the mind is happy, not only the body but the whole world will
> be happy. So one must find out how to become happy oneself.
> Wanting to reform the world without discovering one's true
> self is like trying to cover the whole world with leather to avoid
> the pain of walking on stones and thorns. It is much simpler to
> wear shoes.

source: Matthew 5:15f.

Fulfilling the Law

This is probably the most widely misunderstood passage in the
Gospels. In none of these commandments is Jesus repudiating
the Law, not even in his comment on "an eye for an eye." He is
affirming the Law, but taking it to an even deeper level of compassion.

*"Don't think that my purpose is to destroy the Law; my purpose is not to
destroy the Law but to fulfill it. For I tell you that unless your righteousness is deeper than the righteousness of the scribes, you will never enter
the kingdom of God.*

"You have heard that it was said to our forefathers, You shall not
murder *and* Whoever murders is liable to judgment. *But I tell you
that anyone who hates his brother will be liable to judgment.*

"You have heard that it was said, You shall not commit adultery.
*But I tell you that anyone who harbors lust for a woman has already
committed adultery with her in his heart.*

"You have heard that it was said, You shall not perjure yourselves. *But I tell you, don't take any oaths at all. Let your 'Yes' mean
'Yes' and your 'No' mean 'No.'*

"You have heard that it was said, An eye for an eye and a tooth for a tooth. But I tell you, don't resist a wicked man. If anyone hits you on one cheek, turn the other cheek to him also. And if anyone wants to sue you and take your shirt, let him have your coat as well. And if a soldier forces you into service for one mile, go two miles with him. Give to everyone who asks, and don't refuse anyone who wants to borrow from you.

"You have heard that it was said, You shall love your neighbor. *But I tell you, love your enemies, do good to those who hate you, bless those who curse you, and pray for those who mistreat you, so that you may be sons of your Father in heaven; for he makes his sun rise on the wicked and on the good, and sends rain to the righteous and to the unrighteous.*

"For if you love only those who love you, what credit is that to you: don't even the tax-gatherers do the same? And if you do good only to those who do good to you: don't even the Gentiles do the same? But love your enemies, and give, expecting nothing in return; and your reward will be great, and you will be sons of the Most High, for he is kind even to the ungrateful and the wicked. Therefore be merciful, just as your Father is merciful."

the Law: Professor Sanders, in his important chapter "The Law" in *Jesus and Judaism,* concludes that "there was no substantial conflict between Jesus and the Pharisees with regard to Sabbath, food, and purity laws."

Far from considering the Law oppressive, as Paul did, Jesus' attitude toward the Law in the Sermon on the Mount is the attitude we find in James 1:25 (which refers to "the perfect Law, the Law that makes us free") and in the rapturous praise of Psalm 19:

> The Law of YHVH is perfect,
> reviving the soul.
> The teaching of YHVH is constant,
> making wise the simple.
> The precepts of YHVH are upright,
> rejoicing the heart.
> The commandment of YHVH is lucid,
> lighting up the eyes.

> The word of YHVH is pure,
> abiding forever.
> The statutes of YHVH are true,
> creating justice—
> more precious than the finest gold,
> sweeter than honey from the comb.

righteousness: Jesus, like other Jewish prophets, doesn't use this word in a moralistic sense. By a righteous man he means a man whose whole being is illuminated in God's light, and who therefore naturally acts with justice and compassion.

> It is not the love of righteousness in the abstract that makes anyone righteous, but such a love of fair play toward everyone with whom we come into contact, that anything less than the fulfilling, with a clear joy, of our divine relation to him or her, is impossible.
> (George MacDonald, *Creation in Christ*, ed. Roland Hein, Harold Shaw Publishers, 1976, p. 184)

But I tell you:

> What Jesus presents as his own view is interpretation, not a new law. "Do not kill" means also "do not be angry"; "do not commit adultery" means also "do not look with lust." . . . The vocabulary is that of debate over interpretation and does not point towards an "antithesis" to the law.
> (E. P. Sanders, *Jewish Law from Jesus to the Mishnah*, Trinity Press International, 1990, p. 93)

You shall not murder: Exodus 20:13 and Deuteronomy 5:17.

hates his brother: Literally, "is angry with his brother." Many ancient manuscripts add *eikē*, "without cause," but the word was probably "added by copyists in order to soften the rigor of the precept" (Bruce M. Metzger, *A Textual Commentary on the Greek New Testament*, United Bible Societies, 1975, p. 13). C. H. Dodd paraphrases: "Anyone who nurses anger against his brother."

I have translated this phrase "hates his brother" for the sake of clarity. The problem with the precept as Matthew states it (Was it misunderstood by the disciples? Garbled as it passed from Aramaic into Greek?) is not that it is impossibly rigorous, but that it is mistaken. Anger is a natural emotion, a pure energy, which can be selfish and destructive but can also be generous and life-affirming. And because children feel and express it with complete unselfconsciousness, we can see that it is an invited guest in the kingdom of God. Any attempt to suppress it will lead to emotional and spiritual disaster. Blake said, with great insight:

> Men are admitted into heaven not because they have curbed and governed their passions or have no passions, but because they have cultivated their understandings. The treasures of heaven are not negations of passion, but realities of intellect, from which all the passions emanate uncurbed in their eternal glory. ("A Vision of the Last Judgment")

The point of any genuine spiritual work with anger is not to *not* feel it, but to be fully aware of it as it arises, to express it when that is appropriate, and to let go of it as soon as it passes. It doesn't necessarily arise from the small self, and can even be an angel in disguise. One of the greatest lessons I ever learned came from remaining face to face (when all my impulses told me to run away) with the justified anger of someone who loved me very much: anger so devastating that it felt like an atomic explosion, and so pure that it had no personality sticking to it.

But if the teaching not to be angry at your brother is mistaken, the teaching not to *nurse* that anger, not to hate your brother, is certainly correct. Jesus' point here is that selfish and harmful actions begin in selfish and harmful thoughts. Anyone who is serious about living in the light will have a passionate desire to correct his mistakes at the root.

You shall not commit adultery: Exodus 20:14 and Deuteronomy 5:18.

anyone who harbors lust for a woman: Literally, "anyone who looks at a woman lustfully." Compare the Tenth Commandment, as stated in Deuteronomy 5:21: "You shall not lust after your neighbor's wife."

Again, the problem with the precept as stated in Matthew is not that it is too rigorous, but that it is mistaken. In trying to protect the sanctity of marriage, it makes sexual desire sinful. Thus the cure for adultery becomes as life-threatening as the disease.

Thought leads to action. Just as a disease exists as energy long before it manifests itself in the tissues of the body, so a harmful action exists as a thought long before it is acted out, and in the unconscious mind long before it becomes a thought. Someone who feels strongly tempted to commit adultery has a choice: to indulge the desire, or to realize that it is symptomatic of something lacking in his marriage, and then to address the problem.

Desire for another partner can actually be a sign of health. I have a woman friend who for six months felt intense sexual desire for a certain man she had met; she had no guilt about this feeling and her marriage was strong enough that she could tell her husband as soon as it appeared. Ultimately, after much difficult inner work, both of them began to manifest the kind of sexuality that her desire had pointed her toward.

But thought is only the root of action; it is not action itself. You can't die of a cancer that hasn't yet appeared in your body, nor should you be executed for a murder that you have committed only in your mind. If thought were literally action, we would all be behind bars.

These teachings of Jesus should be considered as preventive medicine. He is not trying to create a society of celibates, as the early church was; he is speaking to everyone, to you and me. If a man is sexually aroused by the sight of a lovely woman, that isn't a sin; in fact, it is an affirmation of life, and rather than "tsk, tsk," we can say "l'hayim!" Lust, like anger, is pure energy, and can be a creative source even for the spiritual life. Jesus' point here is that when sexual desire is misdirected and clung to in the mind, it leads to dangerous actions, actions that can cause great misery to a man's wife and children and to himself.

You shall not perjure yourselves: Leviticus 19:12.

Let your 'Yes' mean 'Yes' and your 'No' mean 'No': "The mature person values sincerity above all things," as Confucius' grandson Tzu-ssu (482–403 B.C.E.) tells us in his wonderful treatise *The Central Harmony:*

> Confucius said, "Sincerity is the way of heaven; arriving at sincerity is the way of man. The sincere person does the right thing without trying, understands the truth without thinking, and acts always in keeping with the Tao."
>
> Sincerity is the fulfillment of our own nature, and to arrive at it we need only follow our true self. Sincerity is the beginning and end of existence; without it, nothing can endure. Therefore the mature person values sincerity above all things.
>
> Sincerity is not only the fulfillment of our own being; it is also the quality through which all beings are fulfilled. When we fulfill our own being, we become truly human; when we fulfill all beings, we arrive at true understanding. These qualities—humanity and understanding—are inherent in our nature, and by means of them we unite the inner and the outer. Thus, when we act with sincerity, everything we do is right.

an eye for an eye: Exodus 21:24.

> We are told that Jesus opposed the concept of "an eye for an eye," found in the legal code of the Hebrew Bible, substituting the law of love for the law of revenge. This is a travesty of the situation in Pharisaism. The Pharisees ... regarded the expression "an eye for an eye" as meaning that in principle any injury perpetrated against one's fellow man should be compensated for in accordance with the seriousness of the injury. Indeed, the legal code of the Hebrew Bible itself provides for such compensation, when it states that loss of employment

and doctor's bills must be paid for by the person responsible for
an injury (Exodus 21:19).

(Hyam Maccoby, *The Mythmaker: Paul and the
Invention of Christianity*, Harper & Row, 1986,
p. 39)

don't resist a wicked man: The career of Gandhi is the best commentary on this verse. As in the previous commandments, Jesus is asking for a deeper level of righteousness here. Not only
are we to compensate our neighbor when we injure him; we
are to compensate him when he injures us. Not only are we to
pay him what is fair; we are to give him what is more than fair:
good in return for evil, love in return for hatred.

This attitude is admirable if it comes from true non-
attachment, as in the following story about the Zen poet Ryōkan:

Ryōkan lived in a small hut at the foot of a mountain. One evening a thief broke in, only to find that there was nothing in the
hut worth stealing.

When Ryōkan returned, he found the thief and said,
"You've probably come a long way, and you shouldn't return
empty-handed. Please take my clothes as a gift."

Shamefaced, the thief took the clothes and left.

Ryōkan sat down naked and looked up at the sky. "Poor fellow," he said, "I wish I could give him this beautiful moon."

(Adapted from Paul Reps, ed., *Zen Flesh, Zen
Bones*, Charles E. Tuttle Co., 1957, p. 27)

There is a similar story about Ramana Maharshi. When
thieves broke into the ashram in 1924, his devotees wanted to
resist, but Maharshi said, "They have their *dharma* [role], we
have ours. It is for us to bear and forbear. Let us not interfere
with them." As the monks filed out of the building, the thieves
beat them with sticks. Maharshi advised the others to put oint-
ment on their bruises.

One of the devotees asked, "What about you?"

Maharshi laughed and said, "I too have received some
puja," punning on a word that can mean either "worship" or
"blows."

When the devotee saw the weal on Maharshi's left thigh, he got angry, picked up an iron bar, and asked permission to go back inside the ashram. Maharshi said, "We are *sadhus* [renunciates]. We shouldn't give up our *dharma*. If you go and hit them, some may die, and that will be a matter for which people will rightly blame not them but us. They are only misguided men, blinded by ignorance. Let us do what is right. If your teeth suddenly bite your tongue, will you knock them out as punishment?"

On the other hand, the refusal to resist may be a disservice to the aggressor, as the refusal to say No is a disservice to a child. If someone violates our limits and we don't tell him, we may be in some sense collaborating in the violation. So standing up to him and saying, "No, this isn't right; you *can't* have my coat; I *won't* go one mile; I *won't* support your being a beggar; I *won't* let you go back on your promise," may be the best way of teaching him, and the greatest act of love.

Nothing could be more abruptly (one is tempted to say "violently") demanding than this and similar suggestions of responses to violent challenges. . . . [I say] this on the basis of having studied the nonviolent tactics of one of Jesus' modern followers, Mahatma Gandhi. Nonviolent behavior must often be shocking in order to shake up the violent opponent's seemingly so normal attitude, to make him feel that his apparently undebatable and spotless advantage in aggressive initiative is being taken away from him and that he is being forced to overdo his own action absurdly. For human violence almost never feels all that "natural," even to the aggressor himself—neither the violence toward children nor that against loved persons nor even that evoked by declared enemies. (Erik H. Erikson, "The Galilean Sayings and the Sense of 'I,'" *The Yale Review* 70, spring 1981, p. 357)

You shall love your neighbor: Leviticus 19:18.

love your enemies: Anyone who has heard the Dalai Lama speak about his enemies the Chinese will understand the depth and exhilaration in this precept when it is truly lived.

> As a free spokesman for my captive countrymen and -women, I feel it is my duty to speak out on their behalf. I speak not with a feeling of anger or hatred toward those who are responsible for the immense suffering of our people and the destruction of our land, homes, and culture. They too are human beings who struggle to find happiness and deserve our compassion. I speak to inform you of the sad situation in my country today and the aspirations of my people, because in our struggle for freedom, truth is the only weapon we possess.
>
> ("The Nobel Peace Prize Lecture" in *A Policy of Kindness: An Anthology of Writings by and about the Dalai Lama*, Snow Lion Publications, 1990, p. 16)

Here there is not a trace of difference between the teaching of Jesus and the teaching of the Buddha.

In this example, too, Jesus is deepening and making explicit a commandment that already appears in the Jewish Bible. This is such an important point that I would like to quote Professor Sanders at length:

> The Jewish Scripture, and consequently most of its interpreters, fixed on specific points in the treatment of enemies. These are the two principal biblical passages:
>
> > If you meet your enemy's ox or his ass going astray, you shall bring it back to him. If you see the ass of one who hates you lying under its burden, you shall refrain from leaving him with it, you shall help him to lift it up. (Exodus 23:4–5)
> >
> > If your enemy is hungry, give him bread to eat; and if he is thirsty, give him water to drink; for you will heap coals of fire on his head [i.e., you will produce in him the pain of contrition—S. M.], and the Lord will reward you. (Proverbs 25:21–22)
>
> Josephus, summarizing and slightly expanding Jewish law, wrote that enemies should be given a decent burial (*Antiquities*

4.265; cf. Deuteronomy 21:22, which refers to condemned criminals). He also noted that Jews are required to give the necessities (shelter, food and fire) to all who ask and to "show consideration even to declared enemies." In his legislation Moses

> does not allow us to burn up their [the enemies'] country, or to cut down their fruit trees, and forbids even the spoiling of fallen combatants; he has taken measures to prevent outrage to prisoners of war, especially women. . . . [He] bade us even in an enemy's country to spare and not to kill the beasts employed in labor. (*Against Apion* 2.211–212)

For the most part, this passage simply summarizes the commandments of Exodus and Proverbs, as well as Deuteronomy 20:19 and 21:10–14, but Josephus has attributed further regulations to Moses: not to despoil corpses nor to kill the enemies' beasts of labor, and to offer one's needy enemy fire as well as bread and water.

Constructively, these commandments can be summarized as "love your enemy," and one can claim no more than that the wording attributed to Jesus is unique. "Love" in biblical usage, both in the New Testament and the Old, refers not so much to an interior emotion as to outward actions. One "loves" someone by treating her or him in the right way. Leviticus 19:18, "love your neighbor as yourself," is a summary of commandments in 19:9–17, which require leaving food in the field for the poor, not stealing, not oppressing one's neighbor or cheating one's servant, and so on. The person who acts in these ways "loves" the neighbor.

(*Studying the Synoptic Gospels*, p. 319)

There are two striking postbiblical Jewish parallels. The first appears in the *Aboth de Rabbi Nathan*: "Who is the mightiest of the mighty? He who makes his enemy his friend"; the second, in the sayings of the eighteenth-century Hasidic rabbi Yehiel Mikhal of Zlotchov: "Pray for your enemies that everything may be well with them. More than all other prayers, this is truly the service of God."

for he makes his sun rise: One of the most beautiful and distinctive sayings of Jesus.

> Jesus . . . did not feel the need of making up artificial illustrations for the truths He wished to teach. He found them ready-made by the Maker of man and nature. . . . Since nature and super-nature are of one order, you can take any part of that order and find in it illumination for other parts. Thus the falling of rain is a religious thing, for it is God who makes the rain to fall on the just and the unjust; the death of a sparrow can be contemplated without despairing of the goodness of nature, because the bird is "not forgotten by your Father"; and the love of God is present in the natural affection of a father for his scapegrace son. This sense of the divineness of the natural order is the major premise of all the parables.
>
> (Dodd, *Parables of the Kingdom*, p. 10)

sends rain to the righteous and to the unrighteous: Philo speaks this central truth with a different emphasis:

> God loves to give, and freely bestows good things on all people, even the imperfect, inviting them to participate in virtue and to love it, and at the same time manifesting his superabundant wealth, which is more than enough for as many as wish to profit from it. He shows this in nature as well. For when he sends rain on the ocean, and causes springs to gush in the most desolate wastelands, and makes sterile soil blossom with grass and flowers, what is he showing but the extravagance of his wealth and goodness? That is why every soul he created has the seed of goodness in it.

your reward will be great: The ninth-century Sufi Master Abu Yazid al-Bistami said, "A single atom of the sweetness of wisdom in a man's heart is better than a thousand pavilions in Paradise." (This and all further sayings of Abu Yazid al-Bistami come from Reynold A. Nicholson, *Translations of Eastern Poetry and Prose*, Cambridge University Press, 1922.)

Therefore be merciful: This is Luke's version. Matthew 5:48 reads, "Therefore be *teleioi* [perfect, whole, complete], just as your heavenly Father is *teleios*." In either version, the saying alludes to Leviticus 19:2: "You should be holy, for I, YHVH your God, am holy."

The first step in becoming perfect is to accept your imperfection, just as the first step in becoming merciful is to treat yourself with mercy.

sources: Matthew 5:17; Matthew 5:20–22; Matthew 5:27f.; Matthew 5:33f.; Matthew 5:37ff.; Matthew 5:43; Luke 6:27, Matthew 5:45; Matthew 5:46f., Luke 6:32f.; Luke 6:35f.

Charity

The rabbis of the Talmud distinguish three levels of charity. The highest level is to give someone work by which he can earn his living for himself. The second is to give money anonymously. The lowest level, which is approved of but not accorded much admiration, is to give money and let people know it.

"Be careful not to do your righteous acts in public, in order to be seen. When you give charity, don't blow a trumpet to announce it, as the hypocrites do in the synagogues and in the streets, so that people will praise them. Truly I tell you, they have their reward. But when you give charity, don't let your left hand know what your right hand is doing, and keep your charity a secret; and your Father, who sees what is secret, will reward you."

source: Matthew 6:1–4

Prayer

This is Jesus' compassionate instruction to beginners. We don't know what his own way of prayer was (except perhaps for the prayer at Gethsemane), or what he would have taught to more mature disciples.

"And when you pray, don't be like the hypocrites, who love to stand and pray in the synagogues and the street corners, so that people will see them. But when you pray, go into your inner room and shut the door and pray in secret to your Father; and your Father, who sees what is secret, will reward you.

"And in your prayers, don't talk on and on, as the Gentiles do; for they think that unless they use many words they won't be heard. Don't be like them, for your Father knows what you need even before you ask him. But pray like this:

> *Our Father in heaven,*
>> *hallowed be your name.*
> *May your kingdom come,*
>> *may your will be done*
>> *on earth as it is in heaven.*
> *Give us this day our daily bread,*
>> *and forgive us our wrongs*
>> *as we forgive those who have wronged us.*
> *And do not lead us into temptation,*
>> *but deliver us from evil.*

For if you forgive others their offenses, your heavenly Father will forgive you."

when you pray: These instructions on prayer are helpful as a regular practice at the beginning stages of spiritual development, and as a reminder later on. But for those who hunger and thirst for God, even the Lord's Prayer is insufficient, as all words ultimately are.

The most direct method of Christian prayer is taught in the excellent fourteenth-century manual *The Cloud of Unknowing*.

Lift up your heart to God with a meek stirring of love; and intend God himself and none of his created things. And be sure not to think of anything but himself, so that nothing may work in your mind or in your will but only himself. And do whatever you can to forget all the creatures that God ever made and all their works. . . .

When you first begin, you find just a darkness and, as it were, a cloud of unknowing, you do not know what, except that you feel in your will a naked intent toward God. This darkness and this cloud, no matter what you do, is between you and your God, and hinders you, so that you can neither see him clearly by the light of understanding in your reason nor feel him in the sweetness of love in your affection. Therefore, prepare to abide in this darkness as long as you must, evermore crying after him whom you love. For if ever you are to see him or feel him in this life, it must always be in this cloud and in this darkness. . . .

But now you ask me, "How shall I think upon God himself, and what is he?" To this I cannot answer you, except to say, "I don't know."

For with your question you have brought me into that same darkness and into that same cloud of unknowing that I want you to be in. For of all other creatures and their works—yes, and of the works of God himself—a man may through grace have fullness of knowing, and he can well think upon them; but upon God himself, no man can think. And therefore I wish to leave everything I can think, and choose for my love that thing which I cannot think. Because he may well be loved, but not thought. By love he may be gotten and held; but by thinking, never.

go into your inner room: This should also be taken metaphorically: go into yourself, into the quietest place in your heart. Inside that inner room you will find your Father.

for your Father knows what you need: Abu Yazid al-Bistami said, "For thirty years I used to say, 'Do this' and 'Give that'; but when I reached the first stage of wisdom, I said, 'O God, be mine and do whatever You want.'"

The same point is made by Isaac of Nineveh (sixth century):

> When we trust God with our whole heart, we don't fill our prayers with "Give me this" or "Take this from me." We don't even think of ourselves when we pray. At every moment we trust our Father in heaven, whose love infinitely surpasses the love of all earthly fathers and who gives us more than we ourselves could ask for or even imagine.

And, in a deeper sense, by Ramana Maharshi:

> God's grace is the beginning, the middle, and the end. When you pray for God's grace, you are like someone standing neck-deep in water and yet crying for water. It is like saying that someone neck-deep in water feels thirsty, or that a fish in water feels thirsty, or that water feels thirsty.

Our Father: I have used Matthew's version of the Lord's prayer because it is such a familiar and beloved part of our Western religious tradition. Luke's version (11:2ff.), which may be more authentic, is as follows:

> Father,
>   hallowed be your name.
> May your kingdom come.
> Give us each day our daily bread,
>   and forgive us our sins
>   for we ourselves forgive all those who have wronged us.
> And do not lead us into temptation.

hallowed be your name: God tells Moses, "My name is *I am*." But in reality, God has no name. Inside that silence all things are holy.

> Man has access to this name, although it is also transcendent. It shines in the beauty and order of the world, and it shines in the interior light of the human soul. This name is holiness itself; there is no holiness outside it; it does not therefore have to be hallowed. In asking for its hallowing we are asking for

something that exists eternally, with full and complete reality, so that we can neither increase nor diminish it, even by an infinitesimal fraction. To ask for that which exists, that which exists really, infallibly, eternally, quite independently of our prayer—that is the perfect petition. We cannot prevent ourselves from desiring; we are made of desire; but the desire that nails us down to what is imaginary, temporal, selfish, can, if we make it pass wholly into this petition, become a lever to tear us from the imaginary into the real and from time into eternity, to lift us right out of the prison of the self.

(Simone Weil, *Waiting for God*, trans. Emma Craufurd, G. P. Putnam's Sons, 1951, p. 217)

May your kingdom come: May we realize that the kingdom of God has already come. By finding heaven in ourselves, may we begin to make heaven on earth.

may your will be done: Meister Eckhart has given the definitive commentary on this verse:

You might ask, "How can I know if something is God's will?" My answer is, "If it were not God's will, it wouldn't exist even for an instant; so if something happens, it *must* be his will." If you truly enjoyed God's will, you would feel exactly as though you were in the kingdom of heaven, whatever happened to you or didn't happen to you.

Dame Julian of Norwich most beautifully expresses the same truth:

And after this I saw God in a point, that is to say in my understanding, by which vision I saw that he is in all things. I beheld with care, seeing and knowing in that sight that he does all that is done. I marveled at that vision with a soft dread, and thought: What is sin? For I saw truly that God does all things, be they ever so little. And I saw truly that nothing is done by chance or by accident, but all by the foreseeing wisdom of God. If it be chance or accident in the sight of man, our blindness and unforesight is the cause. For those things that are in the foreseeing wisdom of God from without beginning, which rightfully and worshipfully and continually he leads to the best end, as they come about fall to us suddenly, without our knowledge; and thus by our blindness and our unforesight we say that these things are by chance and accident.

Thus I understood in this revelation of love, for I well know that in the sight of our lord God there is no chance or accident; wherefore I had to grant that all things that are done are well done, for our lord God does all.

The point of this verse is not that we ask God to do "his" will—as if there were any possibility that God's will would not be done—but that we wholeheartedly assent to it. There is a wonderful Japanese story about a woman who embodied this attitude:

> A hundred and fifty years ago there lived a woman named Sono, whose devotion and purity of heart were respected far and wide. One day a fellow Buddhist, having made a long trip to see her, asked, "What can I do to put my heart at rest?"
>
> Sono said, "Every morning and every evening, and whenever anything happens to you, keep on saying, 'Thank you for everything. I have no complaint whatsoever.'"
>
> The man did as he was instructed, for a whole year, but his heart was still not at peace. He returned to Sono, crestfallen. "I've said your prayer over and over, and yet nothing in my life has changed; I'm still the same selfish person as before. What should I do now?"
>
> Sono immediately said, "'Thank you for everything. I have no complaint whatsoever.'"
>
> On hearing these words, the man was able to open his spiritual eye, and returned home with a great joy.
>
> (Adapted from Zenkei Shibayama, *A Flower Does Not Talk*, Charles E. Tuttle Co., 1970, pp. 189f.)

on earth as it is in heaven: It *is* done on earth as in heaven!
Meister Eckhart said:

> Many people imagine that there is "creaturely being" here and "divine being" in heaven. This is not true. You behold God in your life in the same perfection, and are blessed in exactly the same way, as in the afterlife.

Give us this day our daily bread: Give us what nourishes our spirit; give us not what we want, but what we need. In fact, we always do receive exactly what we need, though we don't always realize it. This prayer makes us participants in the gift.

forgive us our wrongs: God, whose very being is forgiveness, can't forgive a wrong that we commit against a particular person; only that person can. Here the meaning is, "Once we have righted the wrong, help us to forgive ourselves."

as we forgive those who have wronged us: Only by constantly letting go of the self that feels wronged can we forgive others. The more we cling to it, the more paranoid and self-righteous it becomes, blaming the whole world for its sufferings. It is best to treat it like an abused child. As it feels loved and nourished by our compassionate attention, it will no longer act like a separate entity in a dangerous world. Eventually it will feel confident enough to disappear.

> A disciple asked Rabbi Shmelke, "We are commanded to love our neighbor as ourself. How can I do this if my neighbor has wronged me?"
>
> The rabbi answered, "You must understand these words correctly. Love your neighbor like something which you yourself are. For all souls are one. Each is a spark from the original soul, and this soul is wholly inherent in all souls, just as your soul is in all members of your body. It may happen that your hand makes a mistake and hits you. But would you then take a stick and punish your hand because it lacked understanding, and so increase your pain? It is the same if your neighbor, who is of one soul with you, wrongs you because he does not understand. If you punish him, you only hurt yourself."
>
> The disciple asked, "But if I see a man who is wicked before God, how can I love him?"
>
> Rabbi Shmelke said, "Don't you know that the original soul came out of the essence of God, and that every human soul is a part of God? And will you have no mercy on Him, when you

> see that one of His holy sparks has been lost in a maze, and is
> almost stifled?" (Martin Buber, *Tales of the Hasidim: The Early
> Masters*, trans. Olga Marx, Schocken Books,
> 1947, p. 190)

do not lead us into temptation: This prayer Jesus has kindly given
to those at the beginning of the path, who have more than
enough difficulties with the tests that each ordinary day
brings. For himself, and for his more mature disciples, he
might have prayed the opposite: to be put to the test and challenged to the utmost, in order to become a clearer vessel of the
truth.

> Search me, O God; test me
> to the depths of my inmost heart.
> Root out all selfishness from me,
> and lead me in eternal life.
> (Psalm 139:23f.)

but deliver us from evil: Spare us prolonged and unnecessary suffering. And save us from the idea that anyone in the world is intrinsically evil.

For if you forgive others their offenses, your heavenly Father will forgive you: If you hold on to your self and don't forgive others,
God will be reflected in your mirror as an unforgiving father.

When you feel offended, allow yourself to feel offended,
and then let go. As you keep letting go of your self, you also let
go of the capacity to be offended, and eventually you come to
experience the whole universe as grace.

source: Matthew 6:5–14

The Inner Light (3)

"The eye is the lamp of the body. So if your eye is clear, your whole body is luminous; but if your eye isn't clear, your whole body is dark. And if the light in you is darkness, how great that darkness is.

"Can a blind man lead a blind man? Won't they both fall into a ditch? A disciple is not above his teacher, but every disciple who is fully taught will be like his teacher."

The eye is the lamp of the body: The spiritual eye.

if your eye is clear, your whole body is luminous: The Master's eye is so clear that she feels no separation between body and spirit.

Fully embodied wisdom is rare. I know people with very clear spiritual eyes whose physical bodies are anything but luminous; they don't fully inhabit their body because they don't yet accept it with enough love. As a matter of fact, devout Christians, orthodox Jews, Platonists, and other such people of the spirit are often, physically, the most opaque. For someone like this, the ultimate lesson is to see his own body from the Sabbath mind, and to call it "very good."

the light in you: A moving account of a certain mode of inner light appears in the autobiography of Jacques Lusseyran, who went blind through a freak accident at the age of seven. In the following passage, he talks about the discovery he made a few weeks after his accident:

> At that time I still wanted to use my eyes. I followed their usual path. I looked in the direction where I was in the habit of seeing before the accident. . . . Finally, I realized that I was looking in the wrong way. I was looking too far off, and too much on the surface of things. . . . I began to look more closely, not at things but at a world closer to myself, looking from an inner place to one further within, instead of clinging to the move-

ment of sight toward the world outside. Immediately, the substance of the universe drew together, redefined and peopled itself anew. I was aware of a radiance emanating from a place I knew nothing about, a place which might as well have been outside me as within. . . . I felt indescribable relief, and happiness so great it almost made me laugh. . . . Sighted people always talk about the night of blindness, and that seems to them quite natural. But there is no such night, for at every waking hour and even in my dreams I lived in a stream of light. Without my eyes, light was much more stable than it had been with them. As I remember it, there were no longer the same differences between things lighted brightly, less brightly, or not at all. I saw the whole world in light, existing through it and because of it.   (Jacques Lusseyran, *And There Was Light*, trans. Elizabeth R. Cameron, Little, Brown and Co., 1963, pp. 16ff.)

every disciple who is fully taught will be like his teacher: A wonderfully generous statement. Zen Master Kuei-shan goes even farther and says, "Only one whose insight surpasses his teacher's is worthy to be his heir."

sources: Matthew 6:19–23; Luke 6:39f.

Trust

This section includes some of the most important and beautiful of Jesus' sayings.

"Ask, and it will be given to you; seek, and you will find; knock, and the door will be opened to you. For everyone who asks, receives; and he who seeks, finds; and to him who knocks, the door will be opened.

"*What man among you, when his son asks him for a loaf of bread, will give him a stone; or when he asks for a fish, will give him a snake? If you, then, who are imperfect, know how to give good gifts to your children, how much more will your Father, who is perfect, give good things to those who ask him.*

"*Therefore I tell you, don't be anxious about what you will eat or what you will wear. Isn't your life more than its food, and your body more than its clothing? Look at the birds of the sky: they neither sow nor reap nor gather into barns, yet God feeds them. Which of you by thinking can add a day to his life? And why do you worry about clothing? Consider the lilies of the field, how they grow: they neither toil nor spin. And yet I tell you that not even Solomon in all his glory was robed like one of these. Therefore, if God so clothes the grass, which grows in the field today, and tomorrow is thrown into the oven, won't he all the more clothe you? So don't worry about these things and say, 'What will we eat?' or 'What will we wear?' For that is what the Gentiles seek; and your Father knows that you need these things. But first seek the kingdom of God; and these things will be given to you as well.*"

Ask, and it will be given to you: Ask for what you need, not for what you want. What you need will be given to you anyway, but if you ask for it, the gift will go deeper.

seek, and you will find: If you seek and haven't found, just keep seeking, with trust and patience—for another day, another year, twenty years, fifty, a lifetime, fifty thousand lifetimes: ultimately you can't help but find, just as the fruit tree can't help but bear fruit when the right season comes.

> Do you have the patience to wait
> till your mud settles and the water is clear?
> Can you remain unmoving
> till the right action arises by itself?
>
> The Master doesn't seek fulfillment.
> Not seeking, not expecting,
> she is present, and can welcome all things.
> (*Tao Te Ching*, chapter 15)

Abu Yazid al-Bistami said, "This thing we tell of can never be found by seeking, yet only seekers find it."

Look at the birds of the sky: Jesus' love of the natural world, and his trust in the God who can be felt through it, follow in the tradition of the poets who wrote Psalms 104 and 147. To provide the appropriate context, and for your pleasure, here is my adaptation of Psalm 147 (Psalm 104 appears in *The Enlightened Heart*). I have paraphrased the local and historical references to the rebuilding of Jerusalem, though they are lovely and moving in their own right.

> How sweet to sing praises to you,
>   Unnamable God,
>   and to thank you for all your blessings.
> You rebuild what has been ruined
>   and recreate what was lost.
> You heal the brokenhearted;
>   you are medicine for their wounds.
> You lift up the afflicted
>   and give them the courage to endure.
> You count the myriad stars
>   and call each one by its name.
> Infinite is your power,
>   incalculable your wisdom.
> You scatter snow like wool
>   and sprinkle the frost like ashes.
> You strew ice crystals like breadcrumbs;
>   the earth becomes bitter cold.
> You breathe warm winds and the ice melts;
>   you blow and the waters flash.
> You cover the sky with clouds;
>   you send down your rain to the earth,
> making grass grow on the hills
>   and plants to nourish all men.
> You give the wild animals their prey;
>   you feed the young ravens when they cry.
> You delight in the power of the horse
>   and take pleasure in the legs of an athlete.

But most, you rejoice in a pure heart
    and in those who let you shine through them.
You give them joy in your joy,
    and you bless their loves with your love.
You bring peace to their families
    and grant them your infinite wealth.
You send your wisdom to their minds;
    your light runs faster than a thought.
Above all others they are blessed,
    because they can hear you speak
(though your love speaks in all people,
    in the silence of every heart).

first seek the kingdom of God: Gandhi always referred to this verse with the greatest admiration, interpreting it in his own admirable way:

> In my early studies of the Bible, one verse seized me immediately: "Make this world the Kingdom of God, and everything will be added unto you." I tell you that if you will understand, appreciate, and act up to the spirit of this passage, you won't even need to know what place Jesus or any other teacher occupies in your heart. (*The Message of Jesus Christ*, ed. Anand T. Hingorami, Bharatiya Vidya Bhavan, 1963, p. 43)

and these things will be given to you as well: You will always have enough.

sources: *Matthew 7:7–11; Matthew 6:25; Matthew 6:26, Luke 12:24; Matthew 6:27–31; Matthew 6:32f., Luke 12:30f.*

Providence

A teaching intended for those who don't yet understand how infinitely taken care of they are. It is spoken with great tenderness, as if to little children afraid of the dark.

"Aren't two sparrows sold for a penny? Yet not one of them falls to the ground apart from your Father. As for you, every hair on your head is numbered. So don't be afraid: you are worth more than many sparrows."

you are worth more than many sparrows: Like all provisional teachings, this statement has an expiration date stamped on it. It expires as soon as it is said. (It is, of course, untrue from God's viewpoint, or the sparrow's.)

source: Matthew 10:29–31

You Receive Exactly What You Give

These teachings are simple, essential, and worthy of our closest attention.

"Don't judge, and you will not be judged. For in the same way that you judge people, you yourself will be judged.

"Why do you see the splinter that is in your brother's eye, but don't notice the log that is in your own eye? First take the log out of your own eye, and then you will see clearly enough to take the splinter out of your brother's eye.

"So if you don't judge, you will not be judged; if you don't condemn, you will not be condemned; if you forgive, you will be forgiven; if you give, things will be given to you: good measure will be poured into your lap, pressed down, shaken together, and overflowing. For the measure by which you give is the measure by which you will receive.

"Therefore, whatever you want others to do to you, do to them. This is the essence of the Law and the prophets."

Don't judge: This doesn't mean that we shouldn't see people clearly, or recognize where they and we ourselves stand in the moral and spiritual realm. That kind of judgment is as necessary to compassionate action as headlights are to night driving. What Jesus means here is that we shouldn't accuse or condemn, that we should keep our hearts open to everyone. Lao-tzu explains:

> The Tao doesn't take sides;
> it gives birth to both good and evil.
> The Master doesn't take sides;
> she welcomes both saints and sinners.
>
> (chapter 5)

The Master imitates the Tao in being available to everyone. Because she can see into the essential nature of every being, she doesn't get trapped inside her own judgments or delude herself into thinking that people *are* good or evil.

in the same way that you judge people: We attract the same kind of energy that we send out. If we act compassionately toward others, we find that, lo and behold, others are compassionate toward us. If we are judgmental toward others, others are judgmental toward us. This is not a matter of reward and punishment imposed from the outside; it is a law of nature, as pure and impartial as the law of gravity.

if you don't judge, you will not be judged: Jesus doesn't mean that if we judge others we will be judged by God. God's being *is* non-judgment. The more we seduce ourselves into believing that our own judgments, of others or of ourselves, are reality, the farther we are from that being. Judgment is eating from the Tree of the Knowledge of Good and Evil; nonjudgment is eating from the Tree of Life.

the measure by which you give is the measure by which you will receive: Everyone understands cause and effect on the physical plane, but few people see how it applies just as strictly on the moral plane. To use the Hindu and Buddhist term, when you understand how you create your own karma, and recognize that there is absolute justice in your own life, you can begin to make fundamental, enduring changes in yourself. It is possible to understand your karma so meticulously, and on such subtle levels of awareness, that even very entrenched neurotic patterns can be transformed into light.

Emerson may not have known the word *karma*, but he described it accurately when he said:

Justice is not postponed. A perfect equity adjusts its balance in all parts of life. The dice of God are always loaded. The world looks like a multiplication-table, or a mathematical equation, which, turn it how you will, balances itself. Take what figure you will, its exact value, nor more nor less, still returns to you. Every secret is told, every crime is punished, every virtue rewarded, every wrong redressed, in silence and certainty. What we call retribution is the universal necessity by which the whole appears wherever a part appears. If you see smoke, there must be fire. If you see a hand or a limb, you know that the trunk to which it belongs is there behind.

Every act rewards itself, or in other words integrates itself, in a twofold manner; first in the thing, or in real nature; and secondly in the circumstance, or in apparent nature. Men call the circumstance the retribution. The causal retribution is in the thing and is seen by the soul. The retribution in the circumstance is seen by the understanding; it is inseparable from the thing, but is often spread over a long time and so does not become distinct until after many years. The specific stripes may follow late after the offense, but they follow because they accompany it. Crime and punishment grow out of one stem.

Punishment is a fruit that unsuspected ripens within the flower of the pleasure which concealed it. Cause and effect, means and ends, seed and fruit, cannot be severed; for the effect already blooms in the cause, the end preëxists in the means, the fruit in the seed. ("Compensation," *Essays: First Series*)

whatever you want others to do to you, do to them: The Golden Rule. It is stated in its so-called "negative" form by Hillel the Elder (c. 40 B.C.E.–10 C.E.), who, when asked by a Gentile to summarize the Law, said, "What you yourself hate, don't do to your neighbor. This is the whole Law; the rest is commentary. Go now and learn." Four centuries before Hillel, it appears in Tzu-ssu's *The Central Harmony:*

> Confucius said, "To find the Tao, there is nowhere you need to search. If it is not inside you, it is not the Tao." The Book of Songs says,
>
> > When you carve an axe handle,
> > the model is near at hand.
>
> In making the handle of an axe by cutting wood with an axe, the model is indeed near at hand. Thus, in dealing with people, we already have the perfect model of behavior inside us. Just act sincerely, in accordance with your true nature. Don't do to others what you wouldn't want done to you.

The point of the Golden Rule is empathy. Jesus certainly didn't mean it as a projection of egoism, but it has often been taken that way. So the "negative" form is perhaps the more helpful one. I may want others to shower me with attention, while you may prefer to be left alone; if I treat you as I wish to be treated, I do you a disservice. Blake said of a particularly obnoxious do-gooder:

> He has observed the Golden Rule
> Till he's become the Golden Fool.

And Thoreau, who is the essence of sensibility in this matter as in so much else, said:

Absolutely speaking, Do unto others as you would that they do unto you, is by no means a golden rule, but the best of current silver. An honest man would have but little occasion for it. It is golden not to have any rule at all in such a case.

sources: Matthew 7:1–3; Matthew 7:5; Luke 6:37–40; Matthew 7:12

The Narrow Gate

Jesus is not being exclusive here, or dividing humanity into a small group of the elect and a mass of the rejected. He is simply stating a fact: it is difficult to enter the kingdom of God, and it takes a great deal of painful inner work.

"Enter by the narrow gate. For the gate is wide and the way is easy that leads to suffering, and those who go through it are many. But the gate is narrow and the way is hard that leads to true life, and those who find it are few."

the gate is narrow and the way is hard: Spinoza said exactly the same thing in the great concluding lines of the *Ethics:*

> If the way I have pointed out as leading to this result seems exceedingly hard, it can nevertheless be found. It must indeed be hard, since it is found so seldom. For if true freedom were readily available and could be found without great effort, how is it possible that it should be neglected by almost everyone? But all things excellent are as difficult as they are rare.

source: Matthew 7:13f.

Hearing and Doing

The finale of the Sermon on the Mount. Jesus makes the same point here as in his instructions to the scribe who elicits the parable of the Good Samaritan: the only way you can take his teaching to heart is to live it.

"Everyone who hears what I say and does it is like a man who built his house upon rock; and the rain fell and the floods came and the winds blew and beat against that house, and it didn't fall, because it was founded on rock. And everyone who hears what I say and doesn't do it is like a man who built his house upon sand; and the rain fell and the floods came and the winds blew and beat against that house, and it fell; and great was its fall."

who hears what I say and does it: Jesus' brother James (or one of James's disciples), in his compassionate and telling criticism of Paul's teaching about faith and works, says,

> What good is it, my dear friends, for someone to say that he has faith when he doesn't *act* as if he loves God? Can his faith save him? If a fellow human being is naked and hungry, and you say to him, "Keep warm, eat well," and don't give him what he needs, what good is that? So faith, if it doesn't lead to action, is dead. (James 2:14ff.)

source: Matthew 7:24–27, Luke 6:47–49

Jesus' Family (1)

For a discussion of the final sentence in this passage, see pp. 48f.

And when Jesus came down from the hill, he went to the lakeside with his disciples, and large crowds from Galilee followed; and large crowds, hearing of his works, came to him from Judea and Jerusalem as well, and from Idumea and beyond the Jordan and the region of Tyre and Sidon. And he told the disciples to have a boat ready for him, so that he wouldn't be crushed by the crowd, for he had healed many people, and the crippled and sick were all pressing in on him to touch him.

    Then he went into the house; and such a large crowd gathered around them that they didn't even have time to eat.

    And when his family heard about all this, they went to seize him, for they said, "He is out of his mind."

sources: *Matthew 8:1, Mark 3:7f.; Mark 3:9f.; Mark 3:19–21*

Accusations of Sorcery

"When a pickpocket sees a saint, he sees only his pockets." Even the purest of teachers will face bitter criticism from those who feel threatened by him. The temptation (in the early, unripe stages) is to take the criticism personally, to get caught in the substance of the accusation, rather than seeing it as the voice of the accuser's pain. But once a teacher has surrendered all ideas of himself, he has nothing left to defend, and he can react with absolute nonresistance. As with a tai ch'i master, the accuser can't push him off balance, can't even find him, because his ego isn't there. The immature teacher stiffens against adversity; the mature teacher bends in the wind.

And a mute demoniac was brought to Jesus, and he healed him, and the man began to speak. And all the people were amazed.

But certain scribes who had come down from Jerusalem said, "He is possessed by Beelzebul" and "He casts out demons by using the prince of demons."

He casts out demons: At this point, according to Mark (followed by Matthew and Luke), "Jesus" angrily rejects the accusations, becomes defensive, and uses arguments and finally verbal violence against violence, ending with the horrifying statement:

> "Whoever blasphemes against the Holy Spirit will never be forgiven, but is guilty of an eternal sin." (For they had said, "He is possessed by an unclean spirit.") (Mark 3:29f.)

"Jesus" says, in other words, that because the scribes have mistakenly accused him of healing by demonic means, God will never forgive them. This statement, it seems to me, is itself blasphemy against the Holy Spirit, in that it slanders the infinite mercy of God. The truth is that there is no sin too grave to be forgiven; once the sinner truly repents, truly returns, forgiveness is already there, waiting for him. That is why certain ancient rabbis, as well as the early Christian theologian Origen, believed that hell wouldn't exist forever, and that on the last day of time even the devil would return to his original identity as Lucifer, the bringer of light. Robinson Crusoe's man Friday, in his innocence, is also of this opinion:

> I [Crusoe] said, "God will at last punish [the Devil] severely, he is reserved for the judgment, and is to be cast into the bottomless pit, to dwell with everlasting fire." This did not satisfy Friday, but he returns upon me, repeating my words, " 'Reserve at last,' me no understand; but why not kill the Devil now, not kill great ago?" "You may as well ask me," said I, "why God

does not kill you and me, when we do wicked things here that offend Him. We are preserved to repent and be pardoned." He muses awhile at this. "Well, well," says he, mighty affectionately, "that well; so you, I, Devil, all wicked, all preserve, repent, God pardon all."

Jesus' response to the accusations seems to me entirely inauthentic. Could he have been so insecure about the source of his healing power as to lose his composure in this way? I don't believe it.

As a paradigm of a mature response, here is a passage from the Bhaddiyasutta, in which the Buddha answers a similar accusation with the dignity and humor worthy of an enlightened Master:

> Bhaddiya the Licchavi said to the Exalted One, "Sir, some people are saying that you use black magic to entice people to follow you. Is that true?"
>
> The Exalted One answered, "Any good teacher simply points out the correct way of life to his students. He shows them how to cut off greed, hatred, and delusion at the source, and thus helps to free them, in body, speech, and mind, of any acts that arise from greed, hatred, or delusion. That is all."
>
> Bhaddiya said, "How wonderful! Please accept me as a lay disciple."
>
> The Exalted One said, "Bhaddiya, have I said to you, 'Come, be my disciple, and I will be your teacher'?"
>
> "No, sir."
>
> "Bhaddiya, these people are not speaking correctly when they say that I use black magic to entice people to follow me. If there is any magic that I use, it is the magic of the truth. If all good people were enticed to follow me by abandoning their selfishness, it would be for their everlasting advantage and happiness. And if all bad people were enticed to follow me, it would be for their everlasting advantage and happiness. And if all beings in the universe, up to the highest angels and down to the lowest devils, were enticed to follow me, it would be for their everlasting advantage and happiness. Bhaddiya, if these

great sal trees standing here had the ability to think and were enticed to follow me, it would be for their everlasting advantage and happiness—how much more so human beings!"

sources: *Matthew 12:22f., Luke 11:14; Mark 3:22*

Jesus' Family (2)

The second and last time that Jesus' family appears in the authentic passages of the Gospels. See pp. 49ff.

And his mother and his brothers arrived, and standing outside, they sent in a message asking for him.

And people in the crowd sitting around him said to him, "Your mother and your brothers are outside and want to see you."

And Jesus said, "Who are my mother and my brothers?" And looking at those who sat in a circle around him, he said, "These are my mother and my brothers. Whoever does the will of God is my brother, and sister, and mother."

Who are my mother and my brothers:

> Who is your wife, and who is your son?
> Whose son are you, and where do you come from?
> Realize who you are, deluded man,
> realize what is real, and what is not. (Shankara)

> No one belongs to me; I belong to no one.
> There is no "I" or "mine"; all is blissful aloneness.
> (Mahabharata)

source: *Mark 3:31–35*

Two Healings

Here we have the stories of two healings combined, by Mark or some previous compiler, to heighten the drama. Luke adds the story of the widow's son at Nain (7:11–16), a later, idealized version of the second incident.

Once, when Jesus had returned by boat from the other side of the lake, a large crowd gathered around him at the shore. And one of the leaders of the synagogue came to him and prostrated himself at his feet and said, "My little girl is near death; come, I beg of you, lay your hands on her and save her life."

And Jesus went with him. And a large crowd followed and pressed in on him.

And there was a woman in the crowd who had been bleeding for a dozen years, and she had been treated by many doctors, and had spent all her money, and hadn't gotten better but worse. And she had heard about Jesus, and she came up behind him in the crowd and touched his robe, for she thought, "If I touch even his clothes, I will be healed." And immediately the bleeding dried up, and she knew in her body that she was cured of the disease.

And immediately Jesus felt in himself that power had gone forth from him, and he turned around in the crowd and said, "Who touched my clothes?"

And his disciples said to him, "You see the crowd pressing in on you; why do you ask, 'Who touched my clothes?'"

And he looked around to see who had done it.

And the woman, frightened and trembling, knowing what had happened to her, came and prostrated herself before him and told him the whole truth. And Jesus said to her, "Daughter, your trust has healed you. Go in peace, and be cured of your disease."

Before he had finished speaking, some people came to the leader of the synagogue and said, "Your daughter is dead: why bother the rabbi any further?"

But Jesus overheard this, and said to him, "Don't be afraid; only trust." And he wouldn't let anyone go with him except Peter and James and John the brother of James.

And when they arrived at the leader's house, he found a great commotion, and loud sobbing and wailing. And he went in and said to them, "Why all this commotion? The child is not dead but sleeping." And they laughed at him.

But he ordered them all out, and took the child's father and mother and his three disciples, and went in to where the child was. And he took her hand and said, "T'litha, koomi" (which means, "Child, get up"). And immediately the girl got up and began to walk. And they were filled with great astonishment. And he told them to give her something to eat.

Once, when Jesus had returned . . . : There are many stories in rabbinic and Hellenistic literature about philosophers or rabbis raising the dead. The most detailed account features the magician and healer Apollonius of Tyana, a contemporary of Jesus:

> A girl seemed to have died just before her marriage. The bridegroom was following the bier, crying out, and all Rome mourned with him, for the girl came from a family of consular rank. Apollonius, witnessing their grief, said, "Lay down the bier; I will put an end to your mourning." Then he asked what her name was. Everyone thought that he was going to give a funeral oration; but he went over and touched her and whispered over her something that no one could hear distinctly, and woke the girl up from seeming death. She uttered a cry and went back to her father's house.

In a touchingly honest postscript, Philostratus comments:

> Now whether he detected some spark of life in her, which those who were nursing her hadn't noticed, or whether life was really extinct, and he restored it by the warmth of his touch, is a mysterious problem which neither I myself nor those who were present could decide.
>
> (*The Life of Apollonius of Tyana*, vol. 1, trans. F. C. Conybeare, Harvard University Press, 1960, pp. 457ff.)

Gandhi tells a similar story:

> I do not need either the prophecies or the miracles to establish Jesus' greatness as a teacher. Nothing can be more miraculous than his ministry. There is no miracle in the story of the multitude being fed on a handful of loaves. A magician can create that illusion. As for Jesus raising the dead to life: well, I doubt if the people he raised were really dead. I raised a relative's child from supposed death to life, and if I had not been there, she might have been cremated; but that was because the child was not dead. When I saw that life was not extinct, I gave her an enema and she was restored to life. There was no miracle about it. I do not deny that Jesus had certain psychic powers, and he was undoubtedly filled with the love of humanity. But he brought to life not people who were dead, but who were believed to be dead. The laws of Nature are changeless, unchangeable, and there are no miracles in the sense of infringement or interruption of Nature's laws.
>
> (*Message of Jesus Christ*, p. 73)

If the present story has no basis in actual events, it was invented to prove that Jesus was as great as prophets like Elijah and Elisha, who were remembered as being able to resuscitate the dead (I Kings 17:17–24, II Kings 4:18–37).

As for the possibility of such resuscitations, by now there is so much evidence of "near-death experiences" that even skeptics—even doctors—may be tempted to keep an open mind. We also have the testimony of Ramana Maharshi, who was a man of absolute truthfulness, as anyone who knows his teaching will confirm. The incident happened one morning in 1912, when Maharshi was returning from a bath, walking uphill in the hot sun:

> Suddenly the view of natural scenery in front of me disappeared, and a bright white curtain was drawn across the line of my vision and shut out the view. I could distinctly see the gradual process. At one stage I could see a part of the scenery still clear, and the rest was being covered by the advancing curtain. On experiencing this, I stopped walking, so that I wouldn't

fall. When it cleared, I walked on. When darkness and a fainting feeling overtook me a second time, I leaned against a rock until it cleared. And when it came again for the third time, I felt it safest to sit, so I sat near the rock. Then the bright white curtain completely shut out my vision, my head was swimming, and my blood circulation and breathing stopped. The skin turned a livid blue. It was the regular death-like color, and it got darker and darker. Vasudeva Sastri thought that I was dead, held me in his embrace and began to weep aloud and lament my death. His body was shivering. I could at that time distinctly feel his clasp and his shivering, hear his lamentation and understand the meaning. I also saw the discoloration of my skin, and I felt the stoppage of my heartbeat and respiration, and the increased chillness of the extremities of my body. Yet the current of self-effulgence continued as usual in that state also. I was not afraid in the least, nor did I feel any sadness at the condition of my body. I had closed my eyes as soon as I sat near the rock in my usual posture, but was not leaning against it. The body, which had no circulation or respiration, still maintained that position. This state continued for some ten or fifteen minutes. Then I felt a shock passing suddenly through the body; circulation revived with enormous force, and also respiration, and there was profuse sweating all over the body from every pore. The color of life reappeared on the skin. I then opened my eyes, got up casually, and said, "Let's go." We reached Virupaksha cave without further trouble.

[Maharshi added, to correct some stories that were being told about the incident:] I did not bring on the fit purposely, nor did I wish to see what this body would look like at death. Nor did I say that I will not leave this body without warning others. It was one of those fits that I used to get occasionally. But in this instance, it assumed a very serious aspect.

(B. V. Narasimha Swami, *Self-Realization: Life and Teachings of Sri Ramana Maharshi* [8th ed.], Sri Ramanasramam, 1976, pp. 267f.)

one of the leaders of the synagogue: The phrase "named Jairus" is probably a scribal addition to Mark, taken from Luke 8:41.

My little girl is near death: Matthew 9:18 makes the miracle less equivocal and more miraculous by having the father say, "My daughter has just died."

touched his robe: She is too afraid to come up and ask him for help directly. Perhaps her bleeding is menstrual, and she thinks Jesus will refuse a direct request because touching her would make him impure, according to biblical law. But her need and trust are greater than her fear.

power: Jesus' healing energy. Mark uses the phrase *work of power* to mean "miracle."

Who touched my clothes: He becomes aware that the energy is flowing from his body, like milk from a mother's breast. Perhaps he is also aware of the woman's fear.

your trust has healed you: Trust is an attitude toward the world; belief is a structure in the mind. Belief has the instability of yes-or-no. If faith depends on any belief, it is a hostage.

Simone Weil said, "Until God has taken possession of him, no human being can have faith, but only simple belief; and it hardly matters whether or not he has such a belief, because he will arrive at faith equally well through disbelief." She also said, "In what concerns divine things, belief is not appropriate. Only certainty will do. Anything less than certainty is unworthy of God."

rabbi: Didaskale, "Teacher." But the Greek word is itself a translation of the Hebrew/Aramaic "Rabbi," literally, "my great one" or "honored sir," as the Gospel of John makes clear: "They said to him, 'Rabbi' (which, being translated, means Teacher [*didaskale*])" (1:38); "She said to him in Hebrew, 'Rabbouni' (which means Teacher)" (20:16). Jesus is explicitly addressed in Hebrew/Aramaic as "Rabbi" in Mark 9:5, 10:51, 11:21, 14:45, Matthew 26:25, and John 1:49, 3:2, 4:31, 6:25, 9:2, 11:8.

Don't be afraid: This may be an example of Jesus' telepathic awareness, rather than of his confidence in his ability to raise the dead; he can see that the girl is not really dead. But it is possible that this part of the story was added by Mark or a previous editor.

the girl got up and began to walk: Mark says, parenthetically, "She was twelve years old."

he told them to give her something to eat: A wonderfully authentic and touching detail.

————

I am always moved by the confidence Jesus shows here. Like Gandhi in the story quoted above, he was not hypnotized by the crowd into sharing their certainty and grief. He entered the girl's room with a "don't-know" mind, open to all possibilities; thus he was aware enough to notice the faintest sign of life.

If I had felt that this was a story of Jesus' arbitrarily raising the girl from the dead, I wouldn't have included it in this version of the Gospel. I would have felt that it was unworthy of him. Beneath the surface of such "miracles," there is a fear of death and a lack of trust in the goodness and supreme intelligence of God. That is why, in *Parables and Portraits*, I imagined the raising of Lazarus (John 11:1ff.) as a violation, and suggested that Lazarus showed more compassion in answering the call than "Jesus" did in making it:

He had almost reached the end of the tunnel when he heard his friend's voice calling him back. The voice was filled with love, but also with sorrow and pity, and not so much fear of death as resistance to it, as if it were an enemy to be expelled or overcome. He had realized so much, during the four days' journey, that these resonances struck him as odd, coming as they did from a man of such insight; struck him as laughable, as almost childish. All the dramas of his short, intense life were an instant away from being resolved, dissolved, in the light at the end of the tunnel, which was not a physical light—after all, he no longer had physical eyes—but a radiant presence, a sense of completion a million times more blissful than what he had felt even in the company of his beloved friend. And the sweet, seductive drama of master and disciple, how childish that had been too, as if a candle flame needed to warm itself before a fire. He thought of his sisters in the old house in Bethany, of Mary anointing their friend's feet and wiping them with her hair: the tenderness, the absurdity of that gesture.

The voice was still calling. He didn't have the heart to refuse. He knew that, for his friend's sake, he would have to postpone his disappearance, to hurry back down the tunnel and return to his body, left behind so gratefully, which had already begun to stink.

Greater love has no man.

Sorrow at the death of our loved ones is, of course, a natural human response. Who among us, if our child had died, wouldn't give anything on earth to have her brought back to life? And yet, when we take even a small step outside our self, we can recognize this desire as a subtle form of obtuseness, and as a way of not honoring the integrity of the child's life. Rilke said, of those who died young:

> What they want of me is that I gently remove the appearance
> of injustice about their death—which at times
> slightly hinders their souls from proceeding onward.
>
> Of course, it is strange to inhabit the earth no longer,
> to give up customs one barely had time to learn,
> not to see roses and other promising Things
> in terms of a human future; no longer to be
> what one was in infinitely anxious hands; to leave
> even one's own first name behind, forgetting it
> as easily as a child abandons a broken toy.
> Strange to no longer desire one's desires. Strange
> to see meanings that clung together once, floating away
> in every direction. And being dead is hard work

and full of retrieval before one can gradually feel
a trace of eternity.

("The First Elegy," *The Selected Poetry of Rainer
Maria Rilke*, pp. 153–55)

It is possible to grieve for a child's death with all your heart
and at the same time to realize that everything is as it should
be. The world according to God, the world that includes
death, is far more beautiful than the world according to our
desire. What we must constantly keep learning is not to interfere—to receive, to accept, to trust the supreme intelligence of
the universe (*I am what I am*). If Jesus had reversed one death
for one grieving father, that would not teach us anything useful. But for him to show us how to die ("Trust God with all
your heart") and how to accept the death of those we love
("Trust God with all your heart") is a teaching beyond price.

source: *Mark 5:21–43*

Rejection in Nazareth

A bitterly disappointing experience for Jesus, but one he undoubtedly learned from.

*From there he went to Nazareth, his native town, and his disciples fol-
lowed him.*

*And when the Sabbath came, he began to teach in the synagogue, and
many people who heard him were bewildered, and said, "Where does
this fellow get such stuff?" and "What makes* him *so wise?" and "How
can he be a miracle-worker? Isn't this the carpenter, Mary's bastard,
the brother of James and Joseph and Judas and Simon, and aren't his
sisters here with us?" And they were prevented from believing in him.*

And Jesus said, "A prophet is not rejected except in his own town and in his own family and in his own house."

And he was unable to do any miracle there, because of their disbelief.

the carpenter:

Such crafts [as carpentry] were normally hereditary. There is a parable about a son learning his trade by watching his father at work: "A son can do nothing on his own account, but only what he sees his father doing. What the father does, the son does in the same manner. For the father loves his son and shows him everything that he does himself" (all the secrets of the craft). It is perhaps not too bold to find here a reminiscence of the family workshop at Nazareth. There Jesus learned to be a "carpenter"; but the word in Greek (and in the native Aramaic of Galilee) had a wider meaning. His work included, for example, building operations. In one parable he depicts a scene in a carpenter's shop, where two brothers are at work and one of them gets a speck of sawdust in his eye. In another he pillories the jerry-builder who scamps his foundations; and in yet another he notes the importance of drawing up an estimate before operations begin: "Would any of you think of building a tower without first sitting down and calculating the cost, to see whether he could afford to finish it?" The practical craftsman is speaking. Jesus was not only an observer of the workaday scene; he had been busy in it himself. It should perhaps be added that to say he was a craftsman earning his living is not to say that he was uneducated. The level of literacy among the Jews was probably higher than in any comparable community within the Empire. And although superior persons in Jerusalem dismissed him as "this untrained man," he appears to have been quite capable of meeting scholars learned in the Scriptures on their own ground.

(C. H. Dodd, *The Founder of Christianity*, Collier Books, 1970, p. 120)

Mary's bastard: Literally, "the son of Mary." For this phrase as an insulting reference to Jesus' illegitimacy, see pp. 23, 81f.

James: James—in Hebrew, Yaakov (Jacob)—was later to become the head of the Jewish-Christian church at Jerusalem.

Known as "James the Just," he was a devout Jew and strongly opposed Paul's attitude toward the Law and the Gentiles. The Epistle of James, though most scholars consider it a later, pseudepigraphal work, is a fair representation of the Jewish-Christian viewpoint.

And he was unable to do any miracle: Mark (6:5) adds a gloss: "And he was unable to do any miracle there *except that he laid his hands on a few sick people and healed them. And he marveled* because of their disbelief." Matthew (13:58) takes a different editorial tack: "And he didn't do *many* miracles there, because of their disbelief." Both are obviously embarrassed by Jesus' failure at Nazareth.

Luke's solution (4:28–30) is a peculiar one. According to him, the crowd at first "spoke well of [Jesus] and marveled at the gracious words that proceeded from his mouth." Whereupon Jesus, for no discernible reason, says to them, "You will undoubtedly want me to do miracles here, as I have done in Capernaum. But no prophet is acceptable in his own town [or, country]." He then goes on to tell about Elijah's and Elisha's healings of two Gentiles. At this point Luke's version becomes malicious: the crowd suddenly turns into a bloodthirsty mob (the implication is that they are in a typically Jewish xenophobic frenzy), thus eliminating the opportunity for miracles: "And when they heard this, everyone in the synagogue was filled with rage. And they got up and drove him out of the city and took him to the brow of the hill on which their city was built, to throw him over the edge. But he passed through their midst [perhaps he had become invisible] and went away." This is a mere anti-Semitic polemic on Luke's part, free invention with no other source than Mark's account.

sources: Luke 4:16, Mark 6:1; Mark 6:2–6

The Syrophoenician Woman

One of the most touching stories in the Gospels, because it shows us a Jesus who makes a mistake and admits it with humility and good humor, a Jesus who is flexible enough to learn. From a Gentile yet. From a *woman!* If *sin* means "missing the mark," this is an example of a sin immediately and gracefully corrected.

And from there Jesus set out and went to the region around Tyre. And he went into a house, and didn't want anyone to know that he was there, but he couldn't remain hidden. For soon a Gentile woman, a Syrophoenician by race, heard of him, and came and prostrated herself at his feet and said, "Take pity on me, sir; my daughter is possessed by a demon."

And he said to her, "It is not right to take the children's food and throw it to the dogs."

And she said, "True, sir; yet even the dogs under the table eat the children's scraps."

And Jesus answered, "Well said. Now go home; the demon has left your daughter."

And when she went home, she found the child lying in bed, and the derangement was gone.

didn't want anyone to know that he was there: We aren't told why. Perhaps he needed some time for solitary prayer.

And he said to her, "It is not right . . .": According to Matthew (15:24), Jesus first says to the woman, "I was sent only to the lost sheep of the house of Israel." This statement probably circulated as an independent saying. It may have originated from the Jewish Christians of the Jerusalem church in the fierce debates about the Gentile mission that were going on during the first few decades after Jesus' death. But the fact that the verse has survived the anti-Semitic bias of the Gospels argues for its historicity. Compare Matthew 10:5–6 ("Don't travel to the lands of the Gentiles and don't go to any Samaritan towns; but go rather to the lost sheep of the house of Israel"), and the derogatory references to Gentiles in Matthew 5:47, 6:7, 6:32, 20:24, and especially 7:6 ("Don't give what is holy to dogs, or cast your pearls before swine").

The parable of the Good Samaritan is the great and luminous exception in which Jesus speaks reverently of a non-Jew. (The story of the centurion's servant in Matthew 8:5ff. and Luke 7:2ff., a variant of the present story, is probably a creation of the early church.)

to take the children's food and throw it to the dogs: I can never read this verse without a thrill of dismay at Jesus' harshness. The words would be harsh at any time, but especially when said to a mother about her sick child. Jesus' irritability, along with his desire for privacy, may indicate that he was feeling overworked and emotionally drained by the demands of the crowds. But like a young child, he doesn't cling to his mood. He is open to each new moment as it comes, and his harshness can change into delight as easily as a child's tears change into laughter.

True, sir; yet even the dogs under the table eat the children's scraps: She takes the metaphor and returns it to Jesus. What wit, and what presence of mind, even in the midst of her grave worry.

Well said: Jesus is delighted with the woman's answer and softens his tone. This is, if not the admission of a mistake, an acknowledgment that his attitude was too harsh. He honors the woman by learning from her.

Matthew, in making Jesus say, "O woman, great is your faith," misses the point. It's not her faith that Jesus admires, but her chutzpah.

It can't be overemphasized what an important teaching Jesus' willingness to learn is. The rage-filled, defensive Jesus who curses Capernaum or calls his enemies "children of the devil" is a disciple of death, as Lao-tzu would say, while the flexible Jesus of this story is a disciple of life.

> Humans are born soft and supple;
> dead, they are stiff and hard.
> Plants are born tender and pliant;
> dead, they are brittle and dry.
>
> Thus whoever is stiff and inflexible
> is a disciple of death.
> Whoever is soft and yielding
> is a disciple of life.   (chapter 76)

As soon as we blame other people or refuse to acknowledge our own fallibility, we step outside the kingdom of God. Confucius said, "In the archer there is a resemblance to the mature person. When he misses the bull's-eye, he turns and seeks the reason for his failure in himself." There is nothing wrong with making mistakes; the trouble comes with making mistakes about our mistakes.

> The more powerful you grow,
> the greater the need for humility.
> Humility means trusting the Tao,
> thus never needing to be defensive.
>
> When the Master makes a mistake, she realizes it.
> Having realized it, she admits it.
> Having admitted it, she corrects it.
> She considers those who point out her faults
> as her most benevolent teachers.
> She thinks of her enemy
> as the shadow that she herself casts.   (chapter 61)

the demon has left your daughter: It isn't clear whether this is an instance of Jesus' telepathic awareness or a long-distance exorcism. In Matthew it is clearly the latter: " 'Let it be done for you as you wish.' And at that very moment her daughter was healed."

There is a Talmudic story in which the first-century charismatic Hanina ben Dosa performs a long-distance healing:

> When Rabban Gamaliel's son got sick, the Rabban sent two pupils to Rabbi Hanina ben Dosa in his town. Hanina said to them, "Wait till I go to the upper room." He went to the upper room and prayed. Then he came down and said to them, "I have been assured that Rabban Gamaliel's son has recovered from his sickness." They noted the time. It turned out that at that very moment the boy asked for food.
>
> (Palestinian Talmud, Berakhot 9d)

sources: Mark 7:24f.; Mark 7:25, Matthew 15:22; Mark 7:27–30

He Heals a Deaf Man, a Blind Man

These two healings are so similar that some scholars think they are different accounts of the same event.

And Jesus returned from the region of Tyre, and went by way of Sidon to the Sea of Galilee, through the region of the Decapolis.

And they brought him a man who was deaf and could hardly speak, and they begged him to lay his hands on him. And he took him aside, away from the crowd, and put his fingers into the man's ears, and spat and touched the man's tongue; and looking up into the sky, Jesus sighed, and said to him, "Ethpatakh!" (which means, "Be opened!"). And immediately his ears were opened, his tongue was released, and he spoke clearly. And the people were exceedingly astonished.

And a woman in the crowd called out to him, "Blessed is the womb that bore you and the breasts that you sucked."

And Jesus said, "No: blessed rather are those who hear the word of God and obey it."

Another time, in Bethsaida, they brought a blind man to Jesus and begged him to touch him. And he took the blind man by the hand and led him out of the village; and he spat into his eyes, and laid his hands on them, and asked him, "Can you see anything?"

And he looked up and said, "I see men, like trees walking."

And Jesus again laid his hands on his eyes, and the man looked, and his sight was restored, and he could see everything distinctly.

sources: *Mark 7:31–35,37; Luke 11:27f.; Mark 8:22–25; Mark 9:17f.*

An Exorcism

It isn't clear whether this is a case of epilepsy or of insanity.

Still another time, a man in the crowd said to him, "Rabbi, I brought you my son; he is possessed by a mute spirit, and when it attacks him, it throws him around, and he foams and grinds his teeth and gets stiff."

And they brought the boy to him; and immediately he was thrown down violently, and he thrashed around, foaming at the mouth. And Jesus asked the father, "How long has this been happening to him?"

And he said, "Since he was a child. It has tried to kill him many times, and thrown him into the fire or the water. But if it is possible for you to do anything, take pity on us and help us."

And Jesus said to him, " 'If it is possible'! Anything is possible when you believe it is."

And the boy's father cried out, "I believe; help my unbelief."

And Jesus put his hands on the boy and spoke to him. And the boy cried out and went into convulsions, and then became like a corpse, so that most of the people were saying he had died. But Jesus took him by the hand and lifted him, and he stood up.

Anything is possible when you believe it is: The simple truth. But we have to believe in our depths, not just with our conscious mind.

I believe; help my unbelief: An honest and touching statement. By putting his belief first, he is able to acknowledge the presence of his unbelief, and to see that it needs help. What a different statement it would have been if he had said, "I disbelieve; help my belief."

———

Almost all the Gospel accounts of exorcisms are tainted, because their intent is to show that the demons recognize Jesus as the Messiah or the Son of God. This incident and the healing of the Syrophoenician woman's daughter are the only ones without a polemical agenda.

There are two famous ancient descriptions of exorcisms, one Jewish and one Gentile. The first is by Josephus:

And God granted King Solomon knowledge of the art used against demons for the benefit and healing of men. He also composed incantations by which illnesses are relieved, and left behind forms of exorcisms with which those possessed by demons drive them out, never to return. And this kind of cure is of very great power among us [Jews] to this day, for I have seen a certain Eleazar, a countryman of mine, in the presence of [the emperor] Vespasian, his sons, tribunes and a number of other soldiers, free men possessed by demons, and this was the manner of the cure: he put to the nose of the possessed man a ring which had under its seal one of the roots prescribed by Solomon, and then, as the man smelled it, drew out the demon through his nostrils, and, when the man at once fell down, adjured the demon never to come back into him, speaking Sol-

omon's name and reciting the incantations which he had composed. Then, wishing to convince the bystanders and prove to them that he had this power, Eleazar placed a cup or foot-basin full of water a little way off and commanded the demon, as it went out of the man, to overturn it and make known to the spectators that he had left the man. And when this was done, the understanding and wisdom of Solomon was clearly revealed.   (*Jewish Antiquities*, in *Works*, vol. 5, trans.
H. St. J. Thackeray, Harvard University Press, 1934,
pp. 595ff.)

The second description, which includes an account of the aftereffects of the exorcism, is by Philostratus:

The youth was, without knowing it, possessed by a devil; for he would laugh at things that no one else laughed at, and then he would fall to weeping for no reason at all, and he would talk and sing to himself. Now most people thought that it was the boisterous humor of youth which led him into such excesses; but he was really the mouthpiece of a devil, though it only seemed a drunken frolic in which on that occasion he was indulging. Now when Apollonius gazed on him, the devil in him began to utter cries of fear and rage, such as one hears from people who are being branded or racked; and the devil swore that he would leave the young man alone and never take possession of any man again. But Apollonius addressed him with anger, as a master might address a shifty, rascally, and shameless slave and so on, and he ordered him to quit the young man and show by a visible sign that he had done so. "I will throw down yonder statue," said the devil, and pointed to one of the images which were in the king's portico, for there it was that the scene took place. But when the statue began by moving gently, and then fell down, it would defy anyone to describe the hubbub which arose thereat and the way they clapped their hands with wonder. But the young man rubbed his eyes as if he had just woken up, and he looked towards the rays of the sun, and assumed a modest speech, as all had their attention concentrated on him; for he no longer showed himself licentious, nor did he stare madly about, but he returned to his own self, as thoroughly as if he had been treated with drugs; and he gave up his dainty dress and summery garments and the rest of his sybaritic way of life, and he fell in love with the austerity of philosophers, and donned their cloak, and stripping off his old self modelled his life in future upon that of Apollonius.

(Life of Apollonius of Tyana, vol. 1, pp. 391ff.)

There is also a vivid account in the nineteenth-century traveler Charles M. Doughty's *Travels in Arabia Deserta:*

I enquired of Amm Mohammed, "Can you exorcise demons?"

"Indeed," he said, "they are afraid of me. Last year a demon entered into my wife, while we were sitting here as we sit now, I and the woman and Haseyn. I saw it come in her eyes, which were fixed, all in a moment, and she lamented with a laboring in her throat." (I looked over to the poor wife, who answered me again with a look of patience.) "Then I took down the pistol" (commonly such few firearms of theirs hang loaded upon the chamber wall) "and I fired it at the side of her head, and shouted to the demon, 'Aha, cursed one, where are you now?' The demon answered me, by the woman's mouth, 'In her eye.' — 'By which part did you enter her?' — 'Her big toe.' — 'Then by her big toe, I tell you, depart from her.' I spoke the word terribly and the demon left her." But first Mohammed made the demon promise him not to molest his wife any more.

"Are demons afraid of shot?" I asked.

"You are too simple," he said. "It is the smell of the sulphur; they cannot abide it."

(Charles M. Doughty, *Travels in Arabia Deserta*, vol. 2, Cambridge University Press, 1921, p. 191; English modified)

sources: Mark 9:20–24; cf. Mark 9:25; Mark 9:26f.

You Must Become Like Children (1)

Jesus' almost maternal tenderness toward children is one of his most attractive qualities. The only close parallel that I know of among the great spiritual teachers is Ramana Maharshi's affection and respect for dogs, cows, monkeys, squirrels, crows, mongooses, snakes, and assorted other members of God's kingdom.

There is no condescension on Jesus' part. On the contrary, he speaks of children as equals, as patterns, recognizing the natural trust and intelligence that shine through even the most deprived or abused among them. This insight into the nature of blessedness may seem too simple to be true; but the simpler we grow, the more we can live it, and the truer it becomes.

Once, when they were in Capernaum, the disciples asked Jesus, "Who is the greatest in the kingdom of God?"

And he called a child over, and put him in front of them; and taking him in his arms, he said, "Truly I tell you, unless you return and become like children, you can't enter the kingdom of God."

unless you return: To God. To the garden. To your original self.

and become like children: Chapter 55 of the Tao Te Ching reads like a commentary on this verse:

> He who is in harmony with the Tao
> is like a newborn child.
> Its bones are supple, its muscles are weak,
> but its grip is powerful.
> It doesn't know about the union
> of male and female,
> yet its penis can stand erect,
> so intense is its vital power.
> It can scream its head off all day,
> yet it never becomes hoarse,
> so complete is its harmony.

> The Master's power is like this.
> She lets all things come and go
> effortlessly, without desire.
> She never expects results;
> thus she is never disappointed.
> She is never disappointed;
> thus her spirit never grows old.

Chuang-tzu adds:

> The infant cries all day long without straining its throat. It clenches its fist all day long without cramping its hand. It stares all day long without weakening its eyes. Free from all worries, unaware of itself, it acts without thinking, doesn't know why things happen, doesn't need to know.

This mode of being in our body, our original home, at one with the whole world, is still present within us. Who isn't stirred by Thomas Traherne's praise of it?

> Certainly Adam in Paradise had not more sweet and curious apprehensions of the world than I when I was a child. All appeared new, and strange at the first, inexpressibly rare, and delightful, and beautiful. I was a little stranger, which at my entrance into the world was saluted and surrounded with innumerable joys. My knowledge was divine. I knew by intuition those things which since my apostasy I collected again, by the highest reason. My very ignorance was advantageous. I seemed as one brought into the estate of innocence. All things were spotless and pure and glorious: yea, and infinitely mine, and joyful and precious. I knew not that there were any sins, or complaints, or laws. I dreamed not of poverties, contentions or vices. All tears and quarrels were hidden from my eyes. Everything was at rest, free, and immortal. I knew nothing of sickness or death, or exaction, in the absence of these I was entertained like an angel with the works of God in their splendor and glory; I saw all in the peace of Eden; heaven and earth did sing my Creator's praises, and could not make more melody to Adam than to me. All time was eternity, and a perpetual sabbath. Is it not strange that an infant should be heir of the world,

and see those mysteries which the books of the learned never unfold?

The corn was orient and immortal wheat, which never should be reaped, nor was ever sown. I thought it had stood from everlasting to everlasting. The dust and stones of the street were as precious as gold. The gates were at first the end of the world, the green trees when I saw them first through one of the gates transported and ravished me; their sweetness and unusual beauty made my heart to leap, and almost mad with ecstasy, they were such strange and wonderful things. The men! O what venerable and reverend creatures did the aged seem! Immortal cherubims! And young men glittering and sparkling angels, and maids strange seraphic pieces of life and beauty! Boys and girls tumbling in the street, and playing, were moving jewels. I knew not that they were born or should die. But all things abided eternally as they were in their proper places. Eternity was manifest in the light of the day, and something infinite behind everything appeared: which talked with my expectation and moved my desire. The city seemed to stand in Eden, or to be built in heaven. The streets were mine, the temple was mine, the people were mine, their clothes and gold and silver were mine, as much as their sparkling eyes, fair skins and ruddy faces. The skies were mine, and so were the sun and moon and stars, and all the world was mine, and I the only spectator and enjoyer of it. I knew no churlish properties, nor bounds nor divisions: but all properties and divisions were mine: all treasures and the possessors of them. So that with much ado I was corrupted; and made to learn the dirty devices of this world. Which now I unlearn, and become as it were a little child again, that I may enter into the kingdom of God.

(Thomas Traherne, *Centuries of Meditation*, III.1–3)

sources: *Mark 9:33, Matthew 18:1; Mark 9:36, Matthew 18:2f.*

Forgiveness

Jesus' teaching here is not hyperbole. However many times someone wrongs us, we can let go of the wrong. This doesn't mean tolerating it or acting as if nothing has happened. A wrong naturally causes a breach in the relationship, and closes a door in the heart. It is not always in our power to keep the door open. But we shouldn't lock it, or remove it and build a wall. If we keep it unlocked, we are giving our brother the chance to restore the relationship at any time, to knock on the door and wait for us to say, "Come in."

Peter once asked him, "Sir, how often should I forgive my brother if he keeps wronging me? Up to seven times?"

And Jesus said to him, "Not just seven: seventy times seven."

Peter once asked him . . . : The text in the (almost entirely lost) Gospel of the Nazoreans reads as follows:

> Jesus said, "If your brother has sinned against you by a word and apologized, receive him seven times a day."
>
> Simon, his disciple, said to him, "Seven times a day?"
>
> The Lord answered, "Yes, I tell you, and as much as seventy times seven. For even in the prophets, even after they were anointed by the Holy Spirit, there was still found a trace of sin."

This last verse sounds authentic, and is certainly in keeping with Jesus' self-estimation as a prophet (Mark 6:4, Luke 13:33) and as imperfect. *Sin* here means "the capacity to make mistakes."

if he keeps wronging me: The parallel passage in Luke (17:4) reads, "And if he wrongs you seven times in a day, and seven times turns to you saying, 'I repent,' you should forgive him."

source: Matthew 18:21f.

The Good Samaritan

This and the Prodigal Son are deservedly the most famous and beloved of Jesus' parables.

Once a certain scribe stood up and said, "Rabbi, what must I do to gain eternal life?"

And Jesus said to him, "What is written in the Law?"

And the scribe said, "You shall love the Lord your God with all your heart and with all your soul and with all your strength and with all your mind, and You shall love your neighbor as yourself."

And Jesus said, "You have answered correctly. Do this and you will live."

And the scribe said, "But who is my neighbor?"

And Jesus said, "A certain man, while traveling from Jerusalem to Jericho, was set upon by robbers, who stripped him and beat him and left him on the road, half dead. And a priest happened to be going down that road, and when he saw him, he passed by on the other side. And a Levite, too, came to that place and saw him and passed by on the other side. But a Samaritan who was traveling that way came upon the man, and when he saw him, he was moved with compassion, and he went over to him and bound up his wounds, pouring oil and wine on them, and put him on his own donkey and brought him to an inn and took care of him. And on the next day he took out two silver coins and gave them to the innkeeper and said, 'Take care of him; and if it costs more than this, I will reimburse you when I come back.'

"Which of these three, do you think, turned out to be a neighbor to that man?"

And the scribe said, "The one who treated him with mercy."

And Jesus said, "Go then, and do as he did."

a certain scribe: Luke describes this encounter as a hostile one: he has the man stand up "to put [Jesus] to the test" and ask his second question "desiring to justify himself."

Some scholars think that the dialogue between the scribe and Jesus isn't the original framework for this parable. But it seems to me likely that the parable could have arisen, or that Jesus could have repeated it, in just such a situation as this.

eternal life: A synonym for "the kingdom of God": a life lived in such a way that the personality becomes transparent and the light of God shines brilliantly through; a life lived fully in the present moment, beyond time. Philo said, "*Today* means boundless and inexhaustible eternity. Periods of months and years and of time in general are ideas of men, who calculate by number; but the true name of eternity is Today."

You shall love the Lord your God: Deuteronomy 6:5.

You shall love your neighbor as yourself: Leviticus 19:18; *neighbor* here means "fellow human being." Compare Leviticus 19:34: "The stranger who lives in your land with you shall be treated like the native-born, and you shall love him as yourself; for you too were strangers in the land of Egypt." (Deuteronomy 10:18f. gives an almost exactly similar commandment.)

You have answered correctly: In Mark 12:29ff. (which may or may not be the source of the present dialogue), it is Jesus who combines Deuteronomy 6:5 and Leviticus 19:18.

Do this and you will live: The emphasis is on *do*.

But who is my neighbor: There is no reason to suppose, as Luke does, that this question was asked in a hostile way. The scribe simply wants to hear Jesus' teaching on the scope of this essential commandment.

The parable actually answers a slightly different question: "To whom should I be a neighbor?"

a priest:

> The injured man appeared to be dead, and the priest and the Levite are represented as wishing to avoid contracting corpse impurity. . . . The priest and the Levite are not accused of lack

of piety, or of self-service, but of choosing the wrong pious activity. The worship of God would go on even though one priest and one Levite were unable to share in it for a week. In this and similar circumstances the right thing to do was to care for one's brother.   (E. P. Sanders and Margaret Davies, *Studying the Synoptic Gospels*, Trinity Press International, 1989, p. 182)

a Samaritan:

The relations between the Jews and the mixed peoples, which had undergone considerable fluctuations, had become very much worse in the time of Jesus, after the Samaritans, between A.D. 6 and 9 at midnight, during a Passover, had defiled the Temple court by strewing dead men's bones; as a result irreconcilable hostility existed between the two parties. Hence it is clear that Jesus had intentionally chosen an extreme example; by comparing the failure of the ministers of God with the unselfishness of the hated Samaritan, his hearers should be able to measure the absolute and unlimited nature of the duty of love.   (Joachim Jeremias, *The Parables of Jesus*, trans. S. H. Hooke, Charles Scribner's Sons, 1955, p. 204)

oil and wine:

The oil would mollify, the wine would disinfect.

(Ibid.)

two silver coins: Literally, "two denarii." A denarius was an average day's wages (Matthew 20:2). According to Jeremias, "the cost of a day's board would be about one-twelfth of a denarius."

Which of these three: Jesus is making it as simple as possible to get the point. You would have to be a moron not to give the right answer.

The one who treated him with mercy: It would have been enough to say, "The Samaritan"; but the scribe shows a deeper understanding by making the lesson explicit, and an additional gracefulness in referring to the man not by his race but by his action. Jesus can see that he has entered fully into the spirit of the parable.

Go then, and do as he did: The scribe has taken the lesson to heart; now he just needs to act in accordance with his understanding.

source: Luke 10:25–37

The Lost Sheep and the Lost Coin

These simple and moving parables are incarnations of the same lesson taught in the Prodigal Son. Jesus may have told the three separately, or combined them in different ways on different occasions.

Another time, the tax-gatherers and prostitutes were all crowding around to listen to him. And the scribes grumbled, and said, "This fellow welcomes criminals and eats with them."

And Jesus told them this parable. "What do you think: If a man has a hundred sheep and one of them strays, doesn't he leave the ninety-nine on the hills and go looking for the one that strayed? And when he finds it, he is filled with joy, and he puts it on his shoulders and goes home and gathers his friends and neighbors and says to them, 'Rejoice with me: I found my sheep that was lost.'

"Or if a woman has ten silver coins and loses one of them, doesn't she light a lamp and sweep the house and keep searching until she finds it? And when she finds it, she gathers her friends and neighbors and says, 'Rejoice with me: I found the coin that I lost.' In just the same way, I tell you, God rejoices over one sinner who returns."

Another time . . . eats with them: An editorial introduction that places the three parables in an appropriate context, since all three are attempts to make vivid for the pious what they already know: that God will always forgive the truly repentant criminal.

And the scribes grumbled: Here, for a change, Luke's editing reflects the mind of the authentic Jesus. Unlike the "Jesus" of the later accretions, whose hackles are raised at the slightest opposition, Jesus here doesn't take the grumbling personally. He just proceeds, compassionately and with great patience, to explain the truth to the scribes.

one of them strays: This is the clear-minded way of seeing a wicked person: not as someone who "is" wicked, but as someone who through ignorance has lost his way.

doesn't he leave the ninety-nine: The parable shouldn't be read as an allegory. If we equate the shepherd with God, the parable breaks down, since God can never, even for one moment, leave the ninety-nine. (Nor can God leave the one. Even when we are lost, we are found; though only when we realize that we are lost can we begin to be found.)

when he finds it, he is filled with joy: This is the point.

I found my sheep that was lost: Luke adds a moral, "In the same way, I tell you, there will be greater joy in heaven over one sinner who repents [returns] than over ninety-nine righteous people who don't need to repent [return]." This is like saying that more light comes through one window with a little patch wiped clean than through ninety-nine fully transparent windows. On the other hand, as John Tarrant points out, "One repentant sinner's joy fills the whole universe; there is nothing greater because there is nothing else."

silver coins: Literally, "drachmas." A drachma was worth slightly less than a denarius.

God rejoices over one sinner who returns: To be more precise, we have to change metaphors. God is here a mirror reflecting the joy of the person who is found.

sources: *Luke 15:1–3; Matthew 18:12; Luke 15:5f., 8–11*

The Prodigal Son

The heart of Jesus' teaching, and one of the most beautiful stories ever told. The final, overjoyed statement by the father—"For this son of mine was dead, and he has come back to life; he was lost, and is found"—is the only kind of resurrection that Jesus ever spoke about.

And he said, "There once was a man who had two sons. And the younger one said to him, 'Father, let me have my share of the estate.' So he divided his property between them. And not many days afterward, having turned his share into money, the younger son left and traveled to a distant country, and there he squandered his inheritance in riotous living. And after he had spent it all, a severe famine arose in that country; and he was destitute. And he went and hired himself out to a citizen of that country, who sent him to his farm to feed the pigs. And he longed to fill his belly with the husks that the pigs were eating; and no one would give him any food. And when he came to himself, he said, 'How many of my father's hired men have more than enough to eat, while I am dying of hunger. I will get up and go to my father, and say to him, "Father, I have sinned against God and against you, and I am no longer worthy to be called your son. Let me be like one of your hired men."' And he got up, and went to his father. And while he was still a long way off, his father saw him, and was moved with compassion, and ran to him, and threw

*his arms around him, and kissed him. And the son said to him, 'Father,
I have sinned against God and against you, and I am no longer worthy
to be called your son.' But the father said to his servants, 'Quick, bring
out the best robe we have and put it on him; and put a ring on his hand,
and sandals on his feet. And bring the fatted calf, and kill it; and let us
eat and make merry. For this son of mine was dead, and he has come back
to life; he was lost, and is found.' And they began to make merry.*

*"Now the older son had been out in the fields; and on his way home,
as he got closer to the house, he heard music and dancing, and he called
over one of the servants and asked what was happening. And the servant said, 'Your brother has come; and your father has killed the fatted
calf, because he has him back safe and sound.' And he was angry and
would not go in. And his father came out and tried to soothe him; but he
said, 'Look: all these years I have been serving you, and never have I disobeyed your command. Yet you never even gave me a goat, so that I could
feast and make merry with my friends. But now that this son of yours
comes back, after eating up your money on whores, you kill the fatted calf
for him!' And the father said to him, 'Child, you are always with me,
and everything I have is yours. But it was proper to make merry and rejoice, for your brother was dead, and he has come back to life; he was lost,
and is found.' "*

There once was a man who had two sons: It would be more accurate
to call this "The Parable of the Loving Father and His Two
Sons," since in this context its subject is not the younger son
but the older son's reception of him.

he divided his property: The older son was entitled to a double
portion (Deuteronomy 21:17); thus his share would have
been two-thirds of the property.

The legal position was as follows: there were two ways in
which property might pass from father to son: by a will, or by
a gift during the life of the father. In the latter case, the rule was
that the beneficiary obtained possession of the capital immediately, but the interest on it only became available upon the
death of the father. That means: in the case of a gift during the
father's lifetime, (a) the son obtains the right of possession (the

land in question, for example, cannot be sold by the father), (b) but he does not acquire the right of disposal (if the son sells the property the purchaser can take possession only upon the death of the father), and (c) he does not acquire the usufruct, which remains in the father's unrestricted possession until his death. This legal position is correctly depicted in the parable when the elder brother is indicated as the sole future owner, but nevertheless the father continues to enjoy the usufruct.

(Jeremias, *Parables of Jesus*, pp. 128f.)

squandered his inheritance in riotous living: Near the end of the parable, the older son says that the younger son has come back "after eating up your money on whores" (we aren't meant to ask how he found out). The image is of someone who has been reckless and self-indulgent, so swinishly devoted to food and sex that he ends up in an actual pigsty.

The younger son, though he has sinned grievously, is not truly wicked; he is the kind of sinner that a prostitute is, but not wicked like a rapist or a murderer. We aren't told that he has injured other people; he has only cheapened his own life and injured himself. This means that no restitution is necessary and that the father's forgiveness can be simultaneous with the son's repentance.

It would be a different situation if while he was in the distant country he had robbed the poor, murdered his enemies, and committed adultery with his best friend's wife. In that case, the consequences of his sins would have been far more serious, and even sincere repentance would not have been enough, although it would have been a necessary prelude to complete restitution. In fact, for this situation the appropriate parable would be more like the parable of the Lost Son in the Lotus Sutra. In that parable the son is so lost and degraded that he can't "come to himself"; he has forgotten that he is the son of a rich man, and when he happens to wander back to his father's town, he doesn't even know it, doesn't even recognize his father, and is terrified when his father's servants come for him. The father, overjoyed to find his son but heartsick at how low he has sunk, realizes that the truth will be too great a shock for him, and treats him like a mental patient or a wild animal. Over many years, in tiny, gradual stages, he tames him and restores him to the status of a responsible, moral human being. First he gives him a job cleaning manure, then, after several years, a raise and more responsibility, then he makes him a manager, then his chief steward. Finally, twenty years later, when the son is ready, the father summons him to the palace, tells him his true identity, and makes him his heir.

to feed the pigs: An especially degrading job for a Jew.

the husks that the pigs were eating: Literally, "carob pods," which were eaten only by animals and the very poor.

when he came to himself: By realizing what he has done, he becomes himself again—not his true self, but a truer self. This is a very difficult stage of spiritual growth, since the first thing clarity gives rise to is great shame:

> . . . the rending pain of re-enactment
> Of all that you have done, and been; the shame
> Of motives late revealed, and the awareness
> Of things ill done and done to other's harm
> Which once you took for exercise of virtue.
>
> (T. S. Eliot, "Little Gidding," *Collected Poems 1909–1962*, Harcourt Brace Jovanovich, 1963, p. 204)

During this purgatorial stage one is able to burn away a great deal of painful karma. That is why the Buddhists insist that the pain be faced without any palliatives, and why they adopt as their fifth precept the vow not to cloud the mind with any kind of intoxicant or comfort, including religion.

How many of my father's hired men: Since he is starving, his first thought is of his belly. But he also realizes how actively stupid he has been. As a Hasidic rabbi once said, "Never forget that you are the son of a king."

I will get up and go to my father: He has not sunk so low in his self-esteem that he is ashamed to appear before his father.

Father: This is the first word he thinks of saying, and the only word he needs to say. It is already enough.

I have sinned against God and against you: In sinning against himself.

I am no longer worthy to be called your son: Here he shows a touching honesty with himself.

It is important to understand how and when a statement like this is appropriate. For the younger son, in his dawning awareness, the statement is simply a recognition of how morally corrupt he has become. It is not meant to be held up as a pattern of humility, as it is in the "Lord, I am not worthy" of the Mass. At a later stage of spiritual growth, it is just as essential to be able to admit, "I am worthy to be called your son."

And he got up, and went to his father: We don't know how many days or months it took him to arrive from the "distant country." Jesus has compressed the time into this one sentence, as if, once the younger son has come to himself and made his decision, all time disappears.

while he was still a long way off: The Midrash tells the following parable about repentance:

> The son of a king was a hundred days' journey away from his father. His friends said to him, "Return to your father." He said, "I can't; I'm too far away." His father sent to him and said, "Go as far as you can, and I will come the rest of the way to you." Thus the Holy One, blessed be he, said to Israel, "Return to me, and I will return to you" (Malachi 3:7).

his father saw him: Even from a great distance he immediately recognizes him.

and was moved with compassion:

> This is no ideal picture of an imaginary father, of such exceptional saintliness that he can stand for God himself. He is *any*

father worth the name, as the hearers are expected to recognize, and this is how he would behave; and that is what God is like. (Dodd, *Founder of Christianity*, p. 60)

and ran to him:

A most unusual and undignified procedure for an aged oriental, even though he is in such haste.

(Jeremias, *Parables of Jesus*, p. 130)

bring out the best robe: The son is treated as the guest of honor.

was dead: Spiritually dead, as when Jesus says, "Let the dead bury their dead" (Matthew 8:22, Luke 9:60).

the older son: The older son is a figure for the ordinary pious person, not for the truly righteous. He is a good man, but not a wise one; that is, he obeys God's word, but the word hasn't become flesh. Of this kind of person Lao-tzu says:

> When the great Tao is forgotten,
> goodness and piety appear.
> (chapter 18)

he was angry: Professor Dodd thinks, as do most Christian scholars, that the pious "are slyly satirized in the figure of the smug elder brother ('I never once disobeyed your orders!')." But the elder brother is telling the truth, and we are meant to believe him literally, when he says he has never disobeyed his father's command; in a traditional culture, a good son wouldn't even dream of disobedience. Nor is he being at all smug. He feels he has been treated unjustly, and he is speaking from a sense of deep hurt and resentment. After all, he has done everything right, yet he has never felt accepted in the way that he sees his no-good brother being accepted. This is a dangerous situation, as when Cain's offering of fruits is rejected, and it calls for all the father's understanding and love.

Here we mustn't pay *too* close attention to the details of the parable. Realistically, the father has been thoughtless: even in his great joy, he should have had the presence of mind to send one of the servants to call the older son home; there was certainly enough time for that while the fatted calf was being roasted. And during all the years when the older son was being so dutiful, couldn't the father, just once, have given him a goat so that he could feast with his friends? Half a goat? A few chickens? There is a further consideration: Wasn't the father ever aware of the son's dissatisfaction, or concerned that he was working from a sense of duty rather than love? An insightful father would have addressed this problem immediately and not let it fester.

But we aren't meant to listen in this way. The point here is that there are pious people who are feeling hurt and resentful that a repentant sinner has been forgiven and reinstated. How can Jesus help them understand? What can the father say to the older son that will allow him to break free of his resentment and accept his younger brother with open arms?

tried to soothe him: One of the marks of an authentic saying of Jesus is its tolerance and freedom from blame or rancor. We never find a character acting this way in the church's parables. For example, in Luke's version of the parable of the Great Supper (14:16ff.), after the invited guests beg off, the master of the house becomes enraged and vows that none of them will ever taste his banquet (Matthew 22:2ff. is even more violent and punitive).

Child: Such tenderness.

you are always with me: I acknowledge that you have never left me.

But it was proper: Because he has truly risen from the dead.
    The father's statement is as simple as it is profound. He says exactly the same thing to his son and heir as he said to the servants. He is too moved to speak anything but essence.

source: Luke 15:11–32

You Must Become Like Children (2)

Blake once led the painter Samuel Palmer to his window and, pointing to a group of children at play, said, "That is heaven."

And when Jesus had finished saying these things, he left Galilee and entered the territory of Judea. And large crowds gathered around him, and he healed and taught.

And some people were bringing children to him, for him to bless; but the disciples rebuked them. And when Jesus saw this, he was indignant, and said to them, "Let the children come to me, don't try to stop them; for the kingdom of God belongs to such as these. Truly I tell you, whoever doesn't accept the kingdom of God like a child cannot enter it." And he took them in his arms, and put his hands on them, and blessed them.

the disciples rebuked them: The disciples are portrayed as bumblers, as they often are in Mark. They still don't get it.

indignant: This word has been edited out of Matthew and Luke. Of course, it is Mark's editorial comment, but the description rings true.

There is such a thing as anger that doesn't arise from the ego but from compassionate outrage. Blake said, "The voice of honest indignation is the voice of God." The Buddhists call this "Bodhisattva anger," anger for the sake of all beings.

One of the best examples is a story I heard from the Zen teacher Robert Aitken. It seems that Robert Louis Stevenson, out walking one day, saw a man beating a dog. "Stop that immediately!" Stevenson shouted.

The man said, "How dare you, sir! It is my dog. I can treat it as I wish."

"No, sir!" Stevenson shouted. "It is *God's* dog, and I am here to protect it!"

the kingdom of God belongs to such as these: One could say, with equal accuracy, that the child's mind is marked by complete selfishness; at an early age children start to scream "Mine!" and to be caught up in the cycle of greed, hatred, and ignorance. But Jesus' teaching points to the child's presence, trust, openness, love of play, and capacity for wonder.

like a child: Philo, in agreeing with Jesus' insight, gives a slightly different perspective:

> The face of the wise man is not somber or austere, contracted by anxiety and sorrow, but precisely the opposite: radiant and serene, and filled with a vast delight, which often makes him the most playful of men, acting with a sense of humor that blends with his essential seriousness and dignity, just as in a well-tuned lyre all the notes blend into one harmonious sound. According to our holy teacher Moses, the goal of wisdom is laughter and play—not the kind that one sees in little children who do not yet have the faculty of reason, but the kind that is developed in those who have grown mature through both time and understanding. If someone has experienced the wisdom that can only be heard from oneself, learned from oneself, and created from oneself, he does not merely participate in laughter: he becomes laughter itself.

blessed them:

> The antiquity of the custom of blessing the children by laying on of hands is attested by Genesis 48:14. The same passage is the source of the modern Jewish custom of blessing the children, especially in the home and on the Sabbath eve.
>
> (Israel Abrahams, *Studies in Pharisaism and the Gospels*, First Series, Cambridge University Press, 1917, p. 119)

sources: Matthew 19:1f., Mark 10:1; Mark 10:13–16

The Rich Man

This poignant encounter contains two of Jesus' most profound revelations of himself.

And one day, as he was setting out, a man ran up and fell on his knees before him, and said, "Good Rabbi, what must I do to gain eternal life?"

And Jesus said to him, "Why do you call me good? No one is good except God alone. You know the commandments: Do not murder, Do not commit adultery, Do not steal, Do not bear false witness, Do not defraud, Honor your father and mother."

And the man said, "Rabbi, all these I have kept since I was a boy."

And Jesus, looking at him, loved him, and said, "There is one thing that you lack: go, sell everything you have and give it to the poor, and you will have treasure in heaven; then come and follow me."

But when he heard this, his face clouded over, and he went away sick at heart, for he was a man who had large estates.

And Jesus looked around at his disciples and said, "Children, how hard it is for the rich to enter the kingdom of God. It is easier for a camel to go through the eye of a needle than for a rich man to enter the kingdom of God."

ran up and fell on his knees: How emphatic the man's actions are! His question has a passionate urgency to it; he is one of those who hunger and thirst after righteousness.

Good Rabbi: Either the man has previously heard of Jesus and been deeply impressed, or he just now had a glimpse of Jesus' moral radiance. Like recognizes like. Even bad men could see the radiance; how much more so a good man.

Why do you call me good? No one is good except God alone: Literally, "except one: God." This verse goes so much against the grain of the Evangelists' desire to portray Jesus as "sinless" that it must be authentic.

By *good* Jesus means "absolutely good; perfect." This is a touchingly clear statement of how he thought of himself: as fully human and no more than human, as fully capable of making mistakes. Blake said, "It is not because angels are holier than men or devils that makes them angels, but because they do not expect holiness from one another but from God only."

In order to teach people that they are all sons of God, you have to realize that you are the son of God; but in order to teach people that they are only human, you have to realize that you are only human. What makes someone a Master is not that he never makes mistakes; it's that when he makes a mistake, he doesn't *cling* to it.

Matthew (19:16f.) apparently found Jesus' statement so embarrassing that he changed these verses to read: "'Rabbi, what good must I do to have eternal life?' And he said to him, 'Why do you ask me about the good? There is One who is good.'" In his effort to make the verses acceptable, Matthew has turned them into nonsense, since the final sentence has no connection with the preceding one.

You know the commandments: The commandments are a means of simplifying our life and preparing the way for eternal life; they are not eternal life itself. When eternal life breaks through and lives us, we find that the commandments keep themselves.

Honor your father and mother: Could Jesus actually have included this as one of the imperative commandments, while at other times he rejected his mother and advised against burying one's father? If he did include this commandment, was he aware that he himself wasn't yet able to keep it?

all these I have kept: Said with confidence, as a simple matter of fact, and without a trace of pride. Yet there is a current of urgency that runs through this statement and through his question, and no doubt through his whole body. It is as if he were saying, "I have kept all the commandments and done God's will as best I can, and yet I feel that something is missing, that I am not living in God's presence."

And Jesus, looking at him, loved him: This verse is significant as the *only* verse in the Synoptic Gospels in which Jesus is said to love any particular person. The clause is, of course, an editorial comment, but the fact that both Matthew and Luke find it uncomfortable enough to eliminate (both almost always portray scribes and Pharisees in a negative light) may mean that it contains an authentic memory of the event. If it does, it gives us a moving example of Jesus' response to true righteousness. The rich man has answered with sincerity and longing, and Jesus' heart goes out to him.

sell everything you have: Matthew adds, "If you wish to be perfect." This completely misses the point; didn't Jesus just say that even he isn't perfect?

We can't know what quality in the man prompted Jesus to make this radical response. Perhaps, noticing his rich clothing, Jesus intuited that the man's only attachment was to his wealth, and that if he could give it up he would step right into the kingdom of God. (In the Lucan story of Zacchaeus, by contrast, the repentant tax-gatherer has Jesus' approval in giving the poor only half of his ill-gotten wealth.)

"Sell everything" was a teaching for this particular man at this particular moment. If he had immediately said, "Yes, sir, I will," we don't know how Jesus would have responded. I remember a dialogue between Zen Master Seung Sahn and one of his early, hippie disciples, who was very attached to his long blond pony-tail. After a great deal of earnest persuasion, the student finally realized the extent of his attachment. "Okay," he said, "you win, I'll cut it off." At which point Seung Sahn laughed and said, "Now that it's okay to cut it off, you don't need to."

treasure in heaven: Treasure right here and now, in the kingdom of heaven. In fact, the kingdom of heaven *is* the treasure.

Abu Yazid al-Bistami said, "Anyone whose reward from God is deferred until tomorrow has not truly worshiped him today."

come and follow me: In the Gospel of the Nazoreans, there are *two* rich men present. At this point, the second rich man, upset, begins to scratch his head. Jesus says to him,

> How can you say, "I have kept the Law and the prophets?" Isn't it written in the Law, *You shall love your neighbor as yourself*? Yet many of your brothers, sons of Abraham, are dressed in filth and dying of hunger, while your house is filled with many good things, and none of it goes out to them.

This is the same point as Matthew makes in his parable of the Last Judgment:

> Then the king will say, "Come, you who are blessed by my father, inherit the kingdom prepared for you from the beginning of the world. For I was hungry and you fed me, I was thirsty and you gave me drink, I was a stranger and you took me in, I was naked and you clothed me, I was sick and you took care of me, I was in prison and you visited me." And the righteous will answer, "Lord, when did we see you hungry and feed you, or thirsty and give you drink? When did we see you a stranger and take you in, or naked and clothe you? When did we see you sick or in prison and visit you?" And the king will say, "Whatever you did for the poorest of my people, you did for me." (Matthew 25:35–40)

I feel a twinge of sorrow that I can't include these beautiful verses in my version of the Gospel. But they are imbedded in a parable filled with as much hatred as love, as much vindictiveness as compassion.

he went away sick at heart: This reaction testifies to his relative maturity. If he were less mature, he wouldn't be troubled by

Jesus' words and would go back to his life unchanged; if he were more mature, he would realize that there is nothing at all that he lacks, that eternal life has been here all the time, and he would thank Jesus with a bow of deep gratitude.

The man truly wants to gain eternal life, and is caught between his attachment and his longing. This is a spiritual condition that can be as productive as it is painful. The end of the dialogue may be the beginning of a new life for him. We don't know how he will proceed. I hope that Jesus' words prove to be a rich and strange irritant inside him, like a grain of sand in an oyster.

It is easier for a camel: A vivid hyperbole that means "it is extremely difficult for the rich to enter the kingdom of heaven." (Mark 10:26–27 is a later gloss, meant to diminish the radical nature of this statement.)

I feel that a further discussion of wealth and the kingdom of God is called for here, because Jesus' teaching about money, though true, is incomplete.

If we imagine his childhood as one of the most despised and rejected, and his adulthood among the lowest of the low, we can understand how much justified anger he had toward the rich. This is an old and honored Jewish tradition, and not only with the great prophets. We find the same wonderful moral outrage toward the rich and sympathy for the poor throughout the Bible, and at its most passionate in the Book of Job:

> The poor, like herds of cattle,
>   wander across the plains,
> searching all day for food,
>   picking up scraps for their children.
> Naked, without a refuge,
>   they shiver in the bitter cold.
> When it rains, they are drenched to the bone;
>   they huddle together in caves.

> They carry grain for the wicked
> and break their backs for the rich.
> They press olives and starve,
> crush grapes and go thirsty.
>
> (*The Book of Job*, trans. Stephen Mitchell,
> North Point Press, 1987, p. 60)

Jesus is quite correct about how difficult it is for the rich to enter the kingdom of God. But it is difficult at *both* extremes, of wealth and of involuntary poverty. (It is difficult enough in the middle.) It is also true that those who are called to give up all material wealth and security take the most direct path into the kingdom. Here I am not thinking of Christian or Buddhist monks and nuns, who after all have a roof over their heads and the assurance of food in their bellies, but of a more radical kind of renunciate.

We have, first of all, the luminous example of Francis of Assisi. In China there is the less passionate but more balanced example of Layman P'ang (c. 740–808), a wealthy merchant who was later to become a famous and wonderfully funny Zen Master. After his enlightenment, he gave his house away for use as a Buddhist temple, and then wondered what to do with all his money. "Since his wealth was great," an ancient account says, "he worried about it. 'If I give it to other people,' he thought, 'they may become as attached to it as I was. It is better to give it to the country of nothingness.'" So he put all his money and possessions onto a boat in a nearby lake, and sank it. After this, he and his wife, son, and daughter earned their living by making and selling bamboo utensils.

We are also fortunate to have the testimony of Ramana Maharshi about the first time he begged in the streets of Tiruvannamalai after his enlightenment as a boy of sixteen:

> You cannot conceive of the majesty and dignity I felt while begging. The first day, when I begged from Gurukal's wife, I felt bashful about it as a result of the habits of my upbringing, but after that there was absolutely no feeling of abasement. I felt like a king, and more than a king. I have sometimes re-

ceived stale gruel at some house and taken it without salt or any other flavoring, in the open street, in front of great pandits and other important men who used to come and prostrate themselves before me at the ashram, and then I wiped my hands on my head and walked on supremely happy and in a state of mind in which even emperors were mere straw in my sight. You can't imagine it. That is why kings have given up their thrones and taken to this path.

Most religious traditions make a distinction between the path of the householder and the path of the renunciate. This distinction almost always carries with it a judgment (made by renunciates, of course) that the renunciate's path is spiritually superior. But the two are equal, and each has its advantages and pitfalls.

Questioner: Can a householder attain liberation?

Maharshi: Why do you think of yourself as a householder? If you become a wandering monk, a similar thought—that you are a renunciate—will haunt you. Whether you continue as a husband and father, or renounce your family and go to the forest, your small self will still accompany you. The self is the source of thoughts. It creates the body and the world and makes you think that you are really a householder. If you renounce the world, it will only substitute the thought *renunciate* for *householder* and the environment of the forest for that of the household. But the mental obstacles are always there. They even increase in new surroundings. There is no help in the change of environment. The obstacle is the mind. It must be overcome, whether at home or in the forest. If you can do it in the forest, why not in the home? Therefore why change the environment? Your efforts can be made even now, whatever your environment may be.

The Jewish and the Buddhist traditions contain particularly balanced teachings on the subject of wealth. In Mahayana Buddhism there is the archetype of Vimalakirti, a deeply enlightened billionaire disciple of the Buddha, who has a whole sutra written about and named after him. And in Judaism there is, among other examples, the figure of the righteous

Job, the "richest man in the East." Toward the end of the poem, Job reminds God of the great compassion that was a function of his great wealth:

> If I scorned the rights of my slave
>   or closed my ears to his plea—
> what would I do if God appeared?
>   If he questioned me, what could I answer?
> Didn't the same God make us
>   and form us both in the womb?
>
> If I ever neglected the poor
>   or made the innocent suffer;
> if I ate my meals alone
>   and did not share with the hungry;
> if I did not clothe the naked
>   or care for the ragged beggar . . .
> If I ever trusted in silver
>   or pledged allegiance to gold;
> if I ever boasted of my riches
>   or took any credit for my wealth . . .
>
> (*The Book of Job*, pp. 74f.)

The Jewish attitude is well summarized by the eleventh-century Spanish rabbi Bakhya ibn Pakuda:

> If he who trusts in God is rich, he will cheerfully fulfill all the religious and ethical obligations that a rich man has; and if he is poor, he will consider the absence of money as a blessing from God, relieving him of the responsibilities its possession involves, and from the labor of guarding and managing it. The rich man who trusts in God will not find his wealth an obstacle to his faith; for he doesn't place his confidence in his wealth, which is for him a trust he has been assigned for a limited period so that he may apply it for the good of himself, his family, and his society. He doesn't take credit for his generosity, nor does he give charity or do good deeds except anonymously, or require any reward or praise; but in his heart he gives thanks to the Creator who has made him the agent of His beneficence. And if he loses his wealth, he doesn't worry or mourn its loss,

but is grateful to God for taking away what was only entrusted to him, just as he was grateful to God for the original gift, and he rejoices in his portion.

The truth is that when we see money clearly, we can recognize it as neither good nor bad, but as pure energy, and understand that it can be used, like electricity, either for good or for harm. "The unworthy person," said Tzu-ssu in *The Central Harmony*, "develops his wealth at the expense of his character; the mature person develops his character by means of his wealth." When we are in love with God, even money is divine service, as in the following prayer—ecstatic, outrageous, and wonderfully innocent—from the Taittiriya Upanishad:

> May I become famous, may I become richer than the richest, so that I may serve you better, sweet Lord!
>
> May I enter into you, may you enter into me! May I merge with your thousands of shapes, for my purification.
>
> As water flows downward, as the months mingle with the year, may students come to me from everywhere, so that I may serve you better, sweet Lord!

A final story and a prose-poem: A Buddhist friend of mine had entered adulthood with a strongly rooted prejudice against money. He refused to have anything to do with it, except for the bare minimum, and lived on three thousand dollars a year. Then he met a woman of rare insight, who was later to become his wife. Shortly after they met, she began reminding him that aversion is as much of an attachment as desire is, and that in rejecting money he was repressing his own energy, both physical and spiritual. This went on for several years. My friend, who is alert enough to hear the truth when it is said for the seventy-times-seventh time, finally understood, and proceeded to do the painful and, for him, necessary inner work of tracing his aversion to its root. The years came and went; everything grew clear; nothing changed. And then, after seven years, all at once, his work blossomed and the money came pouring in, an outer and visible sign of an inner and spiritual abundance.

This situation fascinated me precisely because my friend had already entered the kingdom of God many years before, and only later did he become rich. Filled with his exhilaration, I reversed Jesus' metaphor and wrote the following piece (it appears in *Parables and Portraits*):

Through the Eye of the Needle

The camel catches his breath, wipes the sweat from his brow. It was a tight squeeze, but he made it.

Lying back on the unbelievably lush grass, he remembers: all those years (how excruciating they were!) of fasting and one-pointed concentration, until finally he was thin enough: thaumaturgically thin, thread-thin, almost unrecognizable in his camelness: until the moment in front of the unblinking eye, when he put his front hooves together. Took one long last breath. Aimed. Dived.

The exception may prove the rule, but what proves the exception? "It is not that such things are possible," the camel thinks, smiling. "But such things are possible for *me*."

source: Mark 10:17–25

Let the Dead Bury Their Dead

These two statements may have circulated as independent sayings. But the original setting of the first statement must have been something like the present one, which is so shocking that it couldn't have been created by the Evangelists. See pp. 44f., 89.

And as they were traveling along the road, he said to a certain man, "Follow me."

And the man said, "Let me first go and bury my father."

But Jesus said to him, "Let the dead bury their dead."

Another man said to Jesus, "I will follow you, sir, but let me first say good-bye to my family."

And Jesus said to him, "No one who puts his hand to the plow and then looks back is ready for the kingdom of God."

Let the dead bury their dead: The most generous interpretation of this saying (we have to stretch it and disregard its harsh tone) would take it beyond the context of funerals. "Of course, your duty is to go bury your father, and you should honor him as best you can. But you shouldn't lose yourself in your grief, like those who don't know any better. Death is just a transition, as is life. Beyond life and death is true life, the only reality. That is what you should be centered in, at every moment, whether your father has just died or you have just gotten married."

John Tarrant comments, "I read in this saying the harshness of a fresh realization of the transitory. In Zen we might say that Jesus is overvaluing the eternal and empty side of things, is dazzled by it."

Another man said to Jesus: Something like this dialogue, which typifies Jesus' attitude toward family, may actually have taken place. But it may just as well be a creation of Luke's. It is meant to show Jesus' superiority to Elijah in I Kings 19:20:

> And Elisha left his oxen and ran after Elijah and said, "Let me kiss my father and mother good-bye, and then I will follow you."
>
> And Elijah said, "Go back; what have I done to stop you?"

I will follow you: John Tarrant comments, "The man needs to ignore Jesus and follow him: to go back and set his affairs in order and *then* leave. In this way, he would honor the great truth of the summons, as well as the smaller but necessary truth of human feeling."

No one who puts his hand to the plow and then looks back: If you look back, you can't see where you're going.

sources: *Luke 9:57,59–62, Matthew 8:22*

First Days in Jerusalem

And as they came near Jerusalem, to Bethany and Bethphage and the Mount of Olives, the large crowds coming for the festival spread their cloaks in front of him on the road, and some people spread brushwood that they had cut in the fields. And those who walked in front of him and those who followed shouted, "Blessed is he who comes in the name of the Lord; praise God in the highest heavens!"

And when he entered Jerusalem, the whole city was stirred up, wondering who he was. And the crowds said, "This is the prophet Jesus, from Nazareth in Galilee."

And he entered the Temple and looked around at everything; but since it was already late, he went out to Bethany with the Twelve.

And every day Jesus would go to the Temple to teach, and at night he would stay on the Mount of Olives. And early in the morning he would go back into the Temple, and all the people gathered around him, and he sat and taught them. And they listened to him with delight.

festival: Josephus mentions that the Romans made special preparations to forestall disturbances at Passover:

> The usual crowd had assembled at Jerusalem for the feast of unleavened bread, and the Roman cohort had taken up its position on the roof of the portico of the Temple; for a body of men in arms invariably mounts guard at the feasts, to prevent disorders arising from such a concourse of people.
>
> (*Jewish War*, in *Works*, vol. 2, trans. H. St. J. Thackeray, Harvard University Press, 1927, p. 411)

when he entered Jerusalem: Jesus' entry into Jerusalem is followed in the Synoptic Gospels by the so-called "cleansing of the Temple" (immediately, according to Matthew and Luke; the next morning, according to Mark; according to John, it happened two years before). I have omitted this incident because, while it may have some basis in actual events, its details and significance are impossible to determine from the accounts that we have.

> How could one person have overcome the resistance to which this action would obviously have given rise? Or, if we suppose that Jesus was assisted by his followers, why did the Temple police or the Roman garrison do nothing to preserve the peace (contrast Acts 4:1ff.), and why was the matter not raised at Jesus' trial? And how did Jesus gather an audience (Mark 11:17) which included those responsible for the desecrations of the Temple? Perhaps the most we can say is that while some definite historical incident may well underlie the story, St. Mark's account is too brief and imprecise to enable us to be sure what it was, or to tell exactly what was in the mind of Jesus.
>
> (Nineham, *Gospel of St. Mark*, p. 301)

As for Jesus' intention: if he meant the action as a protest against current Temple practices, and if the apostles and the other Jewish-Christian disciples knew that, why did they continue in their daily attendance at the Temple, quite contentedly and "of one mind" (Acts 2:46)?

Professor Sanders offers some useful cautions:

> [Many exegetical comments on the "cleansing of the Temple"] are doubtless intended to distinguish the Temple ordained by God—which Jesus did not attack—from the Jewish "abuse" of the divine institution—which Jesus did attack. The way in which the distinction is made, however, implies that it is just the trade itself—the changing of money, the purchase of sacrifices, and probably also the charge for their inspection—which is the focus of the action. The assumption seems to be that Jesus made, and wanted his contemporaries to accept, a distinction between this sort of "practice" and the "real purpose" of the Temple. This seems to owe more to the nineteenth-century view that what is external is bad than to a first-century Jewish view. Those who write about Jesus' desire to return the Temple to its "original," "true" purpose, the "pure" worship of God, seem to forget that the principal function of any temple is to serve as a place for sacrifice, and that

sacrifices *require* the supply of suitable animals. This had always been true of the Temple in Jerusalem. In the time of Jesus, the Temple had long been the only place in Israel at which sacrifices could be offered, and this means that suitable animals and birds must have been in supply at the Temple site. There was not an "original" time when worship at the Temple had been "pure" from the business which the requirement of unblemished sacrifices creates. Further, no one remembered a time when pilgrims, carrying various coinages, had not come. In the view of Jesus and his contemporaries, the requirement to sacrifice must always have involved the supply of sacrificial animals, their inspection, and the changing of money. Thus one may wonder what scholars have in mind who talk about Jesus' desire to stop this "particular use" of the Temple. Just what would be left of the service if the supposedly corrupting externalism of sacrifices, and the trade necessary to them, were purged? Here as often we see a failure to think concretely and a preference for vague religious abstractions.

(Jesus and Judaism, p. 63)

The last word on this incident belongs to Blake, as reported by the deliciously obtuse diarist Henry Crabb Robinson:

Christ, he said, took much after his mother, and in so far was one of the worst of men. On my asking him for an instance, he referred to his turning the money-changers out of the Temple—he had no right to do that. He digressed [*sic!*] into a condemnation of those who sit in judgement on others. "I have never known a very bad man who had not something very good about him." *(The Portable Blake*, ed. Alfred Kazin, Viking Press, 1946, pp. 692f.)

This is the prophet Jesus: There were probably messianic rumors as well.

sources: *Mark 11:1,8, John 12:12; Mark 11:9f.; Matthew 21:10f.; Mark 11:11; Luke 21:37, John 8:2; Mark 12:37b*

The Tax to Caesar

A fine example of Jesus' wit; it is easy to imagine him, as George Bernard Shaw does, laughing to himself over this repartee. Jesus here is an aikido master, using the opponent's own energy to send him sprawling. The point of his response is not to take a position, either for or against obedience to the Roman empire. Rather, it is to say: first things first; if you get caught in politics, it will be hard to enter the kingdom of God; whereas entering the kingdom is the greatest blessing you can bring to your friends, your neighbors, and your country.

One day, as he was teaching in the Temple, some scribes said to him, "Rabbi, is it lawful to pay the tax to Caesar, or not?"

And Jesus said, "Bring me a coin."

And they brought one. And he said, "Whose image is on it?"

And they said, "Caesar's."

And Jesus said, "Give to Caesar the things that are Caesar's, and to God the things that are God's."

One day: Mark reads, "And they [the chief priests, the scribes, and the elders] sent to him certain of the Pharisees and Herodians, to trap him in his words." In the version of this incident in the Gospel of Thomas (Thomas, 100), the questioners are undesignated, and there is no mention of a plot:

> They showed Jesus a gold coin and said to him, "Caesar's men are asking us to pay taxes."
>
> He answered, "Give to Caesar the things that are Caesar's, to God the things that are God's, and to me the things that are mine."

tax:

> The Greek is a transliteration of the Latin *census*, which was a poll tax paid directly into the Roman imperial *fiscus*, or trea-

sury. It was an object of deep resentment to Jews, not only because it was a visible sign of overlordship, but because the coinage carried the name and a representation of the emperor [and thus involved breaking the Second Commandment]. The question therefore—should we pay, or not?—was a "no-win" problem. To answer yes would incur disfavor, and to answer no put the respondent at risk.

(C. S. Mann, *Mark*, Doubleday & Co., 1986, p. 469)

is it lawful to pay the tax: "No" would be the radical answer of the old Quakers, Thoreau, and Tolstoy. "Yes" would be the answer not only of the collaborators, but of those who, in spite of their contempt for a government of brute force, saw it as a necessary evil. The *Ethics of the Fathers* quotes Rabbi Hanina as saying, "Pray for the welfare of the empire, because if it weren't for the fear of it, men would swallow one another alive."

sources: Mark 12:13–17; Luke 20:26

The Greatest Commandment

Many scholars think that the dialogue in Luke 10:25ff., which serves as an introduction to the parable of the Good Samaritan, is a variant of this one. Perhaps. But there are so many differences in the two dialogues that they could easily be accounts of two separate incidents. I have retained both because each has its particular excellence, which would be diluted if they were combined, and because Jesus was probably asked the same question many times in the course of his teaching.

Later, a certain scribe who had been listening to Jesus and had observed how well he answered people's questions asked him, "Which commandment is the greatest of all?"

And Jesus answered, "Hear, O Israel: the Lord our God is one; and you shall love the Lord your God with all your heart and with all your soul and with all your mind and with all your strength. *This is the first and greatest commandment. And there is a second one that is like it:* You shall love your neighbor as yourself. *On these two commandments all the Law and the prophets depend."*

And the scribe said to him, "Excellent, Rabbi! You have said the truth, that God is one and there is no other beside him, and to love him with all your heart and all your understanding and all your strength, and to love your neighbor as yourself, is worth far more than all burnt offerings and sacrifices."

And Jesus, seeing that he had spoken wisely, said to him, "You are not far from the kingdom of God."

a certain scribe: Mark's depiction of this scribe as a sincere seeker of God's kingdom goes so much against the grain of the Gospels' hostility toward scribes and Pharisees that it is very likely to be an authentic memory of the event. Both Matthew and Luke make the encounter into an adversarial one. But according to Mark, the scribe asks his question because he so greatly admires, or is so deeply touched by, Jesus' previous answers. True, it is not a naive question, asked out of ignorance and hunger. And it *is* a kind of test, but a sympathetic one, without a trace of hostility. The scribe wants to know, for his own sake, how well Jesus can do with this essential question.

Hear, O Israel: Deuteronomy 6:4–5.

a second one that is like it: In fact, it is the same as the first.

love your neighbor as yourself: Leviticus 19:18. Rabbi Akiba (c. 50–132) said of this verse, "It is the greatest principle in the Law."

these two commandments: In Luke's incident, it is the scribe who combines the two verses.

And the scribe said to him: This whole second part of the dialogue is omitted by Matthew (and by Luke, if Luke is in fact using Mark), probably because he was offended by Mark's favorable depiction of the scribe.

Excellent, Rabbi: The enthusiasm, the wholeheartedness of his response! "Exuberance is beauty," as Blake reminds us.

worth far more than all burnt offerings and sacrifices: This sentiment is typical of the prophetic tradition in Judaism, which was a check and balance to the priestly tradition. The closest parallels are Hosea 6:6 ("I desire mercy and not sacrifice, / and the knowledge of God more than burnt offerings") and I Samuel 15:22 ("Does God delight in whole-offerings and sacrifices / as much as in obeying his voice? // To do God's will is better than sacrifice, / and to obey is better than the fat of rams").

seeing that he had spoken wisely: Jesus is delighted by the quality of the scribe's response.

You are not far from the kingdom of God: From the scribe's excited, loving approval, Jesus can see into his heart. He is on the brink of the great abyss; he is eight and three-quarters months pregnant with the great joy; he has found the path to the treasure. His present condition is one that a good spiritual teacher will recognize with a smile. Does the scribe need a little encouragement? A quick push? One more step, and he will find that he has been inside the kingdom of God all along.

sources: *Mark 12:28–30, Matthew 22:36f.; Matthew 22:38–40; Mark 12:32–4*

The Woman Caught in Adultery

One of the most moving scenes in the Gospels. See pp. 59ff.

The next morning, as Jesus was teaching in the Temple, the scribes brought a woman who had been caught in adultery, and they stood her in the middle. And they said to him, "Rabbi, this woman was caught in adultery, in the very act. Moses in the Law commanded us to stone such women to death; what do you say?"

But Jesus stooped down and with his finger wrote on the ground.

And as they continued to question him, he stood up and said to them, "Let whoever of you is sinless be the first to throw a stone at her." And again he stooped down and wrote on the ground.

And when they heard this, they went out one by one, the older ones first. And Jesus was left alone, with the woman still standing there.

And Jesus stood up, and said to her, "Woman, where are they? Has no one condemned you?"

And she said, "No one, sir."

And Jesus said, "I don't condemn you either. Go now, and sin no more."

adultery: Jewish horror of adultery is the reverse side of Jewish reverence for marriage. How great this horror was can be seen in the Epistle of James (2:10f.), which implies that adultery is an even greater crime than murder:

> A man who keeps all the commandments and breaks just one is guilty of breaking them all. For he who said, "You shall not commit murder" also said, "You shall not commit adultery." So if you commit murder, you are a breaker of the Law, even though you haven't committed adultery.

Most people remember this scene in terms that would have been alien to its participants: on one side are the petty, legal-

istic, and bloodthirsty scribes (and Pharisees), bent on ston-
ing the woman for a sin that is not all that heinous; and on the
other side is the all-merciful Jesus. But if we are to feel the issue as a first-century Jew would have felt it, it would be more
appropriate to imagine the scribes bringing forward a man
who has just raped and murdered a six-year-old child. How
would we react if in this instance, too, Jesus said, "Let whoever of you is sinless be the first to throw a stone at him"?

they stood her in the middle: It would have been easy to see her ter-
ror. Jesus may also have seen in her eyes a deep shame, and
genuine repentance for her sin. But even if she was unrepen-
tant, his attitude would have been one of compassionate nonjudgment.

Moses in the Law: According to the Law, both the man and the
woman guilty of adultery are to be executed (Leviticus 20:10,
Deuteronomy 22:22ff.).

what do you say: An editor has added the following explanation:
"(They said this to entrap him, so that they might bring a
charge against him.)" The question may have been adversarial. But all talk of plots by the scribes and Pharisees is likely to
be early church propaganda, as Professor Sanders and other
good scholars have shown.

with his finger wrote on the ground: Scholars and theologians have
debated the meaning of this action since the fourth century,
and no one has come up with a convincing explanation. Perhaps Jesus was simply musing. "Sometimes our intuition
leads us to apparently irrelevant actions," John Tarrant says.
"If we trust this, then the time arrives for a deep and true action that wasn't at first possible." Or perhaps the action was a
vivid enactment of his feeling that all judgments are as insubstantial as words written in the dust.

This is the only Gospel scene in which Jesus is asked to act as a judge. He unequivocally refuses, thus practicing what he preached in the Sermon on the Mount.

We can feel the same kind of loving, nonjudgmental attitude in Ramana Maharshi's account of a young prostitute who became his devotee:

> When I was a young man, living under the madukha tree, a twenty-year-old prostitute named Rathnamma saw me one day while going to and from the temple to dance. She grew devoted to me and became disgusted with her profession, and told her mother that she would not eat unless she could give food to the Swami. So both of them brought me food. I was then in deep meditation and opened neither my eyes nor my mouth, even when they shouted. But they somehow brought me out by asking a passerby to pull me by the hand; they then gave me food and left. . . . Since she could not earn a living except by her profession, she confined herself to one man only. What does it matter what community she belonged to? She had great nonattachment and great devotion. Her heart was pure. She never liked her profession and did not want her daughter to follow it.

Let whoever of you is sinless: We may condemn a crime, but not a person. Blame is always a dangerous weapon, and it points both ways. That is why in the Book of Job the negative power in the human cosmos, the cause of all our misery, is called Satan, "the Accuser." Blake said, "The player is a liar when he says angels are happier than men because they are better. Angels are happier than men because they are not always prying after good and evil in one another and eating the Tree of Knowledge for Satan's gratification."

And when they heard this: Certain later Greek manuscripts add an explanation: "And when they heard this, reproved by their own conscience, they went out one by one. . . ."

And Jesus was left alone, with the woman: Perhaps she had already begun to see who he was.

Has no one condemned you: He wants the woman to acknowledge this herself.

No one, sir: Her only words. But they let us feel her wonder and reverence.

I don't condemn you either: Jesus is including himself with the rest.

————

In contrast to Jesus' dignity and restraint in this account, the story of the repentant sinner in Luke 7:36ff. (an elaboration of the simpler, more masculine account in Mark 14:3ff.) seems sentimental, almost mawkish:

> And one of the Pharisees invited him to a banquet, and he went to the Pharisee's house, and reclined for dinner.
>
> And there was a woman of the city who was a sinner; and when she heard that he was having dinner in the Pharisee's house, she brought an alabaster jar of perfume. And she stood behind him, at his feet, crying, and began to wet his feet with her tears. And she wiped them with her hair, and kissed them, and anointed them with the perfume.
>
> And when the Pharisee who had invited him saw this, he said to himself, "If this man were a real prophet, he would have known what kind of woman this is who is touching him: that she is a sinner."
>
> And Jesus said, "Simon, I have something to say to you."
>
> And he said, "Say it, Teacher."
>
> And he said, "There were two people who were in debt to a certain creditor: one owed him five hundred denarii, and the other fifty. When they couldn't repay him, he forgave both their debts. Which of them do you think will love him more?"
>
> And Simon answered, "I suppose, the one for whom he forgave the larger amount."
>
> And Jesus said to him, "You have judged correctly." And turning toward the woman, he said to Simon, "Do you see this woman? I came into your house, and you didn't give me water for my feet, but she wet my feet with her tears and wiped them

with her hair. You didn't give me a kiss, but ever since I came in
she has been kissing my feet. You didn't anoint my head with
oil, but she anointed my feet with perfume. Therefore I tell
you that her sins, which are many, have been forgiven; thus she
has shown much love. But one who is forgiven little, loves little."

And he said to her, "Your sins have been forgiven."

And those who were reclining at dinner with him began to
say among themselves, "Who is this who even forgives sins?"

And he said to the woman, "Your faith has saved you; go in
peace."

In this story there may be some irrecoverable kernel of an actual event; but the story's focus on the person of Jesus, and
"Jesus'" own self-absorption, indicate that it is a creation of
the early church. Jesus himself would have had, I am sure, an
amused contempt for his namesake's desire to be fussed over
with kisses and perfume. And like other legends, it gives "Jesus" what was considered the superhuman power of thought
reading. In addition, in the parable of the two debtors there is
a disparagement of the righteous that I don't find in the authentic words of Jesus. And it is simply not true that the larger
debtor would love more. The love depends on the quality of
the debtor's heart, not on the quantity of the debt. A man with
a relatively pure heart might feel deep gratitude at being forgiven a hundred dollars, while a selfish man might feel nothing but resentment, jealousy, and shame at being forgiven a
hundred thousand dollars.

source: John 8:2–11

Gethsemane

If this scene is historic, it indicates that Jesus had a premonition about the great suffering in store for him. It would hardly take psychic powers to realize the danger of teaching the truth amid the deadly lies of occupied Jerusalem.

And the day before the Passover and the festival of Unleavened Bread, in the evening, he came into the city with the Twelve, and they ate supper. And after they had sung a psalm, they went out to the Mount of Olives, across the Kidron valley, to a garden called Gethsemane.

And Jesus said, "Sit here, while I pray." And going off by himself, he prostrated himself on the ground and prayed. And he said, "Abba, all things are possible for you. Take this cup from me. Nevertheless, not what I want, but what you want."

And when he got up from his prayer and went to the disciples, he found them asleep. And he said to them, "Why are you sleeping? Couldn't you stay awake for even one hour?" And they didn't know what to answer.

the day before the Passover: I am following John's chronology, which makes more sense than the Synoptics'.

going off by himself: Some scholars think that the following prayer must be an invention of Mark's, since no one was there to overhear it. But if Jesus went off to pray at a short distance, one of the disciples could have heard him, and later fallen asleep like the rest.

Abba: See pp. 28ff. Mark adds a translation: "Abba, Father . . ."

all things are possible for you: We simply don't know the limits of the possible. If we think that something is impossible, then it is (for us). When we realize that we don't know, we become open to all possibilities.

Take this cup from me: A touching prayer, and a very human one. Jesus had no conception of his death being sacrificial or redemptive. Like a child, like any natural being, he wanted to avoid suffering, and he asked to be spared the bitter cup of the crucifixion.

Nevertheless, not what I want, but what you want: This is a prayer of great simplicity and beauty. It is the paradigmatic prayer, not only upon confronting suffering, but upon confronting any possibility, joyous or painful. The more we understand how infinitely superior the intelligence of the universe is to our own tiny, conscious mind, the more we can let go into God's will.

Full acceptance can take place only in awareness. We begin the most difficult adventures in life—marriage, for example, or spiritual practice—without knowing the length and breadth of their difficulty; if we knew, we might never begin. As we become more fully aware, we are able to choose again, with open eyes and with all of ourselves, what we have already, half blindly, chosen.

There is an old Jewish myth that the soul, before plunging down into the physical universe at the moment when sperm pierces egg, is granted complete foreknowledge of the life it is about to enter. Not only foreknowledge, but since, for the soul, knowledge and power are one, it is granted complete choice. And since the soul is one with the will of God, God's creation and its creation are one. It sees everything displayed before it, as if on a movie screen, but collapsed into a timeless less-than-a-moment, and it chooses everything: a mother and father whose giant shadows it will have to grow beyond if it can, like a plant reaching for light; a set of core puzzles that may take it a lifetime to resolve; sufferings and joys, opinions, obstacles, illnesses, triumphs, disasters, swirls of events that seem at first or tenth glance trivial or accidental; a particular era and country, with their collective delusions; lovers and children; enemies, friends; the circumstances, terrified or serene, of a death: all of them potential means of becoming mature, that is to say, transparent. And in order to make things more interesting, a split second before sperm pierces egg an angel gives the soul a smack on its non-physical mouth, and it forgets everything.

When Jesus gives his assent to God's will, he gives it not in obedience, as a servant would act toward a master, or a young child toward a parent, but in love, embracing this portion, this point of grief that has been plunged into him, until his will and God's will are two concentric circles around it.

sources: John 13:1, Mark 14:17f.; Mark 14:26,32, John 18:1; Mark 14:32–34; Mark 14:35, Matthew 26:39; Mark 14:36; Luke 22:45f.; Mark 14:37; Mark 14:40

The Arrest

If Jesus was in fact betrayed by Judas Iscariot, this is the only scene that could have had eye-witnesses.

And suddenly Judas came, one of the Twelve, with a battalion of Roman soldiers and some officers from the chief priests, carrying swords and clubs and lanterns and torches. And he went up to Jesus and said, "Rabbi!" and kissed him. And they seized Jesus and bound him, and took him away.

And all the disciples abandoned him, and fled.

Judas: There is an early tradition in which Judas *wasn't* a traitor: Matthew 19:28 includes him on one of the twelve thrones, judging the tribes of Israel; and in I Corinthians 15:5, Paul says that the resurrected Jesus "appeared to Kephas, then to the Twelve." The story of the betrayal, which is probably later, may have been influenced by Psalm 41:9 ("Even my friend, whom I trusted, who ate at my table, / exults in my misfortune"), which John 13:18 quotes as a fulfilled prophecy.

> The later Christians had to explain that Jesus knew all along, or at least in advance, that Judas would betray him (Matthew 26:25, John 6:64, 71 and frequently in John). . . . Luke and Matthew handle the embarrassment caused by Judas' defection differently, Matthew attributing foreknowledge to Jesus and restricting the number of those who saw the resurrection, Luke simply deleting the damaging part of the one saying which presupposes the continuation of the twelve around Jesus.
> (Sanders, *Jesus and Judaism*, p. 100)

We know very little about Judas, except that he was one of the twelve apostles and that he was called Iscariot (explanations of this name are all more or less unsatisfactory). According to John 12:1ff., after Mary, the sister of Lazarus and Martha, anoints Jesus' head at Bethany (in Mark's version of the story, the woman is nameless; in Luke's version, she is "a sinner," perhaps a prostitute), Judas protests that "the perfume could have been sold for three hundred silver coins and the money given to the poor." This is surely a legitimate concern, even a praiseworthy one. But according to John, "He said this not because he cared about the poor, but because he was a thief: he was in charge of the common purse and he used to steal what was put in it." Here the vilification of Judas has proceeded to the point where it is difficult to understand how Jesus could ever have chosen him as an apostle.

None of the Evangelists provides a motivation for Judas' treachery that is even remotely believable. Mark has him betray Jesus spontaneously and for no reason; according to Matthew, greed is the motivation, and Judas goes to the priests to trade information for money; according to Luke, he goes because Satan has entered into him. In John's Gospel, too, Satan enters into Judas, but with the complicity of Jesus himself, and only after Jesus gives Judas a piece of dipped bread at the Last Supper (13:27).

Roman soldiers: Literally, "cohort" (the tenth part of a Roman legion, containing about six hundred soldiers). I am following John's account here.

some officers from the chief priests: It is possible that the priestly authorities were the motivating force behind Jesus' arrest and execution. But the Gospels have an anti-Semitic bias throughout (already strong in Mark, and vicious in Matthew and John), and it is also possible that the Romans arrested him as a preventive measure, without any urging from the priests. Compare Josephus's account of the arrest of John the Baptist:

> To some Jews the destruction of Herod's army seemed to be divine vengeance, and certainly a just vengeance, for his treatment of John, surnamed the Baptist. For Herod had put him to death, though he was a good man and had exhorted the Jews to lead righteous lives, to practice justice toward their fellows and piety toward God, and so doing to join in baptism. . . . When others too joined the crowds about him, because they were aroused to the highest degree by his sermons, Herod became alarmed. Eloquence that had so great an effect on mankind might lead to some form of sedition, for it looked as if they would be guided by John in everything that they did. Herod decided therefore that it would be much better to strike first and be rid of him before his work led to an uprising, than to wait for an upheaval, get involved in a difficult situation and see his mistake. Though John, because of Herod's suspicions, was brought in chains to Machaerus, the stronghold that I previously mentioned, and there put to death, yet the verdict of the Jews was that the destruction visited upon Herod's army was a vindication of John, since God saw fit to inflict such a blow on Herod. (*Jewish Antiquities*, in *Works*, vol. 9, trans. Louis H. Feldman, pp. 81ff.)

If the priests were in fact responsible for Jesus' arrest, their motivation would have been more or less as the Evangelists imagine it: "It was now two days before the Passover and the festival of Unleavened Bread. And the chief priests and the elders gathered in the palace of the High Priest, whose name was Caiaphas. And they said, 'What should we do? This man Jesus has performed many miracles. If we let him continue like this, everyone will follow him, and the Romans will come and take away our position and our country.' So they began to make plans to arrest Jesus secretly, for they said, 'Not during the festival, or there will be a riot among the people' " (Mark 14:1; Matthew 26:3; John 11:47f.; Mark 14:1f.).

> The story is fictitious in detail but true in essence to the situation. . . . [and perfectly sums up] the problem posed for the priests by Jesus, his followers, and their enthusiasm. . . . The Romans, ruling central and southern Palestine at this time, watched [the Temple] as a possible center of trouble, and kept an eye on the rest of the country, intervening with military force to disperse assemblies they thought dangerous. If the Temple were to become the center of a general Jewish uprising, they might close or even destroy it. (It did so in A.D. 66, and was destroyed in 70). (Smith, *Jesus the Magician*, p. 17)

Mark (15:7), using pro-Roman language, mentions that a "rebellion," in which a number of "rebels" had committed "murder," had taken place just before or during Jesus' last days in Jerusalem.

And they seized Jesus: John 18:12 reads, "And the soldiers and their captain and the officers of the priests seized Jesus."

And all the disciples abandoned him, and fled: Who wouldn't be moved by the intense pathos of this sentence?

At the same time, we should understand that Jesus didn't feel, couldn't have felt, abandoned by God. When he entered the Kingdom of God, he understood that even the most painful events happen within God's presence. He saw the crucifixion as a bitter cup, but he also saw that the cup was given to him by God. Only at a relatively immature stage of spiritual awareness, when we are still attached to outer events, are we tempted to say, with the Psalmist, "My God, my God, why have you forsaken me?"

A few more words about Judas, a figure who for twenty centuries has haunted the Christian mind by the gratuitousness of his act.

From what I know of Jesus, it seems to me most likely that there was no betrayal, and that the legend originated in the disciples' need for villains. (We can see a similar demonization happen with the Pharisees, and especially with the "Jews" in the Gospel of John, where "Jesus" becomes so filled with rage and hatred that in verses like John 8:44 he is seething.) If this story is a legend, Judas may have elicited the other apostles' enmity because he differed from them in some essential and threatening way. Did he disbelieve in the resurrection? Did he understand that Jesus' death couldn't and shouldn't cause a change in Jesus' gospel? We'll never know.

On the other hand, if Judas *was* a traitor, that would tell us something significant about Jesus. The philosopher Celsus, in Origen's third-century dialogue, asks the pertinent questions: If Jesus was such a good man, why weren't his disciples loyal to him; and if he was so wise, why did he choose a traitor? My answer to the first question would be either that the apostles, though they may have been the best Jesus could find, were unworthy of him, or that there simply wasn't enough time for him to train them adequately, so that they could ripen into spiritually mature adults. After all, his life as a teacher lasted for only one year, and with all his wisdom, he was still a very young man when he died. (The Buddha, by contrast, had forty-five years to deepen his insight and to refine his teaching and insure its transmission.)

As for the second question, I would say that if there was in fact a betrayal, there must have been some kind of blind spot in Jesus himself. Disciple and teacher are as intimately connected as husband and wife, and whenever there is a divorce, both parties are in some sense responsible. And just as in the growing estrangement between husband and wife, it is not possible for a disciple who is living in close contact with his teacher to nurse resentment or dissatisfaction unless the teacher is insensitive or wilfully unobservant. Any insightful teacher, like an insightful husband or wife, will know instantly, from a facial expression or a tone of voice, that there is something wrong in the other person, and will not let the day pass before the problem is resolved, or at least brought out into the open.

If the Gospel accounts of Judas' betrayal have any basis in fact, there must have been some deep, unacknowledged drama that was played out between disciple and teacher. Was Judas so complicated and deceitful a man that he gave no signs of his mental torment? Did Jesus, with all his openheartedness, have an inadequate insight into human character? Friends of mine at two separate American Zen communities had a bitter experience of the latter possibility in two famous scandals of the 1980s. Each community was founded by an excellent Japanese Zen Master; each Zen Master chose a charming, talented sociopath as his spiritual heir, with disastrous results. My friends assumed that if a teacher had deep insight into the nature of reality, he would also have a clear understanding of people's karma. It ain't necessarily so.

We don't know whether or why Judas was a traitor. But I can understand how certain writers, positing Jesus' foreknowledge and the redemptive value of the crucifixion, have reasoned that only the most selfless of disciples would have, even unconsciously, agreed to become the instrument of Jesus' arrest, and that therefore the "beloved disciple" must have been not John but Judas. Thus Borges, summarizing the conclusions of the fictional theologian Nils Runeberg, says:

> The treachery of Judas was not accidental; it was a predestined deed which has its mysterious place in the economy of the Redemption. Runeberg continues: The Word, when It was made flesh, passed from ubiquity into space, from eternity into history, from blessedness without limit to mutation and death; in order to correspond to such a sacrifice it was necessary that a man, as representative of all men, make a suitable sacrifice. Judas Iscariot was that man. Judas, alone among the apostles, in-

tuited the secret divinity and the terrible purpose of Jesus. The Word had lowered Himself to be mortal; Judas, the disciple of the Word, could lower himself to the role of informer (the worst transgression dishonor abides), and welcome the fire which cannot be extinguished.

> ("Three Versions of Judas," trans. Anthony Kerrigan, in *Ficciones*, Grove Press, 1962, pp. 152f.)

sources: Mark 14:43, John 18:3; Mark 14:45,53,50

Peter's Denial

If this story originated from Peter himself, he showed an admirable honesty in the telling.

And they took Jesus to the High Priest.

And Peter followed at a distance, into the courtyard of the High Priest. And the slaves and attendants had made a charcoal fire, because it was a cold night; and they were standing around the fire, warming themselves. And Peter stood with them and warmed himself.

And one of the slave-girls of the High Priest came. And when she saw Peter, she looked at him closely and said, "You were there too, with that fellow from Nazareth, that Jesus." But he denied it, saying, "I don't know what you're talking about."

And after a while, someone else said to Peter, "You have a Galilean accent; you must be one of them." And he said, "God curse me if I know the man!" And at that moment the cock crowed. And Peter went out and burst into tears.

the cock crowed: As if it awakened Peter from fear into shame. The point of the story as Mark tells it is that Jesus had predicted

that Peter would deny him when the cock crowed twice. But
we don't need the prophecy to feel how appalled Peter was at
his denial.

*sources: Mark 14:53; Mark 14:54; John 18:18; Mark 14:66–68; Mark 14:70,
Matthew 26:73; Mark 14:71f.; Matthew 26:75*

The Trial Before Pilate

I have kept the trial scene to its bare minimum, since the Gospel
accounts are certainly fictional.

*And early the next morning, the chief priests, with the elders and
scribes, bound Jesus and took him away and handed him over to Pilate.
And Pilate sentenced Jesus to death, and flogged him, and handed him
over to his soldiers to be crucified.*

*And they took him out to crucify him, and seized a man named Si-
mon of Cyrene, who was passing by on his way in from the country, and
made him carry the cross.*

early the next morning:

> The Gospels are all influenced by the desire to incriminate the
> Jews and exculpate the Romans. . . . The difficulties with the
> trial scenes are not new ones. Some [scholars], to be sure, still
> defend the scenes as being an authentic portrayal. Many more
> scholars recognize that the earliest Christians knew only the
> general course of events (a Jewish interrogation, the handing
> over to Pilate, the crucifixion), but not the details. . . . All we
> need do is to accept the obvious, that we do not have detailed
> knowledge of what happened when the High Priest and pos-
> sibly others questioned Jesus. We cannot know even that "the
> Sanhedrin" met. Further, I doubt that the earliest followers of

Jesus knew. . . . Once we grant that we do not know what went on inside—that is, when we admit that the long trial scene of Matthew and Mark is not historical—then we must also grant that we do not know (1) if there was a trial; (2) if the whole Sanhedrin actually convened; (3) if there was a formal charge; (4) if there was a formal conviction under Jewish law. . . . The truth is that we do not know the answers to any of the questions just itemized. We share the ignorance of the evangelists. If, as seems highly probable, they were wrong about Jesus' being convicted by a formal Jewish court for blasphemy, we can hardly prove, on the basis of their accounts, that some other charge was sustained. (Sanders, *Jesus and Judaism*, pp. 300f.)

Whatever Pilate's reason for deciding to have Jesus put to death, it is not true that the Jewish crowds shouted out that Jesus should be crucified (Mark 15:12ff.) or that they took his blood upon themselves and their children (Matthew 27:25). Nor did the chief priests tell the prefect, "We have no king but Caesar" (John 19:15). These sentences, which were later written into the account of Jesus' passion, are the products of a bitter polemic between early Christianity and Judaism and have helped to cause the horrors of two millennia of anti-Semitism.

(Thomas Sheehan, *The First Coming: How the Kingdom of God Became Christianity*, Random House, 1986, p. 87)

As for the Barabbas episode,

When viewed objectively, as a reported transaction between a Roman governor, who was supported by a strong military force, and native magistrates and a native mob, the whole account is patently too preposterous and too ludicrous for belief. . . . Such an absurd presentation can be adequately explained in one way only: it resulted from Mark's concern to remove [for his Roman Christian readers] the scandal of the Roman crucifixion of Jesus. His purpose throughout the Barabbas episode is clearly twofold: to show that Pilate recognized the innocence of Jesus; and to exonerate Pilate from responsibility for the crucifixion of Jesus by representing him as compelled by the Jewish leaders and people to order the execution. Mark appears to invoke the episode, as a kind of desperate expedient, to explain away the intractable fact of the Roman cross after he had done all he could in emphasizing the evil intent of the Jewish leaders. . . . [Matthew emphasized Jewish guilt even more, and made the Jews] exclusively guilty of the awful deed. But he little knew, when he represented them as eagerly shouting: "His blood be upon us, and on our children!", what a terrible legacy he was thus imposing upon subsequent generations of his own people. For those fierce words came to be enshrined in the sacred scriptures of the Christian Church, where they were seen as the self-confession of the Jews to the murder of Christ. In the succeeding centuries, down to this present age, those words have inspired hatred for the Jews and justified their cruellest persecutions. (It was only during a session of the Second Vatican Council in 1965 that the Roman Catholic Church formally exonerated subsequent generations of Jews from responsibility for the murder of Christ; even then the decree met with certain opposition.) (S. G. F. Brandon, *The Trial of Jesus of Nazareth*, Stein and Day, 1968, pp. 98, 100, 115)

the chief priests:

The main [political] difference between [the Sadducees and the Pharisees] was that the Sadducees were willing to cooperate *actively* with the Romans, even if this meant handing over troublemakers to them for execution. As an appointee of the Romans, the High Priest was not just a ceremonial official with jurisdiction over the Temple; he was, in effect, a chief of police with his own armed force, his own police tribunal which was concerned with political offenses, and his own penal system, including prisons and arrangements for flogging offenders. In the case of capital offenses, however, such as serious insurrection against the power of Rome, he would hand over the offender to the occupying Roman power rather than attempt to impose sentence himself. The situation can best be understood by comparison with occupied France during the Second World War. (Maccoby, *Mythmaker*, p. 58)

Pilate: Pontius Pilate was procurator (governor) of Judea from 26 to 36 C.E. Far from being the sympathetic figure portrayed in the Gospels (he was later declared a saint by the Coptic church), he is described by Philo as "naturally inflexible and stubbornly relentless," and prone to "acts of corruption, insults, rapine, outrages on the people, arrogance, repeated murders of innocent victims, and constant and most galling savagery." He was finally dismissed as procurator for a brutal massacre of Samaritans.

flogged him:

> Under Roman jurisdiction Jesus was scourged with leather straps fitted with pieces of sharp metal and bone—a punishment commonly administered to those condemned to crucifixion.
> (Sheehan, *First Coming*, p. 87)

to be crucified: Crucifixion was a sentence passed by the Romans on three classes of offenders: rebellious slaves, habitual criminals, and conspirators against Roman rule. (Though it is a Roman form of execution, passages like John 18:31f., Acts 2:23, and I Thessalonians 2:15 try to make "the Jews" responsible.) Cicero called it "that most cruel and disgusting penalty," and Josephus, "the most wretched of deaths."

> Naked and unable to move, the victim was exposed to pain and insult, enduring thirst and finally, sometimes after days, dying from exhaustion, unless mercifully his sufferings were brought to an end by a spear-thrust or a shattering blow.
> (Vincent Taylor, *The Gospel According to Saint Mark*, Macmillan, 1952, p. 589)

> The end came slowly, by exposure, loss of blood, and gradual asphyxiation. The pain and degradation were augmented by blocked circulation and the torment of flies and insects. It is doubtful that any of his closest followers were present at Jesus' final agony.
> (Sheehan, *First Coming*, p. 87)

carry the cross:

> Condemned prisoners were forced to carry a crossbeam, or *patibulum*, weighing some eighty or ninety pounds, to the place of execution outside the city.
> (Ibid.)

The flogging which was a stereotyped part of the punishment would make the blood flow in streams. Presumably Jesus was so weakened by loss of blood that he was unable to carry the beam of the cross to the place of execution; this is also the best explanation of his relatively speedy death.

(Martin Hengel, *Crucifixion*, Fortress Press, 1977, pp. 31f.)

sources: *Mark 15:1; Mark 15:15b; Mark 15:20f.*

The Crucifixion

The final scene, in which all we can know with certainty is the stark fact of the crucifixion. Yet we can be certain that Jesus didn't see his own suffering as tragic, since it happened according to God's will.

And they brought him to the place called Golgotha (which means "the place of the skull"). And some women offered him drugged wine, but he wouldn't take it.

And at about nine o'clock they crucified him.

And above his head the charge against him was written: THE KING OF THE JEWS. And with him they crucified two Zealots, one on his right and one on his left.

And at about three o'clock in the afternoon, Jesus uttered a loud cry, and died.

And some women offered him: Literally, "And they offered him."

The "wine" referred to must have been the concoction which was given to Jews who were about to suffer the penalty of death, in order that they might lose consciousness. The preparation of this drugged wine seems to have been left to the hands of the ladies of Jerusalem, who, doubtless, regarded making and giving it as a deed of piety.

(C. G. Montefiore, The Synoptic Gospels, vol. 1,
Macmillan, 1927, p. 381)

Matthew reads, "They gave him wine mixed with gall to drink, but when he tasted it, he wouldn't drink it." Luke and John make no reference to wine.

but he wouldn't take it: He wanted to die fully conscious.

the charge against him: Even if this is not historical, it is clear that the Romans executed Jesus as a dangerous revolutionary.

two Zealots: The Greek word literally means "bandit" or "robber." Josephus, who collaborated with the Romans, regularly used it in a derogatory sense for the Jewish freedom-fighters known as Zealots, in the same way that Dr. Johnson might have called (perhaps did call) George Washington "a damned rebel."

uttered a loud cry: According to Mark, followed by Matthew, Jesus' last words were a quotation from Psalm 22 ("My God, my God, why have you forsaken me?"); according to Luke, a quotation from Psalm 30 ("Father, into your hands I commend my spirit"). But since the disciples had scattered, it is unlikely that any of them witnessed the crucifixion. Even if they did, they would have been allowed to watch it only from a considerable distance, as Mark says of Mary Magdalene and certain other women (15:40), and they wouldn't have been able to distinguish Jesus' words.

Many scholars think that, like the other borrowings from Psalm 22, these words too were borrowed from the same source, not by Jesus, but by the Evangelist, or by tradition. Jesus died with a "loud cry." What did he say? What had he said? Pious fantasy soon found answers; hence what we now read in Mark and Luke. Jesus was the Messianic hero predicted and represented in the Psalm. Therefore, he is made to quote its opening words, not because those who put the words in his mouth thought that he was, or believed he was, forsaken of God, but because they are the opening words of the Psalm.

(Montefiore, *Synoptic Gospels*, vol. 1, p. 383)

The famous words of Luke 23:34 ("Father, forgive them, for they know not what they do") are missing from many of the most ancient manuscripts and are almost certainly a later addition. As touching as they are, we should realize that they come from a consciousness radically different from Jesus'. Jesus knew that God is our immediate mirror: what we give, we receive; as we judge, we are judged; when we forgive, we are forgiven. There is measure for measure, cause and effect, and no notion of an intercessor. The God whom "Jesus" is addressing in these words is a stern king who acts mercifully only with reluctance, and only after persuasion by the good prince.

and died: The Evangelists add an account of the burial: "And late in the afternoon, since it was Friday and the Sabbath was approaching, Joseph of Arimathea, a respected member of the Sanhedrin, who was himself looking for the kingdom of God, took courage and went to Pilate and asked him for the body of Jesus. And Pilate ordered that it be given to him. And Joseph bought a linen cloth, and took the body down, and wrapped it in the cloth. And he laid it in a tomb that had been cut in the rock. And he rolled a large stone against the door of the tomb, and departed" (Mark 15:41, Luke 23:54; Matthew 27:58; Mark 15:46; Matthew 27:60). These verses may be historical, or they may be apologetic, to prepare for the myth of the empty tomb. Some scholars think it probable that Jesus' body was taken down from the cross by the soldiers and thrown into a mass grave.

I would like to append Nietzsche's deeply insightful account of the crucifixion and of how the apostles used it. (Christian readers may find it easier to forgive his passionate revulsion from the apostles if they can understand his passionate love for Jesus.)

The fate of the gospel was determined by the death—it hung on the "cross.". . . . It was only the death, this unexpected shameful death, only the cross, which was in general reserved for the rabble—it was only this most horrible paradox that brought the disciples face to face with the true riddle: "*Who was that? What was that?*"—The feeling of being bewildered and shocked to their very depths, the suspicion that such a death might be the *refutation* of their cause, the terrifying question mark "Why did this happen?"—this condition is only too easy to understand. Here everything *had* to be necessary, had to have meaning, significance, the highest significance; a disciple's love doesn't recognize the accidental. Only now did the chasm open up: "*Who* killed him? *Who* was his natural enemy?"—this question leaped forth like a lightning bolt. Answer: *ruling* Judaism, its upper class. From this moment they felt themselves in rebellion *against* the social order, in retrospect they understood Jesus as having been *in rebellion against the social order*. Until then this warlike, nay-saying and -doing trait had been *lacking* in his image; even more, he was the contradiction of it. Obviously the little community did *not* understand the main point, the exemplary character of this way of dying, the freedom, the superiority *over* every feeling of resentment:—an indication of how little of him they really understood! Jesus himself couldn't have intended anything by his death except to publicly give the sternest test, the *proof* of his teaching. . . . But his disciples were far from *forgiving* this death—which would have been gospel-like in the highest sense; not to speak of *offering* themselves for a similar death in sweet and gentle peace of heart. . . . Precisely the most ungospel-like feeling, *revenge*, came uppermost again. The matter couldn't possibly be finished with this death: "retribution" was needed, "judgment" (—yet what can be more ungospel-like than "retribution," "punishment," "sitting in judgment"!). Once more the popular expectation of a Messiah came into the foreground; a historic moment appeared: the

"kingdom of God" is coming as a judgment over his enemies. . . . But with this, everything is misunderstood: the
"kingdom of God" as a closing act, as a promise! For the gospel
had been precisely the presence, the fulfillment, the *reality* of
this "kingdom." Just such a death *was* this very "kingdom of
God.". . .

And now an absurd problem arose: "How *could* God have allowed that to happen?" To this, the disturbed reason of the little community found a terrifyingly absurd answer: God gave
his Son for the forgiveness of sins, as a *sacrifice*. All at once the
gospel was done for! The *guilt sacrifice*, and this in its most repulsive, most barbaric form, the sacrifice of the *guiltless* for the
sins of the guilty! What ghastly paganism! — For Jesus had
abolished the very concept of "guilt" — he had denied any separation between God and man, he *lived* this unity of God and
man as *his* "good news". . . . And not as a special privilege! —
From now on, step by step, there enters into the figure of the
redeemer the doctrine of a judgment and a second coming, the
doctrine of his death as a sacrificial death, the doctrine of the
resurrection, with which the whole concept of "blessedness,"
the whole and only reality of the gospel, is conjured away—
in favor of a state *after* death!

(Friedrich Nietzsche, *The Antichristian*)

But because Nietzsche's insight bristles with offense and an-
tagonism, I want to end this commentary by making the same
point in the sweet, serene tones of Lao-tzu:

> The Master gives himself up
> to whatever the moment brings.
> He knows that he is going to die,
> and he has nothing left to hold on to:
> no illusions in his mind,
> no resistances in his body.
> He doesn't think about his actions;
> they flow from the core of his being.
> He holds nothing back from life;
> therefore he is ready for death,

as a man is ready for sleep
after a good day's work.
(chapter 50)

sources: Mark 15:22; Mark 15:25; Matthew 27:37, Mark 15:26; Mark 15:27; Mark 15:34,37

APPENDIXES

Appendix 1: On Jesus

Baruch Spinoza

A correspondent wrote to Spinoza: "People say that you conceal your opinion concerning Jesus Christ, the Redeemer of the world, the only Mediator for mankind, and concerning His incarnation and redemption: they would like you to give a clear explanation of what you think." Spinoza answered:

I do not think it necessary for salvation to know Christ according to the flesh: but with regard to the eternal Son of God, that is, the eternal Wisdom of God, which has manifested itself in all things, and especially in the human mind, and above all in Jesus Christ, the case is far otherwise. For without this no one can come to a state of blessedness, inasmuch as it alone teaches what is true or false, good or evil. And inasmuch as this wisdom was made especially manifest through Jesus Christ, as I have said, his disciples preached it, insofar as it was revealed to them through him, and thus showed that they could rejoice in that spirit of Christ more than the rest of mankind. The doctrines added by certain churches, such as that God took upon himself human nature, I have expressly said that I do not understand; in fact, to speak the truth, they seem to me no less absurd than would a statement that a circle had taken upon itself the nature of a square.

―――――――――

The resurrection of Christ from the dead was in reality spiritual; and to the faithful alone, according to their understanding, it was revealed that Christ was endowed with eternity and had risen from the dead (using "dead" in the sense in which Christ said, "Let the dead bury their dead"), giving by his life and death a matchless example of holiness. Moreover, he to this extent raises his disciples from the dead, insofar as they follow the example of his own life and death.

Thomas Jefferson

My views of the Christian religion are the result of a life of inquiry and reflection, and very different from that anti-Christian system imputed to me by those who know nothing of my opinions. To the corruptions of Christianity I am, indeed, opposed; but not to the genuine precepts of Jesus himself. I am a Christian, in the only sense in which he wanted anyone to be: sincerely attached to his doctrines, in preference to all others; ascribing to himself every *human* excellence; and believing he never claimed any other.

———

The whole history of these books is so defective and doubtful that it seems vain to attempt minute enquiry into it: and such tricks have been played with their text, and with the texts of other books relating to them, that we have a right, from that cause, to entertain much doubt what parts of them are genuine. In the New Testament there is internal evidence that parts of it have proceeded from an extraordinary man; and that other parts are of the fabric of very inferior minds. It is as easy to separate those parts, as to pick out diamonds from dunghills. The matter of the first was such as would be preserved in the memory of the hearers, and handed on by tradition for a long time; the latter such stuff as might be gathered up, for imbedding it, anywhere, and at any time.

———

We must reduce our volume to the simple Evangelists; select, even from them, the very words only of Jesus, paring off the amphibologisms into which they have been led by forgetting often, or not understanding, what had fallen from him, by giving their own misconceptions as his dicta, and expressing unintelligibly for others what they had not understood themselves. There will be found remaining the most sublime and benevolent code of morals which has ever been offered to man. I have performed this operation for my own use, by cutting verse by verse out of the printed book, and arranging the matter which is evidently his, and which is as easily distinguishable as diamonds in a dunghill.

———

You will next read the New Testament. It is the history of a personage called Jesus. Keep in your eye the opposite pretensions: 1, of those who say he was begotten by God, born of a virgin, suspended and reversed the laws of nature at will, and ascended bodily into heaven; and 2, of those who say he was a man of illegitimate birth, of a benevolent heart, enthusiastic mind, who set out without pretensions to divinity, ended in believing them, and was punished capitally for sedition, by being gibbeted, according to the Roman law, which punished the first commission of that offense by whipping, and the second by exile, or death *in furea*.

Do not be frightened from this inquiry by any fear of its consequences. If it ends in a belief that there is no God, you will find incitements to virtue in the comfort and pleasantness you feel in its exercise, and the love of others which it will procure you. If you find reason to believe there is a God, a consciousness that you are acting under his eye, and that he approves you, will be a vast additional incitement; if that there be a future state, the hope of a happy existence in that increases the appetite to deserve it; if that Jesus was also a God, you will be comforted by a belief of his aid and love. In fine, I repeat, you must lay aside all prejudice on both sides, and neither believe nor reject anything, because any other persons, or description of persons, have rejected or believed it. Your own reason is the only oracle given you by heaven, and you are answerable, not for the rightness, but uprightness of the decision. I forgot to observe, when speaking of the New Testament, that you should read all the histories of Christ, as well of those whom a council of ecclesiastics have decided for us, to be Pseudo-evangelists, as those they named Evangelists, because these Pseudo-evangelists pretended to inspiration, as much as the others, and you are to judge of their pretensions by your own reason, and not by the reason of those ecclesiastics.

————

The truth is that the greatest enemies to the doctrines of Jesus are those calling themselves the expositors of them, who have perverted them for the structure of a system of fantasy absolutely incomprehensible, and without any foundation in his genuine words. And the day will come when the mystical generation of Jesus, by the supreme being as his father in the womb of a virgin, will be classed with the fable of the generation of Minerva in the brain of Jupiter. But we may hope that the dawn of reason and freedom of thought in these United States will do away with all this artificial scaffolding, and restore to us the primitive and genuine doctrines of this the most venerated reformer of human errors.

————

His parentage was obscure, his condition poor, his education null, his natural endowments great, his life correct and innocent; he was meek, benevolent, patient, firm, disinterested, and of the sublimest eloquence. . . . But the committing to writing of his life and doctrines fell on unlettered and ignorant men: who wrote too from memory, and not till long after the transactions had passed. . . . The doctrines which he really delivered were defective as a whole, and fragments only of what he did deliver have come to us, mutilated, misstated, and often unintelligible. They have been still more disfigured by the corruptions of schismatizing followers, who have found an interest in sophisticating and perverting the simple doctrines he taught, by engrafting on them the mysticisms of a Grecian sophist, frittering them into subtleties, and obscuring them with jargon, until they have caused good men to reject the whole in disgust, and to view Jesus himself as an imposter. Notwithstanding these disadvantages, a system of morals is presented to us, which, if filled up in the true style and spirit of the rich fragments he left us, would be the most perfect and sublime that has ever been taught by man.

Among the sayings and discourses imputed to him by his biographers, I find many passages of fine imagination, correct morality, and of the most lovely benevolence; and others again of so much ignorance, so much absurdity, so much untruth, charlatanism, and imposture, as to pronounce it impossible that such contradictions should have proceeded from the same being. I separate therefore the gold from the dross; restore to him the former, and leave the latter to the stupidity of some, and roguery of others of his disciples. Of this band of dupes and impostors, Paul was the great coryphaeus and first corrupter of the doctrines of Jesus.

No one sees with greater pleasure than myself the progress of reason in its advances towards rational Christianity. When we shall have done away with the incomprehensible jargon of the Trinitarian arithmetic, that three are one, and one is three; when we shall have knocked down the artificial scaffolding, reared to mask from view the simple structure of Jesus; when, in short, we shall have unlearned everything which has been taught since his day, and got back to the pure and simple doctrines he inculcated, we shall then be truly and worthily his disciples: and my opinion is that if nothing had ever been added to what flowed purely from his lips, the whole world would at this day have been Christian.

We find in the writings of his biographers matter of two distinct descriptions. First, a ground work of vulgar ignorance, of things impossible, of superstitions, fanaticisms, and fabrications. Intermixed with these again are sublime ideas of the Supreme Being, aphorisms and precepts of the purest morality and benevolence, sanctioned by a life of humility, innocence, and simplicity of manners, neglect of riches, absence of worldly ambition and honors, with an eloquence and persuasiveness which have not been surpassed. These could not be inventions of the grovelling authors who relate them. They are far beyond the power of their feeble minds. They show that there was a character, the subject of their history, whose splendid conceptions were above all suspicion of being interpolations from their hands. Can we be at a loss in separating such materials, and ascribing each to its genuine author? The difference is obvious to the eye and to the understanding, and we may read, as we run, to each his part; and I will venture to affirm that he who, as I have done, will undertake to winnow this grain from its chaff, will find it not to require a moment's consideration. The parts fall asunder of themselves as would those of an image of metal and clay. . . .

That Jesus did not mean to impose himself on mankind as the Son of God physically speaking, I have been convinced by the writings of men more learned than myself in that lore. But that he might conscientiously believe himself inspired from above, is very possible. The whole religion of the Jews, inculcated in him from his infancy, was founded in the belief of divine inspiration. . . . Elevated by the enthusiasm of a warm and pure heart, conscious of the high strains of an eloquence which had not been taught him, he might readily mistake the coruscations of his own fine genius for inspirations of a higher order. This belief carried therefore no more personal imputation than the belief of Socrates that himself was under the care and admonitions of a guardian daemon. And how many of our wisest men still believe in the reality of these inspirations, while perfectly sane on other subjects. Excusing therefore, on these considerations, those passages in the Gospels which seem to bear marks of weakness in Jesus, ascribing to him what alone is consistent with the great and pure character of which the same writings furnish proofs, and to their proper authors their own trivialities and imbecilities, I think myself authorized to conclude the purity and distinction of his character in opposition to the impostures which those authors would fix upon him.

William Blake

The diarist Henry Crabb Robinson put to Blake "the popular question, concerning the imputed Divinity of Jesus Christ." Blake answered: "He is the only God" — *but then he added* — "And so am I and so are you." *He had before said—and that led me to put the question—that Christ ought not to have suffered himself to be crucified.* "He should not have attacked the Government. He had no business with such matters." *On my representing this to be inconsistent with the sanctity of divine qualities, he said Christ was not yet become the Father.*

———

Christ, he said, took much after his mother, and in so far was one of the worst of men. On my asking him for an instance, he referred to his turning the money-changers out of the Temple—he had no right to do that. He digressed into a condemnation of those who sit in judgement on others. "I have never known a very bad man who had not something very good about him."

Speaking of the Atonement in the ordinary Calvinistic sense, he said, "It is a horrible doctrine; if another pay your debt, I do not forgive it."

———

There is not one moral virtue that Jesus inculcated but Plato and Cicero did inculcate before him. What then did Christ inculcate? Forgiveness of sins. This alone is the gospel and this is the life and immortality brought to light by Jesus, even the covenant of Jehovah, which is this: if you forgive one another your trespasses, so shall Jehovah forgive you, that he himself may dwell among you.

Ralph Waldo Emerson

Jesus Christ belonged to the true race of prophets. He saw with open eye the mystery of the soul. Drawn by its severe harmony, ravished with its beauty, he lived in it, and had his being there. Alone in all history he estimated the greatness of man. One man was true to what is in you and in me. He saw that God incarnates himself in man, and evermore goes forth anew to take possession of his World. He said, in this jubilee of sublime emotion, "I am divine. Through me, God acts; through me, speaks. Would you see God, see me; or see thee, when thou also thinkest as I now think." But what a distortion did his doctrine and memory suffer in the same, in the next, and the following ages! There is no doctrine of the Reason which will bear to be taught by the Understanding. The Understanding caught this high chant from the poet's lips, and said, in the next age, "This was Jehovah come down out of heaven. I will kill you, if you say he was a man." The idioms of his language and the figures of his rhetoric have usurped the place of his truth; and churches are not built on his principles, but on his tropes. Christianity became a Mythus, as the poetic teaching of Greece and of Egypt, before. He spoke of miracles; for he felt that man's life was a miracle, and all that man doth, and he knew that this daily miracle shines as the character ascends. But the word Miracle, as pronounced by Christian churches, gives a false impression; it is Monster. It is not one with the blowing clover and the falling rain.

————

Historical Christianity has fallen into the error that corrupts all attempts to communicate religion. As it appears to us, and as it has appeared for ages, it is not the doctrine of the soul, but an exaggeration of the personal, the positive, the ritual. It has dwelt, it dwells, with noxious exaggeration about the *person* of Jesus. The soul knows no persons. It invites every man to expand to the full circle of the universe, and will have no preferences but those of spontaneous love.

———

I cannot but think that Jesus Christ will be better loved by being less adored. He has had an unnatural, an artificial place for ages in human opinions—a place too high for love. There is a recoil of the affections from all authority and force. In the barbarous state of society it was thought to add to the dignity of Christ to make him king, to make him God. Now that the scriptures are read with purged eyes, it is seen that he is only to be loved for so much goodness and wisdom as was in him, which are the only things for which a sound human mind can love any person.

———

Is it not time to present this matter of Christianity exactly as it is, to take away all false reverence for Jesus, and not mistake the stream for the source? God is in every man. God is in Jesus, but let us not magnify any of the vehicles as we magnify the Infinite Law itself. We have defrauded him of his claim of love on all noble hearts by our superstitious mouth-honor.

———

If Jesus came now into the world, he would say—You, YOU! He said to his age, I.

———

The fear of degrading the character of Jesus by representing him as a man indicates with sufficient clearness the falsehood of our theology. The inexhaustible soul is insulted by this low, paltering superstition, no more commendable in us than in the mythology of other heathens.

———

We think so meanly of man that 'tis thought a profanity to call Jesus one.

———

Christ preaches the greatness of Man, but we hear only the greatness of Christ.

———

The world is divided on the fame of the Virgin Mary. The Catholics call her "Mother of God," the skeptics think her the natural mother of an admirable child. But the last agree with the first in hailing the moral perfections of his character, and the immense benefit his life has exerted and exerts.

———

[The publisher James] Munroe seriously asked me what I believed of Jesus and the prophets. I said, as so often, that it seemed to me an impiety to be listening to one and another, when the pure Heaven was pouring itself into each of us, on the simple condition of obedience. To listen to any second-hand gospel is perdition of the First Gospel. Jesus was Jesus because he refused to listen to another, and listened at home.

Henry David Thoreau

It is remarkable that the highest intellectual mood which the world tolerates is the perception of the truth of the most ancient revelations, now in some respects out of date; but any direct revelation, any original thoughts, it hates like virtue. The fathers and the mothers of the town would rather hear the young man or young woman at their tables express reverence for some old statement of the truth than utter a direct revelation themselves. They don't want to have any prophets born into their families, — damn them! So far as thinking is concerned, surely original thinking is the divinest thing. Rather we should reverently watch for the least motions, the least scintillations, of thought in this sluggish world, and men should run to and fro on the occasion more than at an earthquake. We check and repress the divinity that stirs within us, to fall down and worship the divinity that is dead without us. I go to see many a good man or good woman, so called, and utter freely that thought which alone it was given to me to utter; but there was a man who lived a long, long time ago, and his name was Moses, and another whose name was Christ, and if your thought does not, or does not appear to, coincide with what they said, the good man or the good woman has no ears to hear you. They think they love God! It is only his old clothes, of which they make scarecrows for the children. Where will they come nearer to God than in those very children?

―――――

It is necessary not to be Christian to appreciate the beauty and significance of the life of Christ. I know that some will have hard thoughts of me, when they hear their Christ named beside my Buddha, yet I am sure that I am willing they should love their Christ more than my Buddha, for the love is the main thing, and I like him too.

Leo Tolstoy

The true Christian teaching is very simple, clear, and obvious to all, as Jesus said. But it is simple and accessible only when man is freed from that falsehood in which we were all educated, and which is passed off upon us as God's truth.

Nothing needful can be poured into a vessel full of what is useless. We must first empty out what is useless. So it is with the acquirement of true Christian teaching. We must first understand that all the stories telling how God made the world six thousand years ago; how Adam sinned and the human race fell; and how the Son of God, a God born of a virgin, came on earth and redeemed mankind; and all the fables in the Old Testament and in the Gospels, and all the lives of the saints with their stories of miracles and relics—are nothing but a gross hash of superstitions and priestly frauds. Only to someone quite free from this deception can the clear and simple teaching of Jesus, which needs no explanation, be accessible and comprehensible. That teaching tells us nothing about the beginning, or about the end, of the world, or about God and His purpose, or in general about things which we cannot, and need not, know; but it speaks only of what man must do to save himself, that is, how best to live the life he has come into, in this world, from birth to death. For this purpose it is only necessary to treat others as we wish them to treat us. In that is all the Law and the prophets, as Jesus said. And to act that way, we need neither icons, nor relics, nor church services, nor priests, nor catechisms, nor governments, but on the contrary, we need perfect freedom from all that; for to treat others as we wish them to treat us is possible only when a man is free from the fables which the priests give out as the truth, and is not bound by promises to act as other people may order. Only such a man will be capable of fulfilling, not his own will nor that of other men, but the will of God.

The reader should understand that the belief that the Gospels are the inspired word of God is not only a profound error, but a very harmful deception. He should remember that Jesus himself did not write a book, nor did he transmit his teaching to learned or even to educated men, but spoke for the most part to illiterate people, and only long after his death were his life and teaching described.

The reader should also remember that a large number of such descriptions have been written, from which the church selected at first three, and later a fourth Gospel, that out of the great mass of literature about Jesus they accepted much that was inaccurate, and that there are nearly as many faulty passages in the canonical Gospels as in the rejected writings. Nor does it follow, because the teaching of Jesus is inspired, that all the descriptions are inspired. He should remember that these official Gospels are the work of many human minds; that over the centuries they have been selected, enlarged, and commented upon; and that the most ancient copies which have come down to us are only from the fourth century. The reader must remember all this in order to disengage himself from the idea, so common among us, that the Gospels, in their present form, have come to us directly from the Holy Spirit. If he does so, he will admit that, far from it being blamable to disencumber the Gospels of useless passages, and to illuminate passages the one by the other, it is unreasonable *not* to do this and to consider every one of these verses sacred.

On the other hand, I pray my readers to understand that, if I do not consider the Gospels to be sacred books, coming directly from the Holy Spirit, even less do I regard them as mere monuments in the history of religious literature. I am conscious of both their theological and historical significance, but I do not consider either of these important. What I see in Christianity is not a divine revelation nor a mere historical phenomenon, but a teaching that gives us the true meaning of life.

When, at the age of fifty, I first began to study the Gospels seriously, I found in them the spirit that animates all who are truly alive. But along with the flow of that pure, life-giving water, I perceived much mire and slime mingled with it; and this had prevented me from seeing the true, pure water. I found that, along with the lofty teaching of Jesus, there are teachings bound up which are repugnant and contrary to it. I thus felt myself in the position of a man to whom a sack of garbage is given, who, after long struggle and wearisome labor, discovers among the garbage a number of infinitely precious pearls. This man knows that he is not blameworthy in his distaste for the dirt, and also that those who have gathered these pearls along with the rest of the sackful, and who thus have preserved them, are no more to blame than he is, but, on the contrary, deserve his love and respect.

When I perceived that only light enables men to live, I sought the source of this light. And I found it in the Gospels, despite the false teachings of the church. And when I reached this source of light, I was dazzled by its splendor, and I found in it answers to all my questions about life, answers which I recognized as being in complete harmony with all the known answers gained among other nations, and, to my mind, surpassing all other answers.

I sought a solution to the problem of life, not to a theological question. And that is why I did not care about knowing whether Jesus is God, or whom the Holy Spirit proceeds from, etc. For me, the only important concern was this light, which for eighteen hundred years has been shining upon mankind, which has been shining upon me as well, and which shines upon me still. But to know, in addition to this, how I ought to name the source of this light, what elements compose it, and what kindled it, did not interest me in the least.

———

Up to the present time, some people, conceiving Jesus to be the second person of the Trinity, accept his teaching only as it accords with that pseudo-revelation of the Holy Spirit which they find in the Old Testament, the Epistles, the Edicts of the Councils, and the Patristic writings, and preach a strange creed founded on these, which they assert to be the teaching of Jesus. Other people, who do not believe that Jesus is God, understand his teaching by the interpretation of Paul and others. But even though they believe that he was a man, they would deprive him of the right every man may claim, of being answerable for his own words, and in trying to explain his teaching, they credit him with what he would never have dreamed of saying.

Friedrich Nietzsche

What is "the good news"? That true life, eternal life, has been found—it is not something promised, it is already here, it is *within you*: as life lived in love, in love without subtraction or exclusion, without distance. Everyone is the child of God—Jesus

———

definitely claims nothing for himself alone—and as a child of God everyone is equal to everyone else.

———

Jesus' faith doesn't prove itself, either by miracles or by rewards and promises, and least of all "by scripture": it is, at every moment, its own miracle, its own reward, its own proof, its own "kingdom of God."

———

In the whole psychology of the "Gospel" the concept of guilt and punishment is lacking; also the concept of reward. "Sin"—any distance that separates God and man—is abolished: *precisely this is the "good news."* Blessedness is not promised, is not tied to any conditions: it is *the only reality.*

The deep instinct for how one would have to *live* in order to feel oneself "in heaven," to feel "eternal," while in every other condition one certainly does *not* feel oneself "in heaven": this alone is the psychological reality of "redemption."—A new way of living, *not* a new belief.

———

The word "son" expresses the entrance into the feeling of the total transfiguration of all things (blessedness); the word "father" expresses *this feeling itself*, the feeling of eternity, of perfection.

The kingdom of heaven is a condition of the heart—not something that comes "above the earth" or "after death." The whole concept of natural death is *lacking* in the Gospel: death is not a bridge, not a transition; it is lacking because it belongs to an entirely different, a merely apparent world, useful only insofar as it furnishes symbols. The "hour of death" is *not* a Christian concept—an "hour," time, physical life and its crises simply don't exist for the teacher of the "good news." The "kingdom of God" isn't something that one waits for; it has no yesterday and no tomorrow, it doesn't come in "a thousand years"—it is an experience that takes place inside the heart; it is everywhere, it is nowhere.

George Bernard Shaw

I must now make a serious draft on the reader's attention by facing the question whether, if and when the medieval and Methodist will-to-believe the Salvationist and miraculous side of the gospel narratives fails us, as it plainly has failed the leaders of modern thought, there will be anything left of the mission of Jesus: whether, in short, we may not throw the gospels into the waste-paper basket, or put them away on the fiction shelf of our libraries. I venture to reply that we shall be, on the contrary, in the position of the man in Bunyan's riddle who found that "the more he threw away, the more he had." We get rid, to begin with, of the idolatrous or iconographic worship of Christ. By this I mean literally that worship which is given to pictures and statues of him, and to finished and unalterable stories about him. The test of the prevalence of this is that if you speak or write of Jesus as a real live person, or even as a still active God, such worshippers are more horrified than Don Juan was when the statue stepped from its pedestal and came to supper with him. You may deny the divinity of Jesus; you may doubt whether he ever existed; you may reject Christianity for Judaism, Mahometanism, Shintoism, or Fire Worship; and the iconolaters, placidly contemptuous, will only classify you as a freethinker or a heathen. But if you venture to wonder how Christ would have looked if he had shaved and had his hair cut, or what size in shoes he took, or whether he swore when he stood on a nail in the carpenter's shop, or could not button his robe when he was in a hurry, or whether he laughed over the repartees by which he baffled the priests when they tried to trap him into sedition and blasphemy, or even if you tell any part of his story in the vivid terms of modern colloquial slang, you will produce an extraordinary dismay and horror among the iconolaters. You will have made the picture come out of its frame, the statue descend from its pedestal, the story become real, with all the incalculable consequences that may flow from this terrifying miracle. It is at such moments that you realize that the iconolaters have never for a moment conceived Christ as a real person who meant what he said, as a fact, as a force like electricity.

Mohandas K. Gandhi

It was more than I could believe that Jesus was the only incarnate son of God, and that only he who believed in him would have everlasting life. If God could have sons, all of us were his sons. If Jesus was like God, or God Himself, then all men were like God and could be God Himself. My reason could not believe literally that Jesus, by his death and by his blood, redeemed the sins of the world. Metaphorically, there might be some truth in it. Again, according to Christianity, only human beings had souls, and not other living beings, for whom death meant complete extinction; while I held a contrary belief. I could accept Jesus as a martyr, an embodiment of sacrifice, and a divine teacher, but not as the most perfect man ever born. His death on the cross was a great example to the world, but that there was anything like a mysterious or miraculous virtue in it, my heart could not accept.

———

My Christian friends have told me on more than a few occasions that because I do not accept Christ as the only son of God, it is impossible for me to understand the profound significance of his teachings. I believe that this is an erroneous point of view, and that such an estimate is incompatible with the message that Jesus gave to the world. For he was certainly the highest example of one who wished to give everything, asking nothing in return, and not caring what creed might happen to be professed by the recipient. I am sure that if he were living here now among men, he would bless the lives of many who perhaps have never even heard his name, if only their lives embodied the virtues of which he was a living example on earth: the virtues of loving one's neighbor as oneself and of doing good and charitable works among one's fellow men.

What then does Jesus mean to me? To me he was one of the greatest teachers humanity has ever had. To his believers he was God's only-begotten Son. Could the fact that I do or do not accept this belief make Jesus have any more or less influence in my life? Is all the grandeur of his teaching and of his doctrine to be forbidden to me? I cannot believe so.

To me it implies a spiritual birth. My interpretation, in other words, is that in Jesus' own life is the key to his nearness to God; that he expressed, as no other could, the spirit and will of God. It is in this sense that I see him and recognize him as the son of God.

Ramana Maharshi

When Jesus worked his miracles and spoke his wonderful words, he was utterly unconscious of being a separate, finite personality. He was pure light, pure life, cause and effect working in perfect concert. "The Father and I are one." He had given up all ideas of "I" and "mine." Can the body possess anything? Can the mind possess anything? Both of them are lifeless, unless the light of God shines through.

Appendix 2: On Healing

I asked my friend Laura, who is a healer, and for whose insight I have the deepest respect, to comment on Jesus' healings. She said:

I feel that Jesus touched people from a place of great presence and love. He was in contact with the essence of these sick people, and they recognized that. And if they were open to him, they could receive that love and use it to heal themselves.

The people he healed were ready to let go of something. There was an opening in them which was probably there before they saw him, but when they saw him there was a deeper opening that allowed them to move through pain or suffering in order to be healed. These healings are described as instantaneous, but they weren't necessarily instantaneous. There were probably many steps along the way which led to the healing. If someone is completely ready to be healed, and if the healer can hold the space of wholeness and love for her, then it's possible at that moment for her to open up and heal herself through the healer. But with some of my patients, most of what I do is lay groundwork. Every moment of laying groundwork is just as important as that one moment when everything opens up. That *seems* more miraculous because you can see and feel the cure. But actually every moment along the way is just as miraculous.

The curing of physical symptoms is only one aspect of healing. A disease begins as a certain energy before it goes into the physical body. Once it manifests itself on the gross level of the tissues, healing it is a slower process, because the body is a lot denser, it vibrates more slowly than other energy levels. Though even with physical symptoms, love can accelerate the healing process.

But healing can be deeper than that. It can be a transformation of the whole person: not just a physical healing but an emotional and spiritual opening as well. When you embrace an illness, and really learn what it's trying to communicate to you, your whole life can be transformed, from the inside out.

When I'm doing a healing with someone, I don't try to *direct* the energy out through my hands. I *allow* it to flow out. If someone is open to me and letting the healing happen on a deep level, my feet feel strongly connected to the ground, the whole upper part of my body feels connected to the heavens, and I feel connected to everything, and there's a flow of energy in my body that heals me also. It's a very pleasurable experience, very calm. When the energy is flowing, I feel that everything in the universe is perfect the way it is, that everything is just as it should be. There's a deep calm, and a quiet sense of joy. The energy flows through my body, and it flows out through my hands. It is highly intelligent, so it moves to wherever the person needs healing, on whatever level.

Basically, what happens is that the energy which is connected to everything else, the energy of the Tao, or "source energy" I sometimes call it, fills my whole body, and it moves out my hands also, and the person I'm working with remembers that energy in her body. Because that's who we are. We all come from that place. So she remembers that, and her energy comes up to meet it, and in the course of coming up to meet it, the physical illnesses and the emotional blocks that she's holding on to are easier to let go of. Most of the time we identify ourselves with our body or our personality, we feel that we are our illnesses and neuroses. And if these things are who we are, then letting go of them seems like committing suicide. So it's very hard to let go. But when someone can feel this energy moving through her body, and remembers who she *really* is, then it's a lot easier to let go.

On the healing of the leper

This healing may have been instantaneous, but from the Gospel account it's impossible to know whether it was complete. If it wasn't complete, then whatever manifested itself as leprosy would have manifested itself again—in a week, a month, a year—as another disease or an accident or some other kind of difficulty. If the healing was complete, nothing would have been left unresolved, and the illness wouldn't have had to be expressed in another way. It could be that Jesus' love was so strong, and entered the leper's body so deeply, that he felt completely accepted by it, and this allowed him to let go of all the manifestations of feeling unaccepted and unloved.

On the healing of the woman with the flow of blood

It seems like the woman was feeling enormous reverence for Jesus and a strong belief that he could heal her. So she was very open to anything that could happen. It helps to have great trust in the healer and it helps even more to trust your own ability to heal. Sometimes trusting the healer can open a pathway to trusting yourself.

The flow of Jesus' healing force, when he "felt in himself that power had gone forth from him," seems to be a response he had to the woman without consciously knowing it. When the energy flows, it's not as if it somehow goes out of me and leaves me drained, it flows *through* me. It feels like it's more present for me as well.

After the healing, the woman in the story seems to be filled with gratitude as well as fear. With that kind of healing, she must have felt that she had been given back to herself and that things were all right in the universe. And with that feeling of peace and well-being inside her, there must have been a sense that what she had done really wasn't so terrible. But she knew that she hadn't been straightforward, and she was afraid that Jesus was going to scold her.

It's good that Jesus said to her, "Your trust has healed you." It's clear that her trust was enormous, to the point that even touching his robe could heal her. There was a great openness in her; without that openness nothing would have happened. He's saying, "Don't think that I actually did anything to you; your own trust is what healed you."

On the raising of the dead girl

This incident reminds me of when I watched my grandmother die. I felt her presence there in the room, after she died. I saw that her spirit—or however you want to call it, the essence of who she was—hadn't really separated from her body. She wasn't *in* her body, but hovering somewhere above it. Then, gradually, she was less and less present, and after maybe twenty or thirty minutes she was gone.

I think that when the spirit really separates from the body, death is irreversible. But if this girl had actually died, she had been dead for such a short time when Jesus arrived that she could still have returned. It's possible that the force of his conviction, or his very presence, could have brought her back. My question is whether it was *appropriate* to bring her back. Sometimes it's not a bad thing to die. Sometimes that's the best healing.

Maybe there was something unfinished in the girl's life and she was just checking out of her body. Some people die because they just don't want to deal with very painful karma. Of course, they have to do it all over again, but they're not aware of that. I can't tell from this account whether Jesus' act was an act of love. If she felt complete with her life and was ready to die and had no desire to come back, and if he was calling her back because of the father's grief or the needs of the family, then it wasn't an act of love, and it wasn't a healing either. But if she really wanted to come back and he was there helping her with his presence, then it was an act of love.

On the healing of the blind man

I like this story a lot. I like the blind man's description of "men like trees walking," because it sounds so real, like it wasn't made up by some editor. Only someone who had been blind would say that. And I also like the fact that Jesus did the healing in two parts: he did a first healing and the man got partly better, and then he did another, and the man could see clearly. So it happened in steps. Most healing does. Usually the instantaneous healing is glorified, but most growth in life, most changes, happen gradually. We take in as much light as we can, and we digest it and assimilate it, and then we go on to the next step and then the next; and there's something very beautiful about that. Whenever people transform their lives and do really deep healing, that's a miracle. It's not any more miraculous to get rid of physical symptoms all in one step.

Appendix 3: On Miracles

Sharafuddin Maneri

When God confers miracles upon those who love him, submission and docility increase in their hearts, at the same time that docility and courtesy, along with dread and fear, are also enhanced. The king of mystics, Abu Yazid al-Bistami, at one stage on his journey came to the edge of a large expanse of water that needed a boat to be crossed. He did not have one, but he began to experience that he was crossing it without a boat. In this state, he traversed a path that appeared in the water until, coming to his senses, he exclaimed, "Fraud! Fraud!" and returned. There is a delicate mystery here, and it is this: Genuine sanctity is connected with rejecting all that is not the Friend. Everything must be abandoned for the sake of God.

William Blake

Commenting on Watson's An Apology for the Bible, *a criticism of Thomas Paine's* The Age of Reason:

Jesus could do no miracles where belief hindered, hence we must conclude that the man who holds miracles to be ceased puts it out of his own power to ever witness one. The manner of a miracle being performed is in modern times considered as an arbitrary command of the agent upon the patient, but this is an impossibility, not a miracle, neither did Jesus ever do such a miracle. Is it a greater miracle to feed five thousand men with five loaves than to overthrow all the armies of Europe with a small pamphlet? Look over the events of your own life, and if you do not find that you have both done such miracles and lived by such, you do not see as I do. True, I cannot do a miracle through experiment and to domineer over and prove to others my superior power, as neither could Christ. But I can and do work such as both astonish and comfort me and mine. How can Paine the worker of miracles ever doubt Christ's in the above sense of the word miracle? But how can Watson ever believe the above sense of a miracle, who considers it as an arbitrary act of the agent upon an unbelieving patient? Whereas the Gospel says that Christ could not do a miracle because of unbelief.

If Christ could not do miracles because of unbelief, the reason alleged by priests for miracles is false, for those who believe want not to be confounded by miracles. Christ and his prophets and apostles were not ambitious miracle-mongers.

George Bernard Shaw

Possibly my readers may not have studied Rousseau's *Letters Written from the Mountain*, which may be regarded as the classic work on miracles as credential of divine mission. Rousseau says, in effect, there is nothing in making a lame man walk: thousands of lame men have been cured and have walked without any miracle. Bring me a man with only one leg and make another grow instantaneously on him before my eyes, and I will be really impressed; but mere cures of ailments that have often been cured before are quite useless as evidence of anything else than desire to help and power to cure.

Jesus, according to Matthew, agreed so entirely with Rousseau, and felt the danger so strongly, that when people who were not ill or in trouble came to him and asked him to exercise his powers as a sign of his mission, he was irritated beyond measure, and refused with an indignation which they, not seeing Rousseau's point, must have thought very unreasonable. To be called "an evil and adulterous generation" merely for asking a miracle worker to give an exhibition of his powers, is rather a startling experience. Mahomet, by the way, also lost his temper when people asked him to perform miracles. But Mahomet expressly disclaimed any unusual powers; whereas it is clear from Matthew's story that Jesus (unfortunately for himself, as he thought) had some powers of healing. It is also obvious that the exercise of such powers would give rise to wild tales of magical feats which would expose their hero to condemnation as an impostor among people whose good opinion was of great consequence to the movement started by his mission.

But the deepest annoyance arising from the miracles would be the irrelevance of the issue raised by them. Jesus' teaching has nothing to do with miracles. If his mission had been simply to demonstrate a new method of restoring lost eyesight, the miracle of curing the blind would have been entirely relevant. But to say "You should love your enemies; and to convince you of this I will now proceed to cure this gentleman of cataract" would have been, to a man of Jesus' intelligence, the proposition of an idiot. If it could be proved today that not one of the miracles of Jesus actually occurred, that proof would not invalidate a single one of his didactic utterances; and conversely, if it could be proved that not only did the miracles actually occur, but that he had wrought a thousand other miracles a thousand times more wonderful, not a jot of weight would be added to his doctrine. And yet the intellectual energy of skeptics and divines has been wasted for generations in arguing about the miracles on the assumption that Christianity is at stake in the controversy as to whether the stories of Matthew are false or true. According to Matthew himself, Jesus must have known this only too well; for wherever he went he was assailed with a clamor for miracles, though his doctrine created bewilderment.

Seung Sahn

Many people want miracles, and if they witness miracles they become very attached to them. But miracles are only a technique.

They are not the true way. If a Master used miracles, people would become very attached to this technique of his, and they wouldn't learn the true way. If a doctor gave a sick person medicine that cured his sickness but gave him another sickness, would you call him a good doctor? It is true that people might be attracted to meditation practice if a Master were to walk on water. But if they came for this reason, they would find actual meditation practice too difficult, or too boring, or too unmiraculous, and they would soon leave.

There is a story about the great ninth-century Zen Master Huang-po. He was traveling with another monk, and they came to a river. Without breaking stride, the monk walked across the water, then beckoned to Huang-po to do the same. Huang-po said, "If I had known he was that kind of fellow, I would have broken his legs before we reached the water."

A keen-eyed Zen Master understands people's karma. The Buddha said, "Karma that you have made for yourself can disappear only if you want it to. No one can make you want it to." He also said, "I have good medicine, but I can't take it for you." The Buddha has already given instructions for someone who is blind or disabled. But most people want easy solutions. They want someone else to do their work for them.

It's like a mother teaching her child. If a mother does everything for the child, the child will come to depend on her. A good mother makes the child do things for itself. Then it will grow up strong and independent.

Nowadays there is a man in Korea who has proclaimed himself as the Christ. Many people believe in him. After he washes his face and his feet, they take the water and drink it as medicine. And indeed, their sicknesses are miraculously cured. But it is their minds that are curing their bodies. They believe in this man so completely that he can do miracles. If they didn't believe, he wouldn't be able to do miracles. In the same way, when a boy and a girl are in love, the first time they kiss, their lips are filled with magical energy. This man can touch his followers and it is as if his fingers were flowing with electricity. There are many religious leaders like this in India.

But this is not good teaching. It keeps the disciples dependent on the teacher. They cannot understand how their own minds are creating the miracles. And it becomes difficult for them to act for themselves. Magic alone can't make bad karma disappear; it is only a technique. Did Jesus solve anything by raising Lazarus from the grave? Lazarus still had the same karma as before, and he still had to die.

One of the Buddha's disciples, Maudgalyayana, was a great miracle-worker. One day, as he was meditating, he saw that the Kapila kingdom would soon be destroyed by a war. He thought, "If I don't do something, a week from today, at eleven A.M., our whole country will be in ruins." So he went to the Buddha and said, "Lord, do you know that next week many of your people are going to be killed?"

"Yes."

"Then why don't you save them?"

"I can't."

"But you have psychic powers and can do miracles. Why can't you save them?"

The Buddha said, "It is impossible to make merited karma disappear."

But Maudgalyayana didn't believe him. He got very angry, because he thought that the Buddha wasn't being compassionate. So he went and shrunk the whole kingdom and put it into an eating bowl. Then he got the bowl to the highest heaven, where all is peace and serenity, and he left it there for seven days, in the middle of the palace that stood in the middle of the highest heaven. After the allotted time had passed, Maudgalyayana breathed deeply and said to himself, "Ah, everything is all right now." So he got the bowl and brought it back to earth. But when he took off the cover and looked inside, he saw that the miniature country had been devastated by a miniature war.

Magic is only a technique. Some people know how to do card tricks. It looks as if they have done something magical, but it is really a trick; we don't see what is actually happening. What we call magic is the same. It is taking a person's consciousness and manipulating it. This can indeed be very powerful. There was once a Chinese general who was a great magician. During a civil war, he conjured up an enormous army of gods, and sent it flying through the air. The opposing army was terrified, and many soldiers were killed by this god-army. But the opposing general happened to be a wise man, and he understood what was going on. So the next day he called his troops together before a large crystal ball that he had put up on a high post. "You must all gaze intently at this crystal," he said, "and keep your minds clear of all thinking. Then you will be safe. But if you look around or begin to think, you will certainly be killed by the gods." So all the soldiers kept their minds clear and couldn't be manipulated by magic. Soon the army of gods appeared. They hung in the air for a moment; then all that could be seen was a bunch of dry leaves floating down to the ground.

If someone wants to be able to do miracles, it is possible to learn how. But this is not the correct way. Keen-eyed Zen Masters don't use magic or miracles, because these can't help people find the true way. The only way to make karma disappear is for your consciousness to become clear and open. Then there are no miracles. Then there are only correct views and correct practice. This is the true miracle.

Sources

p. 277, People say that you conceal: Oldenburg to Spinoza, November 15, 1675.

p. 277, I do not think it necessary: Letter LXXIII.

p. 277, The resurrection of Christ: Letter LXXV.

p. 278, My views of the Christian religion: To Dr. Benjamin Rush, April 21, 1803.

p. 278, The whole history of these books: To John Adams, January 24, 1814.

p. 279, We must reduce our volume: To John Adams, October 12, 1813.

p. 279, You will next read the New Testament: To Peter Carr, August 10, 1787.

p. 280, The truth is that the greatest enemies: To John Adams, April 11, 1823.

p. 280, His parentage was obscure: To Dr. Benjamin Rush, April 21, 1803.

p. 281, Among the sayings and discourses: To William Short, April 13, 1820.

p. 281, No one sees with greater pleasure than myself: To Timothy Pickering, February 27, 1821.

p. 282, We find in the writings of his biographers: To William Short, August 4, 1820.

p. 283, The diarist Henry Crabb Robinson put to Blake: Henry Crabb Robinson, *Reminiscences*, in *The Portable Blake*, ed. Alfred Kazin, Viking Press, 1946, p. 680.

p. 283, Christ, he said, took much after his mother: Ibid., pp. 692f.

p. 283, *There is not one moral virtue:* "The Everlasting Gospel" (spelling and punctuation modified).

p. 284, *Jesus Christ belonged:* "An Address, delivered before the Senior Class in Divinity College, Cambridge, July 15, 1838," in *Nature, Addresses, and Lectures.*

p. 284, *Historical Christianity has fallen into the error:* Ibid.

p. 285, *I cannot but think that Jesus:* Edward Waldo Emerson and Waldo Emerson Forbes, eds., *Journals of Ralph Waldo Emerson*, vol. 3, Houghton Mifflin Co., 1910, p. 223.

p. 285, *Is it not time to present:* Ibid., p. 324.

p. 285, *If Jesus came now into the world:* Ibid., vol. 4, p. 277.

p. 285, *The fear of degrading the character of Jesus:* Ibid., p. 444.

p. 286, *We think so meanly of man:* Linda Allardt, ed., *The Journals and Miscellaneous Notebooks of Ralph Waldo Emerson*, vol. 12, Harvard University Press, Belknap Press, 1976, p. 256.

p. 286, *Christ preaches the greatness of Man:* Ibid., p. 410.

p. 286, *The world is divided on the fame:* Ralph H. Orth and Alfred R. Ferguson, eds., *The Journals and Miscellaneous Notebooks of Ralph Waldo Emerson*, vol. 13, Harvard University Press, Belknap Press, 1977, p. 322.

p. 286, *[The publisher James] Munroe seriously asked me:* Ibid., p. 406.

p. 286, *It is remarkable that the highest intellectual mood:* H. G. O. Blake, ed., *The Writings of Henry David Thoreau*, vol. 7, Riverside Press, 1894, pp. 280f.

p. 287, *It is necessary not to be Christian:* *A Week on the Concord and Merrimack Rivers.*

p. 287, *The true Christian teaching:* "Letter to a Non-Commissioned Officer," trans. Aylmer Maude, *Tolstoy's Writings on Civil Disobedience and Non-Violence*, Bergman Publications, 1967, pp. 166f.

p. 288, *The reader should understand: Christ's Christianity*, trans. anonymous, Kegan Paul, Trench and Co., 1885, pp. 319ff. (English modified).

p. 290, *Up to the present time:* Ibid., p. 326.

p. 290, *What is "the good news":* *The Antichristian.*

p. 291, *Jesus' faith doesn't prove itself:* Ibid.

p. 291, *In the whole psychology of the "Gospel":* Ibid.

p. 291, *The word "son" expresses the entrance:* Ibid.

p. 292, *I must now make a serious draft:* Preface to *Androcles and the Lion.*

p. 293, *It was more than I could believe:* Mohandas K. Gandhi, *The Message of Jesus Christ*, ed. Anand T. Hingorami, Bharatiya Vidya Bhavan, 1963, p. 11.

p. 293, *My Christian friends have told me:* Mohandas K. Gandhi, *All Religions Are True*, ed. Anand T. Hingorami, Bharatiya Vidya Bhavan, 1962, pp. 65f.

p. 294, *When Jesus worked his miracles:* B. V. Narasimha Swami, *Self-Realization: Life and Teachings of Sri Ramana Maharshi* (8th ed.), Sri Ramanasramam, 1976, p. 121.

p. 301, *When God confers miracles:* Paul Jackson, S.J., trans., *Sharafuddin Maneri: The Hundred Letters*, Paulist Press, 1980, p. 41.

p. 301, *Jesus could do no miracles where belief hindered:* Annotations to *An Apology for the Bible* (spelling and punctuation modified).

p. 302, *Possibly my readers may not have studied:* Preface to *Androcles and the Lion.*

p. 303, *Many people want miracles:* Stephen Mitchell, comp. and ed., *Dropping Ashes on the Buddha: The Teaching of Zen Master Seung Sahn*, Grove Press, 1976, pp. 99ff.

Acknowledgments

I am grateful to many people for their share in this book:

to John Grubb for finding, and to Paul and Anna Hawken for renting me, an ideal work space;

to Robert Aitken, Chana Bloch, Linda Brown, Thomas Farber, Robert Hass, Jane Hirshfield, Huston Smith, and Brother David Steindl-Rast, O.S.B., for their many invaluable suggestions;

to John Tarrant for helping the book find its true shape;

to David Bullen for yet another beautiful design;

to Hugh Van Dusen, my editor, and William B. Shinker, my publisher, for their unfailing support;

to Michael Katz, my agent, for his keen insight into almost every aspect of the book;

and, as always, to my dear impeccable Vicki: wife, teacher, partner on the path.